MUSIC, SOUND AND MULTIMEDIA

Music and the Moving Image

Series Editor
Kevin Donnelly

Titles in the series include:

MUSIC, SOUND AND MULTIMEDIA
From the Live to the Virtual

Edited by

Jamie Sexton

EDINBURGH UNIVERSITY PRESS

© in this edition Edinburgh University Press, 2007
© in the individual contributions is retained by the authors

Edinburgh University Press Ltd
22 George Square, Edinburgh

Typeset in 10/12.5 Adobe Sabon
by Servis Filmsetting Ltd, Manchester, and
printed and bound in Great Britain by
Antony Rowe Ltd, Chippenham, Wilts

A CIP record for this book is available from the British Library

ISBN 978 0 7486 2533 8 (hardback)
ISBN 978 0 7486 2534 5 (paperback)

The right of the contributors
to be identified as authors of this work
has been asserted in accordance with
the Copyright, Designs and Patents Act 1988.

CONTENTS

ACKNOWLEDGEMENTS

I would like to thank: Kevin Donnelly for encouraging me to edit this volume and for advising on certain issues along the way; Sarah Edwards for a lot of good advice and for being a helpful editor; Kay Dickinson for suggesting that I should edit this volume; and Kate Egan for being generally supportive during the process of editing and writing.

ILLUSTRATIONS

NOTES ON CONTRIBUTORS

Randolph Jordan holds an MA in film studies from the Mel Hoppenheim School of Cinema at Concordia University in Montreal, Canada, and is currently a doctoral candidate in Concordia's Interdisciplinary PhD Humanities programme. His research focuses on the intersections between film sound theory, electroacoustic music and acoustic ecology. His dissertation examines films which express ecological concern through creative approaches to the relationship between sound and image on screen. For more information, visit www.randolphjordan.com.

Angelina I. Karpovich is a lecturer in multimedia technology and design at Brunel University. Her research concerns media fandom, the social significance of media texts, and the varying uses of media technologies by professionals and non-professionals.

Jem Kelly is senior lecturer and research coordinator in the Department of Performing Arts, University of Chichester. Jem's academic writing includes *Auditory Space: Emergent Sounds and Affective Practices in Steve Reich and Beryl Korot's* Three Tales (Intellect 2005), and forthcoming chapters in *Devising with Technology* (Routledge), *Telematic and Tactile: Devising Practices of Station House Opera* (Intellect) and *They Did It My Way: Intermediality and Liveness in* Sinatra Live!, The Musical (CTR). Jem also composes music for theatre and television, producing albums with the Lotus Eaters and the Wild Swans.

Kieran Kelly is a senior lecturer at the University of the West of England, Bristol, based in the School of Cultural Studies. His doctoral thesis was a study of the business and economic history of the systems and networks associated with the port of Bristol. Kieran is a joint author of the Routledge volume *New Media: A Critical Introduction*, shortly to enter into its second edition.

Dan Laughey is senior lecturer in media and popular culture at Leeds Metropolitan University. He is the author of *Music and Youth Culture* (2006) and *Key Themes in Media Theory* (2007). Dan's PhD (completed in 2003) involved ethnographic research on young people's music use and consumption. His current research is focused on music audiences and histories of popular music in everyday life.

Dana Milstein teaches humanities courses at Baruch College (CUNY) and various online institutions in the United States. While her primary specialization is nineteenth-century Europe, she lectures and writes extensively on the relationship between the arts. Her current interests are underground music culture and the apex of Symbolism with Mallarmé and Debussy.

Rod Munday worked in television post-production for seventeen years before taking his degree. He is currently a doctoral student at the University of Wales, Aberystwyth. His research interests include Peircean semiotics, virtual reality, new media and massively multiplayer online games.

Jamie Sexton is a lecturer at the University of Wales, Aberystwyth. His other research interests include experimental and cult media. He is the co-editor (with Laura Mulvey) of *Experimental British Television* (2007) and co-author (with Ernest Mathijs) of *Cult Cinema: An Introduction* (forthcoming).

Lee Tsang is lecturer in music at the University of Hull. His research interests span music analysis, timbre perception, expressionism, world cinema (especially the films of François Ozon), animation, music as social enterprise and performance studies. He held the post of information officer for the Society for Music Analysis during the period 2000–3 and that of events officer in 2004, and directed the Hull University Music Analysis Conference 2003 in association with the Society. In 2005, he was awarded the University of Hull Vice Chancellor's Prize for his practice-based research, educational and outreach work with Hull Sinfonietta.

Zach Whalen is a PhD candidate in the Department of English at the University of Florida, where he studies video games and digital media. He has published articles in *Game Studies: The International Journal of Computer Game*

Research, *Works & Days* and *M/C: A Journal of Media and Culture*, and has contributed chapters to several edited collections. He is the production editor for the journal *ImageTexT: Interdisciplinary Comics Studies* and edits, maintains and writes for the game studies resource site *Gameology.org*. His dissertation in progress is a study of typography and textual practices in video games.

INTRODUCTION

Jamie Sexton

Critical analysis of music has been dominated by a focus on sonic matter as a unitary object of analysis. In other words, music is predominantly appreciated as a singular media experience, separated from other media forms, which it may often interact with. To some extent, this approach decontextualises and idealises musical matter. Whilst it has been common to contextualise music culturally and historically – as interacting with the social and as emerging out of cultural traditions – it has not been so frequently analysed in its materiality, in terms of the ways it is transmitted and received, and how it often intersects with other media modes. A core reason for this general analytic trend is that, in order to understand music properly and take it seriously, critics have tended to demarcate it from other media. Understandable though such an approach is, it has led to a relative lack of scrutiny of music's incorporation into broader media forms. I don't want to overstate such neglect: there is plenty of work now being produced on the role of music and other sounds within films, as well as the intersection of audio-vision within music videos. Nevertheless, audio interactions with other media forms have only been partially explored. And, as digital technologies feed into what has generally been referred to as a converging mediascape, the need to address the myriad ways in which sonic matter interacts with other media becomes increasingly pressing.

As I have indicated, the tendency to idealise music is not totally widespread, although musical analysis will often downplay how sounds interact with their material conditions of transmission/reception. Such interactions, however, can deeply influence how sonic matter is perceived, and can thus constitute important semantic filters. Music, as Nicholas Cook has pointed out, is never alone: it has long been associated with other media – with the visual in live performance, and with words in programme notes, on record sleeves, and in the conversational flow of interval chatter. Musical meaning, therefore, emerges from its relationships with other media (Cook 1998: 121–2).

Previous to the advent of recording technologies music was automatically associated with some kind of visual accompaniment. As the production of musical sounds was always produced live, co-present spectators would witness how the movements of the musicians fed into the emanating sounds. In the early days of the phonograph such lack of accompanying visual information was considered rather distressing, as sounds became disembodied and therefore took on a somewhat spectral air. Thus, according to Mark Katz, Edison's company was involved in many strategies to help visualise music. They invented devices such as the Stereophone and the Illustrated Song Machine, both introduced in 1905, which attached to cylinder-playing phonographs and rotated images in time with the music (Katz 2004: 19). Concentration on sound without (visual or other sensory) interference, then, is a relatively modern phenomenon, engendered by recording technologies. Yet the recording age has far from banished music's intermeshing with other media: if headphones could be seen as providing an opportunity to reduce other sensory modes and enhance concentration upon sonic matter in and of itself, new ways of listening to music in conjunction with other sensory modes have also proliferated. So, for example, listening is often accompanied by a diverse array of visual forms, whilst media predominantly associated with other sensory registers often contain sonic information that feeds into the integrated media experience.

Defining (Multi-)Media

Before describing some important ways in which audio culture is intersecting with other media forms, it is important to stress just how I am using the term 'multimedia'. In so doing, it is also pertinent to think about how we use the actual term 'media'. For 'media', as Cook has pointed out (2000: 262–3), can apply to a number of things: it can refer to the medium within which information is embedded (perhaps its most common meaning), but it can also refer to the sensory impression of different modes (such as words, sounds, images), as well as the manner in which material may be cognitively processed in different ways. Cook, though, makes a case for describing multimedia in a manner that is not reductive to these notions of media, even though he acknowledges that these are valid ways in which the term 'medium' may be understood. So, for example, the 'media as carrier' definition is fraught with problems, as – and this is increasingly common – a film or television programme, for example, may be experienced across a broad range of media forms (the cinema, the television, the computer) without radically changing the experience or meaning of the work.[1] If we think about 'medium' in sensory terms, sound and speech can both fall under the auditory mode. Likewise, two different modes of cognitive processing may be involved in listening to different types of music. Therefore, argues Cook, the term 'multimedia' cannot be a straightforward multiplication of any of these single 'media' definitions. Instead, multimedia should be defined structurally on the idea of variance. That is, 'multimedia' is applicable when separate media forms are combined and constitute 'independent "dimensions" of variance' (2000: 263).

Cook therefore argues that ballet is an instance of multimedia, whereas a classical guitar performance is not. In ballet, music and dance constitute independent forms of media: these two media are autonomous to a degree and intersect to create meaning. In a classical guitar performance, on the other hand, whilst there is the visual dimension of physical performance and the sonic dimension of the music, the two forms are not considered to be independent because the 'physical gesture is massively determined by the sound' (2000: 263). In other words, the physical gestures are an outcome of having to place fingers in a certain position in order to produce the desired sounds. I would have to take issue with Cook's argument here as I believe that he underplays the variance admitted to the musical performance: in this example he only pays attention to the physical movements of the player, which excludes a number of other visual elements such as costume, facial gestures, surrounding performance environment, to name but the most obvious examples. He does admit for variation in musical performance, but argues that these do not constitute an 'independent dimension of variance'. An example he gives of musical performance going beyond routine determination and creating an instance of multimedia interaction is the performances of Jimi Hendrix, but by citing this example Cook seems to indicate that it is exceptional. On the contrary, I would argue that any performance is an example of multimedia to an extent, though there are different degrees to which the importance of the visual within musical performance plays a part in its overall meaning. In any performance the image of the performer will contribute information of some kind: at the most basic level, this semantic contribution may be minimal, whilst at the other end of the scale the visual element of performance may provide a much greater proportion of the performance's overall meaning. Cook's criterion for multimedia seems too rigidly tied to a model of variation, as well as a demand that different media elements play a largely equal role in the overall meaning of a work. This seems somewhat idealistic: real-world multimedia instances will combine media of different kinds in different ways, but why should these elements be at variance, and why should they all partake in a proportionate semantic contribution to the overall work?[2] This rather prescriptive conception of musical multimedia has previously been criticised by Annette Davidson, who has argued that a definition of multimedia which excludes works where different media are entirely conformant 'does not seem altogether useful' (Davidson 2003: 351).

The rigidity of Cook's account is inevitable considering that his book is an attempt to build a model of multimedia interactions that is widely applicable to different instances of multimedia. His attempt to build a general model that can be used for all instances of musical multimedia also seems somewhat hindered by the fact that he only applies it to a few examples (primarily two film segments, a music video and a television advertisement). In contrast to Cook's overly abstract approach to musical multimedia, this book contains a number of more concrete investigations of particular areas in which the sonic interacts with other media forms. Whereas Cook was attempting to expand musicological analysis beyond music itself, stressing the ways in which music intersects with other media, this volume takes the existence of sonic multimedia more for granted. Nevertheless, there is still awareness that the centrality of music and other sounds, and the roles that they play within broader media forms, need to be more thoroughly investigated.

One benefit of Cook's analysis, though, is his conception of multimedia in broader terms than is sometimes evident in definitions of the term. It is a term that has sometimes been solely applied to interactive, computer-based applications that combine sensory modes – what is often referred to as 'digital multimedia' (see Chapman and Chapman 2000 for an overview). Yet, whilst the advent of computer-based technologies, including CD-ROMs and the World Wide Web, has led to a focus on digital multimedia, the term is by no means confined to digital applications. As Packer and Jordan have pointed out, 'the concept of integrated, interactive media has its own long history, an evolution that spans over 150 years' (Packer and Jordan 2002). They themselves trace multimedia to Richard Wagner's concept of the *Gesamtkunstwerk* ('total artwork'), which was 'one of the first attempts in modern art to establish a practical, theoretical system for a comprehensive integration of the arts' (ibid.). Instances of multimedia may be traced much further back than this, though it may be the case that Wagner was one of the first artists to reflect discursively on the integration of media.

In this book the term 'multimedia' is, admittedly, applied rather loosely. Rather than attempting to come up with a strong definition of the word, the book instead allows writers to interrogate specific instances where sound and/or music are integrated into broader media systems. If we allow for the fact that, following Cook, music is never alone, then it could be argued that all music is part of a broader multimedia environment. I would go along with this, though some may argue that, if such a broad conception of multimedia is admitted, it effectively renders the term useless. I would counter that there are different instances of multimedia interactions, but that at the basic level most forms of media are also forms of multimedia. If we think of media as combining sensory, technological and cognitive aspects, then we cannot really think of one medium as ever totally distinct. We rarely encounter music 'pure' because such encounters are laden with preconceptions that have been gleaned through other forms of media. For example, when we listen to music we generally will relate this to other things that we have heard, read and seen; all of these inter-media experiences influence 'musical encounters'.

The concept of multimedia in this volume serves a largely heuristic purpose: it allows the writers of individual chapters to focus on any area of music in a manner that is sensitive to the ways in which the sonic interacts with other media instances. In other words, there are no prescriptive guidelines as to what extent inter-media mixing must occur, or the ways in which such media must interact. Nevertheless, the chapters are mostly concerned, to some extent, with digital forms of multimedia. This is because I want to present chapters that reflect upon more recent developments. At the same time, many of these developments are contextualised so that pre-digital instances often inform certain chapters.

DIGITAL TRENDS

As this book primarily (though not exclusively) focuses upon digital media I shall briefly discuss a few issues related to the ways in which mediated sound, and its relation to other media, have been affected by the increasing digitisation of the mediasphere. Without doubt, the most important development over the past decade or so has been the growth of the Internet and its permeation into everyday life (at least for many people). Alongside increasingly fast network speeds and expanding computer capacities, we can now access a vast range of multimedia sites over the Internet, as well as engage in networked exchanges with others. In its earlier years, the web was largely text-based, due to storage and connection speed limitations; however, it has increasingly become capable of delivering a mixture of various media components and offering a much broader range of experiences. For example, the web contains a mixture of sites providing information about music: these relate to print-based music periodicals but extend their content provision through the addition of music and moving images; they also occasionally enhance interactive possibilities. Music webzines, then, often do not just feature writing about music, but can also link to music being written about (via downloads, streaming music or podcasts); there may also be links to other related materials such as streaming music videos, or interviews with musicians.

It is clear that the Internet is impacting upon the state of music culture in a number of ways. Information about music, as well as music itself, is becoming increasingly easier to access for those who are connected. Whilst general books on new media/digital media tend to limit musical coverage to file sharing, there

is a lot more going on than this (admittedly highly important) cultural phenomenon. In terms of talk about music – mainly criticism but also other kinds
of music-related chat – it is now much easier to consume, as well as produce,
such information. There are a number of sites, for example, that provide criticism for free, and this proliferation of critical discussion means that there are
more people producing such criticism. This, in one sense, blurs distinctions
between the consumer and producer of information, as well as the distinctions
between the amateur and the professional critic. Such blurring, however, should
not be overstated, for it is also the case that professionalism carries over from
traditional media forms onto the web. Hence, it is more difficult for new
webzines to establish a presence on the web than it is for those that have already
built up a readership; and yet, it is possible for such webzines to establish a
steady readership and gain a reputation through word of mouth; hence the popularity of sites such as *Pitchfork* and *Stylus*.[3] In terms of personal criticism, it
is again more difficult for non-institutionally affiliated writers with no track
record of music journalism to establish a presence, but once again this difficulty
is not absolute: there is now more chance for individuals to send reviews to,
and establish themselves at, music webzines; there is also a slim chance of individuals gaining a reputation for music criticism through personal blogs, via
word of mouth or through discovery via blog aggregator sites.

The blog has also enabled professional music journalists to create unedited
and unpublished ruminations on the web. Free from the shackles of their paid
vocational work, they can bypass the commercial restrictions of their day jobs
to create more personal reflections on the art of music. Rob Young has argued
that whilst traditional music criticism is prey to 'narrowing markets and strict
advertising targets', the blog has rejuvenated such cultural discourse. He
further argues:

> What they add up to is a fertile breeding ground for a new style of music
> writing – just when the trade needs it most. The ludic quality of music
> criticism merges with a serious approach to the subject rarely found in a
> mainstream that treats music as entertainment rather than art. Add ency-
> clopaedic knowledge, genre-crossing frames of reference and a disregard for
> celebrity, and you have the key traits of the music blog. (Young 2003: 10)

There is, then, a more connected, interactive musical culture emerging in
those parts of society where broadband access is prevalent. Views on music,
information relating to music, as well as music itself, can be posted on the web
or exchanged through numerous file-sharing services (both legal and of dubious
legality). Whilst most views about such developments are generally positive
(excepting those disputing illegal activities) there are, however, some who
lament the passing of information scarcity. Whilst data about, and access to,

music are unprecedented in terms of availability, information overload can result, which may lead to quantity overwhelming and blunting quality. If music is so easy to access, the desire for consumption may, as it did for *Stylus* writer Nick Southall, result in an addiction to accumulating music at the expense of actually having much time to listen to it. Southall writes of this in terms of ennui, the boredom of plenty:

> There is a compulsion to consume, and it's getting worse. So eager are we to sample everything, quickly and in quantity, that we take no time to taste what it is that we're consuming, never let our stomachs feel full or our palettes be sated. And so we stuff ourselves indiscriminately with everything we come across and end up bloated, sluggish, and tired. (Southall 2005)

Without wishing to play down the undoubted benefits of new trends in music collecting, there are also developments that may lead to a sense of loss and nostalgia for information scarcity. With the accumulation of so much to listen to, one has less time to experience each piece of music in a single collection. Previously, a purchased record or CD may have been given more listening time, both because it had less audio competing for playtime and because the monetary investment in the object would have commonly led to a patient willingness to become familiar with its content. Now, if one is freely downloading a large amount of music, there may be less investment and a greater tendency to skim and select (though, of course, this is not always so). And, in a culture of plentiful information about and criticism of music, it may also be the case that the listener/collector is accumulating and checking off those recordings that have been raved about by others in the virtual community that the self tends to inhabit, rather than fully experiencing them in any depth.

The Internet, though, is not all about consumption: as previously noted it can also lead to an increase in the production of cultural artefacts – not just writing about music, but also constructing graphics, films, or music itself. Once again, both legally and illegally, people can download and make use of a broad array of software that aids the manipulation of existing artefacts. There is a large variety of existing software (some free, some not) which allows people to record, manipulate, edit and generally transform sounds in a variety of ways.[4] On a basic level, a person can extract a favourite song and instantly transform it through adding echo and delay, for example. On a more advanced level, a person can cut bits of the audio, rearrange them and piece them together with other audio fragments to create an audio collage. One particularly notable way in which consumption has transformed into production is through the audio mashup, wherein people layer elements of songs over one another in order to create a hybrid work. Though the mashup predates digital technologies, it is now – with the free distribution of software that enables people to create mashups with relative ease – entering a new stage of popularity. Digital software also aids the production of original music. Whilst the variety of software ranges from simple to extremely complex, and from free to expensive, there is no doubt that it is now easier than ever before for many individuals or small groups to gain access to production software. It is possible for people to produce music on their own software and then to self-distribute that music over the web. It is certainly not particularly easy to gain any kind of recognition through doing this, but there is a new culture of self-produced, self-distributed musicians emerging in networked space, and the importance of this culture is likely to grow in importance as people continually strive to bypass traditional mediating forces.

Music is undergoing a process of increasing manipulability and visualisation. Digital software production and editing tools allow for sound to be visualised in the form of waveforms that can be magnified and precisely edited, or in the form of other visual representations that aid careful organisation of musical units. The ability to manipulate music – through cutting, pasting, treating, merging separate units, undoing 'mistakes' – is far greater than was previously achievable through analogue technologies. This process fits in with Lev Manovich's argument that digital media is *programmable media*, which allows for easier automation and variation. For example, because it is now so simple to copy digital media and manipulate its underlying code, it is now more common to manipulate pre-existing sounds, so that variation becomes a core theme of digital music. Manovich writes that whereas old (analogue) media was characterised by the creation of an object, which was then duplicated on a mass scale (standardisation), new media objects are characterised by the numerous ways in which they become modified: 'Instead of identical copies, a new media object typically gives rise to many different versions. And rather than being created completely by a human author, these versions are often in part automatically assembled by a computer' (Manovich 2002: 36). Of course, variation is not something new: cover versions, remixes and cutting/pasting sounds have long been practised in different sound cultures, though the degree to which manipulation of pre-existing sounds occurs has undoubtedly increased in an exponential fashion.

Visualisation is relevant to a number of areas of music culture, in addition to its centrality within production and editing. If, as Katz argues, early records gave rise to a strange sense of lack because of the absence of musicians playing sounds, then the visual has undoubtedly returned with a vengeance in more recent times. Much music now is accompanied by visual images in some form or other, a process that has been increasingly central to music culture since the rise of MTV in the 1980s. Now there is a variety of visual-related musical artefacts: music DVDs, for example, are growing in popularity, particularly with the rise of 5.1 home television systems; also emerging are audio DVDs, which contain 5.1 audio and music videos (an example being the Flaming Lips' 2004 DVD audio release of their 2002 album *Yoshimi Battles the Pink Robots*, which also features accompanying abstract imagery – or 'frequency waveform cartoons' – designed by George Salisbury); whilst audio played on computers is often accompanied by abstract imagery in the form of 'visualisations' offered by media players such as Microsoft's Media Player. Both of these later examples represent a kind of simplified, automated continuation of abstract visual films based upon music principles (such as films by Oskar Fischinger, Len Lye and Harry Smith, for example, who all were drawn to creating 'musical' abstract forms, sometimes based upon theories of synaesthesia).

The media phenomenon of 'convergence' has undoubtedly led to a stage in which media interactions have increased. Distinctions between different media forms certainly still exist, but their boundaries now seem more porous and difficult to demarcate. Within the domestic space, for example, machines used for previously separate media experiences are often interlinked or combined. With a digital television linked to a 5.1 speaker system and DVD player, we may listen to music CDs, watch and listen to music DVDs, or listen to radio on our television sets. In the 1980s this might not have seemed a very attractive prospect because the sound quality of television sets at this point was not particularly impressive (though, of course, we may have watched music on television, for the loss of audio quality was compensated by the added visual dimension). The computer now allows us to listen to music alone or with visual accompaniment in a range of formats alongside its other multimedia functions.

Outside of domestic space convergence has also impacted upon mobile media. In particular, the mobile phone is increasingly becoming a more generalised multifunctional device, which can also be used as an MP3 player, a camera, a radio, a video player and a gaming device, for example. Electronic media are now much more likely to accompany us on the move. Whilst the history of such media stretches further back, it was undoubtedly the arrival and subsequent popularity of Sony's Walkman in 1980 that heralded the modern age of personalised mobile gadgets. It was also a device that gave rise to extensive commentary, many fearing that it would damage sociality by cocooning the individual in his or her own solipsistic sound world (see Hosokawa 1984: 165). Today's MP3 players now extend the capacities of the Walkman, allowing people to take what sometimes amounts to their entire record collections with them wherever they go; and the MP3 player is not merely a device that is used 'in between' spaces, but is also used in spaces such as the home, at work and in the car (Bull 2005: 345). In addition to the ways in which the personal music device is increasingly capable of other media functions, it can also be said to transform the objective landscape into a media-like audio backdrop (and here it is following in the footsteps of the analogue Walkman): the surrounding world can become, for some users, aestheticised and heightened, so that – as one iPod user comments – 'I feel as though life is a movie and is playing especially for me' (quoted in Bull 2005: 348).

The atomisation of media users predicted by doomsday critics when the Walkman became a cultural phenomenon has, perhaps, now been extended with the proliferation of mobile gadgets, but at the same time there has also been an increase in connectivity (between different media as well as between people, who can link with other individuals in different ways). Atomisation has not destroyed connectivity; rather the two have grown in tandem with one another. We can use our multimedia devices to withdraw from, but also to tune into, a broader social fabric. Likewise, music is becoming increasingly 'invisible' (with the proliferation of virtual files), but is also attaching itself to different media devices and visual forms. In an ever-mutating media landscape, where once-separate media levels are interconnecting in novel configurations, the need to address the state of audio culture and its broader place within a multimedia landscape is more pressing than ever.

The sheer variety of music-related multimedia forms pervading contemporary culture has led to my being selective in terms of what I cover in this collection. In order to strike a balance between variety and focus, I have structured the chapters into four broader sections, which pertain to specific areas of musical multimedia interactions. The first two sections are less general than the latter two, hence the inclusion of two chapters in each of these and three in the latter sections. The first section focuses upon fandom and music videos. Whilst there has been a lot of academic work upon 'traditional' music videos, there has not been a great deal of attention paid to music videos made by fans, which is a cultural form that – despite having its roots in the 'analogue' era – has grown in importance and popularity in line with the proliferation of digital technologies. In the first chapter Angelina Karpovich provides an overview of 'fan vids', which are 'non-professional' forms of music videos that often appropriate existing, previously separate visual and sonic elements to create a fresh cultural object. Disputing Henry Jenkins's previous assertions about this cultural form, she points out the difficulty of actually demarcating the 'professional' music video and the fan video in any simple manner, a process that has been muddied further by digital developments. In the second chapter Dana Milstein focuses more concretely on a specific generic category of the 'fan vid' (or, as she terms them, 'unofficial music videos' or UMVs): anime music videos (AMVs), which limit their video footage to anime-related media. In tandem with the international cult interest in anime, AMVs now themselves constitute a particularly interesting subsection of fan videos. Milstein focuses closely on the aesthetic traits that characterise such videos and goes on to mention how the influence of AMVs is now seeping into other forms of anime-related media. In this sense, not only does fan production pilfer from 'official' culture, but the reverse also takes place, so that the lines between the 'official' and the 'unofficial' are never easy to distinguish clearly.

The second section addresses the role of music (and other sounds) within video games, now one of the most popular forms of entertainment media. Whilst this increasingly important cultural form is now the subject of growing academic research, the role of sound has not gained extensive attention. It would be a mistake to say that no work has been done in this area, but more work certainly needs to be done. In Chapter 3 Rod Munday provides an overview of how video-game music can be approached. By outlining some of the functions of music within video games, Munday warns against musicological approaches as they tend to overlook how music can contribute to the emotional experience of the gamer, and also define music itself rather restrictively (so that some essential sounds would be rejected as 'non-musical'). For Munday, music in video games functions in three important ways: environmentally (contributing to the construction of game space), immersively (contributing to a player becoming emotionally involved in the gaming experience) and diegetically (contributing to a game's narrative). In the next chapter, Zach Whalen looks at some of the similarities and differences between video-game music and film music, using *Silent Hill* as a case study through which to explore such issues. Whalen rejects rigidly semiotic and narratological approaches to video-game music, preferring instead a 'unit operations' approach that theorises video-game music in the context of the gaming environment as it interacts with a number of other codes.

In section three a broader theme is covered: performance and presentation within musical multimedia. Many performances of music can be considered to be multimedia events in terms of the live presentation of musical performers and also, on occasions, the use of other visual material such as film and video accompaniment. In addition, sonic information often plays an important – yet rarely scrutinised – role within the presentation of cultural objects, such as within galleries and museums. My own chapter looks at the theme of sonic art, in which sound objects are often presented within gallery spaces or as site-specific installations. The chapter presents an overview of this contested term, focusing on historical developments and specific concepts that have been addressed within such works. It goes on to consider how digital technologies impact upon sonic art, particularly through interactive networks and the emergence of virtual sound objects. In Chapter 6 Jem Kelly discusses the 'inter-medial' pop concert, where live performance is combined with virtual representations of some kind, and how these can impact on what actually constitutes a live performance. Through looking at instances of inter-medial performances by the Velvet Underground, Madonna and – in more extensive detail – Gorriliaz, Kelly analyses how such concerts raise a number of questions related to issues such as authenticity, presence and authorship. Contrastingly, Randolph Jordan analyses a very different theme in live performance in Chapter 7: the presentation of 'acousmatic' music, where sounds are produced to be listened to intently and 'in their own right', without any visual associations. In many ways such an ideal runs counter to musical multimedia; however, Jordon goes onto stress how such an ideal is difficult to achieve within a visually dominant culture. Building on the writings of R. Murray Schafer and Hildegard Westerkamp amongst others, he goes onto analyse the ways in which such music can be presented live without attempting to deny non-sonic elements.

Section four of the volume looks at the area of production and consumption, particularly in relation to a new range of musical multimedia that has grown in tandem with the growth in digital technologies. In Chapter 8 Lee Tsang focuses on the use of sound and music in websites, a generally underresearched component in the visually dominated field of web research. Tsang considers the types of sounds used in websites and draws on psychological studies of sound response to look at how website designers may harness sound in the light of the types of content they are providing and their intended target audience. He goes onto look at some of these issues through analysing McDonald's international websites (which in particular allows him to focus on cross-cultural issues) and other examples in order to explore sonic-aesthetic problems faced by website producers. In Chapter 9 Dan Laughey focuses on how young people use music in everyday life, in an empirical study. Surveying a range of ways in which young people not only listen to music, but also gain information about it and attain access to it, he focuses less upon 'alternative' music consumption (which has tended to dominate such studies) than upon more 'ordinary' uses. He notes how music use often bridges the private and public spaces of young people's lives, and also looks at how different technologies are often associated with different uses. Finally, in Chapter 10 Kieran Kelly employs a political economy approach to scrutinise the phenomenal success of the Apple iPod. Whilst many chapters in this book focus on how technologies are taken up by users, Kelly reminds us that the ways in which technologies are designed and manufactured nevertheless frame how they are taken up, even if they do not determine such uses. Countering hyperbolic coverage of the iPod as an innovative technology, Kelly stresses how integration and competition, rather than innovation, are key to a product's success within a capitalist economy.

Whilst this volume cannot cover all instances of musical multimedia or the different methodological approaches to studying the field, it does present a diverse array of subjects and methodological approaches. This is in keeping with my belief that an area as broad as this, which is constantly in transition, requires a flexible approach. I am not convinced that all aspects of musical multimedia can be encompassed by a restricted methodological approach, because of the sheer variety of instances that can be related to such a broad field. This volume will be useful for those interested in the ways sonic culture is embedded within a variety of media instances. As this is a relatively underresearched area, I hope that it will also stimulate further research into related topics.

Notes

1. Of course, the different contexts within which a work is encountered *will* affect the type of experience, and hence its meaning. I don't think, however, these can be said to alter the meaning of the work *radically* in the same way as, for example, a live performance of a song can be radically different from a recorded work. Of course, it may be the case that the scale of image, the sound quality, and the individual's position in relation to the screen and speakers will alter experiences of the same film from one medium to another. At the same time, watching the same film in the same position at the same cinema will also result in a different experience, if only in the sense that the individual experiencing the film cannot interact in exactly the same way twice.
2. Of course, even determining the respective semantic contribution of different elements is fraught with problems, as it may be the case that different semantic levels will be concentrated on by some more than others.
3. Their site addresses are: http://www.pitchforkmedia.com and http://www.stylusmagazine.com. It should be noted that *Stylus* also covers film, though more space is devoted to music.
4. Audio editors include software such as GoldWave Digital Audio Editor, ProTools and SoundForge. Sequencing/programming software includes a variety of different programs including Ableton Live, Cakewalk, Cubase and Reason.

References

Bull, M. (2005), 'No Dead Air! The iPod and the Culture of Mobile Listening', *Leisure Studies*, Vol. 24, No. 4, October, pp. 343–55.

Chapman, N., and Chapman, J. (2000), *Digital Multimedia* (Chichester and New York: Wiley).

Cook, N. (1998), *Music: A Very Short Introduction* (Oxford: Oxford University Press).
—— (2000), *Analysing Musical Multimedia* (Oxford: Oxford University Press).

Davidson, A. (2003), 'Music and Multimedia: Theory and History', *Music Analysis*, Vol. 22, No. 3, pp. 341–465.

Hosokawa, S. (1984), 'The Walkman Effect', *Popular Music*, Vol. 4, pp. 165–80.

Katz, M. (2004), *Capturing Sound: How Technology Has Changed Music* (Berkeley, CA: University of California Press).

Manovich, L. (2002), *The Language of New Media* (Cambridge, MA: MIT Press).

Packer, R., and Jordan, K. (2002), 'Overture', in R. Packer and K. Jordan (eds), *Multimedia: From Wagner to Virtual Reality* (New York and London: Norton). Online at http://www.artmuseum.net/w2vr/overture/overture.html (accessed January 2007).

Southall, N. (2005), 'Soulseeking', *Stylus Magazine*, 9 September, http://www.stylusmagazine.com/articles/weekly_article/soulseeking.htm (accessed January 2007).

Young, R. (2003), 'Like Falling off a Blog', *Guardian*, 19 November, p. 10.

SECTION ONE:

FANDOM AND MUSIC VIDEOS

1. REFRAMING FAN VIDEOS

Angelina I. Karpovich

Our relationship with pop songs is, in some ways, markedly different to our relationships with other forms of popular culture. First, this relationship is becoming less and less material: the rapidly expanding market in portable digital music players has ensured that popular music is increasingly becoming obtained, stored, and otherwise traded purely as data files, rather than as tangible physical property. Music is ideally suited to electronic storage and playback, unlike other entertainment forms, where true portability is still some way off. Films and television programmes, for example, are still largely rooted to the domestic setting, with portable video technology encumbered by either unsatisfyingly small screens or lack of true portability due to size and short battery life. Music is also freely available 'on the move', most commonly through radio broadcasts, in a way in which other forms of popular culture are not; music radio can and does serve as 'background noise' to other activities, while the parallel activities of watching television, reading newspapers or magazines, or even browsing the Internet, demand their audiences' full attention.

Secondly, the notion of authorship in popular music appears far more diffused than it is in other popular culture forms.[1] The emergence of such phenomena as cover versions, remixes, karaoke and most recently, mashups, points to popular music having a far more transient relationship with the notion of an identifiable single 'author' than other media, with the writer(s), performers, publishers and record companies all having varying sets of institutional, legal and associative claims to the individual songs. Pop music, in particular, can be said to dispense with the singular figure of the 'author' altogether, replacing it with the far more marketable figure of the 'performer', who may then take on aspects of authorship through the performance. For example, Lewis (1993) illustrates the explicit distinction between 'ownership' and 'authorship' of pop songs in her discussion of Cyndi Lauper's reworking of the original lyrics of 'Girls Just Wanna Have Fun'. Public perceptions and commercial considerations regarding the authorship of pop songs frequently diverge: an obvious example being one of the most successful pop songs of the 1990s, 'Baby One More Time'; despite the song's immense popularity, the name of its writer/ producer, Max Martin, is almost unknown within mainstream popular culture, while the name of its original performer, Britney Spears, is ubiquitous. Pop songs are remixed or covered (in both cases, essentially remade) far more frequently than any other popular cultural form. These practices destabilise the notion that any one version of a pop song can ever be 'definitive', and with it, the attendant notion of the song having a singular 'author'.

Thus, the notion of authorship has long been in flux in popular music, or at least in the way popular music has been perceived by its public. Music video continues this tradition, by focusing ever more closely on the figure of the performer, who in most cases becomes central to the video. In the majority of cases, the performer is not only highly visible within the video, but actually lip-synchs the song, thus not only achieving what seems like a direct mode of address to the viewer, but also verifying his or her claim to the 'authorship' of the song. While a number of music video directors have achieved prominence with a 'signature' style which may be discussed in terms of cinematic auteurism (most notably, perhaps, Hype Williams, but also Nigel Dick, Mark Romanek, Stephane Sednaoui), and a smaller number have indeed made a successful transition from music video to feature film (David Fincher, Spike Jonze, Michel Gondry, McG), music videos remain firmly associated with the song and its performer rather than with the creator of the visual imagery. Thus, Goodwin (1993a) makes the distinction between 'authorship' and 'auteurism' in relation to the music video, arguing that the latter term is particularly irrelevant to the form. In some cases, multiple music videos are produced for the same song (for different national markets, or for the reissue of a single, or, in rarer cases, for pre- and post-watershed versions of controversial or graphic songs), which further destabilises the notion of the music video as a singular authorial text. Notably, the transience of authorship in music video is underscored by the director Mark Romanek: 'If I make a music video a hit, if it makes it into heavy rotation and becomes entrenched in the culture, I still don't own it or stand a chance to reap anything from it. I don't like that at all' (cited in Reiss and Feineman 2000: 213).

At first glance, the emergence of fan videos appears to be closely linked to the development of the music video. Like other forms of fan production, fan videos (or 'vids' for short) are produced by non-professionals who have been inspired by the source media texts, and are primarily intended for and circulated within the social networks of fandom. Typically, a fan video is a relatively complex montage, in which short visual excerpts from one or more source media texts are edited together to the soundtrack of a (usually well-known) song, most often one which had not previously been associated with the source media text. The visuals are decontextualised from their original source: a vid can focus on a secondary character, giving them a prominence which they may not have had in the original narrative; it can dramatically juxtapose the characters' actions with the lyrics of the song, reframing the characters and their relationships and thus altering their significance; or it can bring together characters from multiple sources in a way which would never have been possible in the original media texts. A vid can explore 'alternative universes', where, for example, characters who were killed off in the source text are still alive and still part of the ongoing narrative. A popular genre is the 'ship' (shortened version of 'relationship') vid, in which footage of two characters who may or may not be romantically involved in the source texts is edited to suggest a romantic relationship between them; these videos tend to be accompanied by songs whose lyrics are centred on love and longing.

Of course, not all fan videos are such radical reworkings of the original narrative themes: some fan video creators, or 'vidders', choose to produce videos in which narratively significant moments from the source texts are edited together to emphasise the most spectacular or dramatic aspects of the source narrative, or ones which have been deemed to have the greatest significance for the fan communities. Another popular vid genre is that of the 'character study', in which, as the name suggests, the focus is usually on a single character's journey through the narrative; these videos distil the character's development over the course of the entire narrative (which, in the case of a television series, can run to several years) into a three-minute clip, or, alternatively, expand upon a character's single, perhaps brief, narrative action, once again using the sonic and lyrical elements of the accompanying song to illustrate the character's emotional state.

Fan Videos and Technology

Technologically enabled by the rise of domestic video recording technology, which largely coincided with the launch of MTV in 1981, fan videos were a new form of creative expression for fans of film and television programmes. Contemporary fan videos are made using different methods and techniques to the undeniably cumbersome process of using one or more domestic VHS recorders and laser disk players to select, edit and synch the relevant footage from the source texts (first described by Jenkins 1992). Even with such basic tools, however, some vidders attempted to alter not only the order but also the structure of the original sequences, manipulating and modding the VHS machines to speed up or slow down the footage and to create more advanced editing effects such as freeze-frame, jump-cuts and reverse-motion. Subsequently, the videos were distributed through fan networks via word of mouth and at fan conventions. With new advances in computer hardware and software, contemporary fan video artists draw upon a range of domestic, semi-professional and professional technologies in order to create their works.

Fan video production is just one example of media-literate fans using the Internet to disseminate and obtain technical knowledge which had previously been considered 'specialised', and adapting existing technologies and skills to sustain and promote fan communities (Karpovich 2006). Instead of video recorders, vidders now select their source clips from DVDs and from television shows available for download via both official sources and peer-to-peer sharing networks. Clips are then edited using a range of software programs, from the widely available consumer programs such as Windows Movie Maker and iMovie to the professional-standard editing packages like Adobe Premiere and Final Cut Pro. The completed videos are made available in a range of ways: via peer-to-peer networks, as direct downloads from the vidders' personal web-sites, as files uploaded to online vidding communities and archives, and as files shared on free video hosting sites such as YouTube.com.

In recent years, the rate of production of fan videos has increased exponentially, enabled by technological advances as much as by the increasing numbers of participants in fan vid communities. Hundreds of new fan vids are created every year, which means that the current rate of production of amateur fan videos matches, if not in fact surpasses, the rate of production of professional music videos. As well as becoming ever more prominent at media fan conventions, fan video creators have organised their own annual convention: VividCon, established in Chicago in 2002 and currently lasting three days, showcases new and 'classic' vids and enables vidders and other fans to discuss individual vids, exchange creative ideas and technical tips, show off their skills, and participate in informal workshops on the interplay between the aesthetic and technical dimensions of the form.

Despite such considerable technological advances, vids have retained many, if not all, of their original formal characteristics. In this type of montage, the visuals tend not only to follow closely, but to match, the verbal cues contained in the lyrics of the song. As Jenkins points out, using the example of a vid which combines the visuals from the original series of *Star Trek* with the song 'You Needed Me', the line 'I cried a tear' shows Spock crying, or 'You held my hand' shows Kirk and Spock holding hands' (1992: 244). However, such instances are not merely literal. Rather, as Jenkins argues, they contain the particular pleasures of the form, which focus 'on the fascination in watching familiar images wrenched free from their previous contexts and assigned alternative meanings.

The pleasure comes in putting words in the characters' mouths and making the series represent subtexts it normally represses' (pp. 227–8). The characters' glances and gestures, remembered from the original media texts, become 'decontextualised' and whole sequences 'assume new significance when they are stripped of their original narrative context and divorced from the delivered dialog' (p. 228). Although Jenkins is too concerned with the fan relationship to the visuals from the source media texts to consider the audiences' potential perceptions of the songs used in fan vids, it is fair to assume that they too may be granted a new significance through recontextualisation.

Fan Video and Music Video: Coincidence or Convergence?

The creators of fan videos are simultaneously working within at least three arenas which are traditionally seen as distinct within contemporary popular culture. They are, to use Jenkins's term, 'poaching' the content of films and television programmes; they are also reusing popular songs, paying particular attention to the rhythm of the beat while recontextualising them through juxtaposition, in a manner which is conceptually similar to audio remixing and the more recent phenomenon of 'mashups';[2] and they appear to be approximating some of the conventions of the music video format.

However, according to Jenkins, fan video artists 'insist that their works bear little or no direct relationship to MTV's commercial music videos' (1992: 232). In Jenkins's view, the difference between fan vids and music videos lies in the entirely different approaches to the role and image of the song's performer within the video:

> If MTV treats the performer's voice as the central organizing mechanism, nondiegetic performers play little or no role within fan videos. Fan viewers are often totally disinterested in the identity of the original singer(s) but are prepared to see the musical performance as an expression of the thoughts, feelings, desires, and fantasies of the fictional character(s). . . . The performer's personality must be effaced so that the singer may speak more effectively on behalf of the fictional character. (pp. 235–6)

Although there is obviously some truth to Jenkins's assertions regarding the different emphases of the fan vid and the music video, his view of the latter is based on such outdated sources as Fiske (1987) and Kaplan (1985, 1987), both of whom wrote about MTV and music videos predominantly in terms of 'non-narrativity' and 'postmodernism', resulting in what has since been recognised as a frustratingly myopic and ahistorical framework. Subsequent scholarship has attempted a more nuanced approach to music video, recognising that the format draws upon, or at least allows for, a far more diverse range of styles and modes of address than had previously been imagined.

For example, Gow (1992) draws upon the work of Bordwell and Thompson (1986) in order to trace different formal systems of the music video, arguing that music videos can contain narrative, associational and abstract elements, though in his sample of the most popular videos of the 1980s, these elements still tended to be secondary to the performative aspects of the videos. Goodwin (1993a) opposes the prevalent description of intertexuality, or 'the incorporation of other texts into music video' (p. 160), as postmodern pastiche. Rather, he outlines a continuum of possible positions within music video, which includes social criticism, parody, self-reflexivity, pastiche, promotion, and homage to the texts being 'cited' in the video. Meanwhile, Vernallis (2004) argues that music videos have tended to be interpreted as 'failed narratives' only because they have been analysed according to the criteria of traditional film theory, rather than as a complex synergy of both cinematic and sonic features which addresses the spectator/listener in a way which is particular to the form. Finally, Mundy (1999) points out that the music video format itself pre-dates MTV, tracing its roots from both the popularity of promotional clips in the television chart shows of the mid-1960s, and the extensive cinematic and televisual adventures of the Beatles and subsequently, the Monkees. Indeed, the origins of the form may be traced even earlier, for example to the much-publicised and controversial television appearances of Elvis Presley in the 1950s. The development of colour television throughout the 1950s and 1960s coincided with the arrival of the first broadcast-standard video recorder in 1956, which allowed pre-recorded promotional music clips to be broadcast during chart and variety shows. Mundy makes an explicit link between this emergence of the new format and technological advances in film and video production, 'with a reduction in cost and increase in availability' (p. 206). Once we accept that music videos are thus more complex and less generalisable than Jenkins, following Fiske's and Kaplan's analyses, allows for, we can begin to readdress the relationship between the music video and the fan video forms, since a comparison of their similarities may be just as illuminating as a comparison of their differences.

Aside from the apparently near-identical role played by new technologies in enabling new visual forms (the growing availability of domestic video recorders in Jenkins's account of the emergence of fan videos in the early 1980s and new advances in film and video, which, according to Mundy, enabled the emergence of the music promo in the mid-1960s), most of these similarities are aesthetic and conceptual, rather than technological. The interrelationship between music video and film and television is very firmly established in popular culture, primarily through extensive intertextual referencing of the latter forms in music videos. In most cases, this is achieved through appropriating a distinct and recognisable visual iconography, rather than the narrative elements of the original media texts; examples of such referencing are very common.[3] Moreover, the intertextual references are not restricted to fictional narratives: R.E.M.'s 'Everybody Hurts', Eminem's 'My Name Is' and Placebo's 'Pure Morning' all feature the iconography and conventions of television news bulletins. These are just a few of the more straightforward examples, and do not include videos that address a whole genre, rather than a single text, as in R. Kelly's 'Down Low', which follows the visual conventions of the gangster film, Michael Jackson's 'Thriller', which pastiches the horror genre, the Beastie Boys' 'Sabotage', which recalls 1970s police shows, and Bjork's 'It's All So Quiet', which employs some of the visual conventions of the Technicolor-era musicals, or those videos that address a text whose significance goes beyond the strictly cinematic, as in Meat Loaf's 'I Would Do Anything For Love', which is clear in its allusion to the story of Beauty and the Beast, but doesn't specifically reference any of the individual Beauty and the Beast film adaptations. Even more tangential, yet still recognisably cinematic, is the use of imagery associated with surveillance (e.g., Duran Duran's 'A View to a Kill', Justin Timberlake's 'Cry Me a River') or with dreaming (e.g., A-ha's 'Take on Me', Busted's 'What I Go to School For'); these are amongst the most commonly used themes in music videos (Kinder 1987).

At the same time, as Mundy (1999) points out, popular songs have become a key part of film marketing strategy, so that the resultant music videos promote not only the musical artists but also the films associated with their songs. Film clips become a part of the music video, both decontextualised and fixed within a new context, especially if the song's performer also features in the film (as in the case of Whitney Houston's 'I Will Always Love You' and a large proportion of Madonna's video oeuvre). Similarly, even when not promoting their own films, film actors have often featured (as 'guest stars') in music videos, further blurring the line separating the two visual formats. And of course, actors can and have actually become pop singers, and vice versa (Dickinson 2001). At the same time, the visual influences began to travel in the opposite direction, with films and television programmes drawing inspiration from the so-called 'MTV aesthetic'; in her definition of the term, Dickinson (2001) focuses on 'the submission of editing to the customary tempi of popular music, a presentation of shots which defies the standard broadcast rhythm of around three seconds minimum each'. The secondary characteristics of the 'MTV aesthetic' may be described as an emphasis on visual spectacle, self-consciously rapid editing, and the use of rock (or pop) music to accentuate tension. These elements were combined in the mid-1980s in *Miami Vice* (1984), the creators of which were explicitly using techniques associated with MTV in order to appeal to a younger audience; indeed, the working title of the programme during its development was *MTV Cops* (Mundy 1999). Subsequently, the stylistic influence of music video and, by extension, of MTV can clearly be seen in such diverse and yet successful cinematic and televisual texts as *Top Gun* (1986), *CSI* (2000), *William Shakespeare's Romeo + Juliet*

(1996) and *The Fast and the Furious* (2001). Moreover, if we accept Mundy's contention that the origins of the music video can be traced at least as far back as the 1960s, then a similar point could be made in relation to the use of music in film and television. Non-diegetic music had been used for dramatic effect and had dictated the pace of the editing long before the emergence of a recognisable 'MTV aesthetic'; an obvious example is the famous sequence from the final episode of *The Prisoner* (1968), in which a stylised machine-gun battle is juxtaposed with the Beatles' 'All You Need Is Love'. This heavy interdependence of popular music and film and television, and at least some of the stylistic elements which are now recognised as parts of the 'MTV aesthetic', actually pre-date the emergence of MTV, but MTV has foregrounded a range of elements of visual style and focused the attentions of audiences (and analysts) upon them.

Thus, visual intertextuality is prevalent, if not inherent, in the music video; the use of intertextual references to films and television programmes appears to cut across song styles and musical genres. In most cases, there is no obvious link between the style or lyrical content of a song and the media text referenced in the music video. However, the visual referencing serves a variety of purposes, from practical ones such as showcasing the skills of the video's director and ensuring that the musicians enjoy the shoot, to conceptual ones, like raising the musicians' profiles and providing the pleasure of recognition for the audience. In this latter instance, the 'rhetorical dimensions' of the music video, its particular modes of communication and the ways in which it 'invite[s] the viewer to construct meanings' (Gow 1992: 41) find a direct parallel with Jenkins's account of the experience of watching recontextualised images in fan videos: '[The] videos play upon the reader's ability to see these images as simultaneously contributing to a new narrative and bearing memories of their status in a very different context. . . . The pleasure of the form centers on the fascination in watching familiar images wrenched free from their previous contexts and assigned alternative meanings' (1992: 227).

ARE FAN VIDEOS UNIQUE?

In his account of fan videos (and of fan culture in general) Jenkins uses Bakhtin's notion of heteroglossia and his rejection of the notion of original authorship in favour of a conception of the writer as always already confronting a history of previous authorship: 'Fan music videos vividly illustrate the aesthetic regulation of heteroglossia. Using home videotape recorders . . . fan artists appropriate "found footage" from broadcast television and re-edit it to express their particular slant on the program, linking series images to music similarly appropriated from commercial culture' (1992: 225). What makes fan videos unique is their double appropriation and reworking of texts: '[N]either the sights nor the sounds found in most videos originate with the fan artists;

the creator's primary contribution, in most cases, comes in the imaginative juxtaposition of someone else's words and images' (p. 225).

Once again, despite its claim for the uniqueness of the fan video form, this account is strikingly similar to the founding principles of music video, as articulated by MTV's first vice-president of programming, Robert Pittman, back in 1981: 'It's ridiculous to think that you have two forms of entertainment – your stereo and your TV – that have nothing to do with one another. What we're doing is marrying those two forms so that they work together in unison. . . . We're talking about creating a new form using existing technologies' (cited in Goodwin 1993b: 50).

Thus, upon closer examination of the music video form, there appear to be some significant formal and conceptual parallels between fan videos and music videos, which apparently have not been acknowledged by either fandom scholars or the fans themselves. Leaving aside the question of the validity of Jenkins's apparent extrapolation from the opinions of two vidders to fandom as a whole, the denial of a link between fan vids and music videos can be explained as any one of several rhetorical and conceptual manoeuvres. First, the disavowal of music videos allows fan vids a claim to the far more flattering status of an original, rather than derivative, form, within which the relationship between fan vids and the source media texts can thus be framed as a radical reworking or a playful yet sophisticated pastiche, rather than as a straightforward derivation. Here, the disassociation from music videos is employed as a potential marker of the relative complexity and sophistication of fan videos as a distinct cultural form. Secondly, the popular perception of music television, and particularly of MTV, as one of the most lowbrow and disposable contemporary cultural products, and one apparently aimed predominantly at teenagers (Sun and Lull 1986), may have prompted fan vidders to try to dissociate themselves from an area which attracted even greater socio-cultural stigma than that of fandom itself (Jensen 1992). Within this framework, the insistence on the dissociation from the music video can be read as more of a defensive manoeuvre, intended to protect the status of media fans and fandom from any further potential accusations of lowbrow excess. Thirdly, there is little doubt that the early music videos were unambiguous promotional vehicles for the musical artists and the song; the aesthetic emphasis on memorable visuals, striking composition and narrative was a later development of the form. Although in this respect, the aims of fan videos were, and remain, quite different, it would be wrong to dismiss music videos as entirely commercial and therefore devoid of the kind of meaning that is invested in fan videos by fan producers and fan audiences. As Sandvoss (2005) notes, music fans can be just as emotionally invested in their fandom as fans of film and television, if not more so; a music video featuring a favourite performer, then, can be a meaningful and significant addition to their fandom for some viewers, while remaining a crass commercial object for others.

It should be noted that the actual techniques of juxtaposing 'found' (that is, not originally produced by the video-maker) visuals with the soundtrack of a popular song appear to be shared by several distinct practices: along with fan videos, similar techniques were used in the 'scratch video' genre, which was briefly in vogue among British visual artists in the early 1980s (Abt 1987), and are currently popular as domestic entertainment in, for example, Morocco, where compilations of locally edited videos set to local and Western hits are distributed commercially (Langlois 2004).

If fan videos differ from these other 'non-professional' video texts, and indeed from professional music videos, it is not primarily because of differences in production practices or industrial contexts, which are challenged by new video editing and distribution technologies (it could be argued that some of the industrial and budgetary differences between music videos and fan vids are already rendered irrelevant by the indiscriminate nature of online distribution, when, for example, they inevitably appear side by side on YouTube.com). Rather, of all the audiovisual forms mentioned above, fan videos are the only form which originates and flourishes within a fan community – a community based on strong emotional investment in the visual imagery from which the video is assembled. In fan videos, the figure of the musical performer, and in most cases the song itself, recede into the background, while the visuals gain thematic supremacy, as both the motivation for, and the focus of, the overall fan artefact. Fan videos break down the visual and narrative flow of the 'original' TV show, and, for the most part, tend to dispense with the dialogue or at the very least recontextualise it.

Yet at the same time, the music takes some precedence over the image, in the sense that the visuals are edited to fit in with the pace and timbre of the music. Thus, in the creation of fan vids, the music is chosen before the visuals and dictates which visual segments are used at which point. Inasmuch as the genre of the music dictates the theme, and genre, of the video ('romantic' videos are made to the soundtrack of ballads, humourous videos are produced to the soundtrack of parodic songs), the music can be said to *articulate* emotions which may not be sufficiently articulated (or indeed apparent) in the original text. This would fit with both Feuer's (1982) and Laing's (2000) analyses of the role of the musical numbers in classic Hollywood musicals, where, they argue, music is used to convey an emotional level which would be impossible to express through dialogue or through any other cinematic element. If we consider André Bazin's observation that the use of montage editing declined, and eventually disappeared, from film with the introduction of sound, then, as Vernallis (2004) argues, the essentially 'silent' image track of the music video easily lends itself to the classic montage technique in which meaning is created through the juxtaposition of unrelated images, rather than being contained within them. As Bazin originally put it, 'The combinations are infinite. But the only thing they have in common is the fact that they suggest an idea by means of a metaphor or by an association of ideas' (2004: 26).

Having emerged at roughly the same time, and sharing a similarly complex relationship with the media of film and television, music videos and fan videos have more in common than has previously been acknowledged by either the fan video producers or theorists of fan culture. Although the practices of the production, distribution and consumption of fan videos remain distinct from those of mainstream media production, the rush to claim them as 'unique' betrays a disregard for the multiple ways in which images and sounds are used and reused within a media-saturated world. Film and television fans, as highly media-literate consumers of the visual media, have at their disposal the capacity to absorb, internalise and critically evaluate the full range of cinematic codes used in conveying meaning in mainstream media texts. Fan videos are not only a creative expression of fandom and a means of sustaining fan communities by contributing new content, but also the result of their creators' cumulative media experience, in which aesthetic and conceptual influences from a variety of texts, genres and forms result in multi-layered texts that are steeped not only in the immediate context of the source media text, but in the very same audiovisual aesthetic that has also produced, among other forms, the music video.

NOTES

1. Although the notion of authorship in other media forms is by no means concrete, it is comparatively easier to establish authorship in, for example, film (where auteur theory conventionally locates it with the director) or popular serial and series television (where, conversely, it has tended to be identified with the figure of the writer-producer, e.g. Gene Roddenberry, Aaron Spelling, Steven Bochco, David E. Kelley, Dick Wolf, Joss Whedon, J. J. Abrams, etc. in the US, and more recently, Phil Redmond, Russell T. Davies, Paul Abbott, etc. in the UK) than in pop music.
2. 'Mashups' are unofficial and unsanctioned remixes, in which two or more songs are mixed together (see Gunderson 2004).
3. For instance, the Pretenders pretended to be in an episode of *The Avengers* in 'Don't Get Me Wrong'; Blur employed the iconographies of *Last Year in Marienbad* in 'To the End' and *A Clockwork Orange* in 'The Universal'; Madonna referenced *Gentlemen Prefer Blondes* in 'Material Girl', *Looking for Mr Goodbar* in 'Bad Girl' and, more tangentially, *Metropolis* in 'Express Yourself'; Maroon 5 remade *The Graduate* in 'She Will Be Loved'; Dr Dre and Tupac Shakur referenced *Mad Max* in 'California Love'; the Smashing Pumpkins performed a homage to *Voyage to the Moon* in 'Tonight, Tonight'; Weezer physically inserted themselves into the original footage of *Happy Days* in 'Buddy Holly'; Texas utilised both the iconography and the disjointed narrative style of *Chunking Express* in 'Halo'; and Will Young performed a pastiche of *Top Gun* in 'Switch It On'.

REFERENCES

Abt, D. (1987), 'Music Video: Impact of the Visual Dimension', in J. Lull (ed.), *Popular Music and Communication* (London: Sage).

Bazin, A. (2004), *What Is Cinema?* (Berkeley, CA: University of California Press).

Bordwell, D., and Thompson, K. (1986), *Film Art: An Introduction* (2nd edn) (New York: Knopf).

Dickinson, K. (2001), 'Pop, Speed and the "MTV Aesthetic" in Recent Teen Films', *Scope*, June, http://www.nottingham.ac.uk/film/journal/articles/pop-speed-and-mtv.htm (accessed November 2006).

Feuer, J. (1982), *The Hollywood Musical* (London: Macmillan).

Fiske, J. (1987), *Television Culture* (London and New York: Routledge).

Frith, S., Goodwin, A., and Grossberg, L. (eds) (1993), *Sound and Vision: The Music Video Reader* (London and New York: Routledge).

Goodwin, A. (1993a), *Dancing in the Distraction Factory: Music Television and Popular Culture* (London: Routledge).

—— (1993b), 'Fatal Distractions: MTV Meets Postmodern Theory', in S. Frith, A. Goodwin and L. Grossberg (eds), *Sound and Vision: The Music Video Reader* (London and New York: Routledge).

Gow, J. (1992), 'Music Video as Communication: Popular Formulas and Emerging Genres', *Journal of Popular Culture*, Vol. 26, No. 2, Fall 1992, pp. 41–70.

Gunderson, P. A. (2004), 'Danger Mouse's *Grey Album*, Mash-Ups, and the Age of Composition', *Postmodern Culture*, Vol. 15, No. 1, September, http://muse.jhu.edu/journals/pmc/v015/15.1gunderson.html (accessed November 2006).

Jenkins, H. (1992), *Textual Poachers: Television Fans and Participatory Culture* (London: Routledge).

Jensen, J. (1992), 'Fandom as Pathology: The Consequences of Characterisation', in L. A. Lewis (ed.), *The Adoring Audience: Fan Culture and Popular Media* (London: Routledge).

Kaplan, E. A. (1985), 'A Post-Modern Play of the Signifier? Advertising, Pastiche, and Schizophrenia in Music Television', in P. Drummond and R. Patterson (eds), *Television in Transition* (London: BFI).

—— (1987), *Rocking Around the Clock: Music Television, Postmodernism, and Consumer Culture* (London: Methuen).

Karpovich, A. I. (2006), 'The Audience as Editor: The Role of Beta Readers in Online Fan Fiction Communities', in K. Helleksen and K. Busse (eds), *Fan Fiction and Fan Communities in the Age of the Internet: New Essays* (Jefferson: McFarland).

Kinder, M. (1987), 'Music Video and the Spectator: Television, Ideology, and Dream', in H. Newcombe (ed.) *Television: The Critical View* (4th edn) (Oxford: Oxford University Press).

Laing, H. (2000), 'Emotion by Numbers: Music, Song and the Musical', in B. Marshall and R. Stilwell (eds), *Musicals: Hollywood and Beyond* (Exeter: Intellect).

Langlois, T. (2004), 'Music, Images and Technology in Morocco', paper presented at the 'Off-Screen Spaces: Regionalism and Globalised Cultures', conference, University of Ulster, Coleraine, 29 July.

Lewis, L. A. (1993), 'Being Discovered: The Emergence of Female Address on MTV', in S. Frith, A. Goodwin and L. Grossberg (eds), *Sound and Vision: The Music Video Reader* (London and New York: Routledge).

Mundy, J. (1999), *Popular Music on Screen: From Hollywood Musical to Music Video* (Manchester: Manchester University Press).

Reiss, S., and Feineman, N. (eds) (2000), *Thirty Frames Per Second: The Revolutionary Art of the Music Video* (New York: Abrams).

Sandvoss, C. (2005), *Fans: The Mirror of Consumption* (Cambridge: Polity).

Sun, S.-W., and Lull, J. (1986), 'The Adolescent Audience for Music Videos and Why They Watch', *Journal of Communication*, Vol. 36, No. 1, Winter, pp. 115–25.

Vernallis, C. (2004), *Experiencing Music Video: Aesthetics and Cultural Context* (New York: Columbia University Press).

2. CASE STUDY: ANIME MUSIC VIDEOS

Dana Milstein

When on 1 August 1981 at 12:01 a.m. the Buggles' 'Video Killed the Radio Star' aired as MTV's first music video, its lyrics parodied the very media presenting it: 'We can't rewind, we've gone too far, . . . put the blame on VTR.' Influenced by J. G. Ballard's 1960 short story 'The Sound Sweep', Trevor Horn's song voiced anxiety over the dystopian, artificial world developing as a result of modern technology. Ballard's story described a world in which naturally audible sound, particularly song, is considered to be noise pollution; a sound sweep removes this acoustic noise on a daily basis while radios broadcast a silent, rescored version of music using a richer, ultrasonic orchestra that subconsciously produces positive feelings in its listeners. Ballard was particularly criticising technology's attempt to manipulate the human voice, by contending that the voice as a natural musical instrument can only be generated by 'non-mechanical means which the neruophonic engineer could never hope, or bother, to duplicate' (Ballard 2006: 150). Similarly, Horn professed anxiety over a world in which VTRs (video tape recorders) replace real-time radio music with simulacra of those performances. VTRs allowed networks to replay shows, to cater to different time zones, and to rerecord over material. Indeed, the first VTR broadcast occurred on 25 October 1956, when a recording of guest singer Dorothy Collins made the previous night was broadcast 'live' on the *Jonathan Winters Show*. The business of keeping audiences hooked 24 hours a day, 7 days a week, promoted the concept of quantity over quality: yesterday's information was irrelevant and could be permanently erased after serving its money-making purpose.

MTV chose in its defining moment to air a video that disapproved of the ineluctable transition from talent to marketability, to the extent that the band blows up a television in the video's closing moments. Horn remarks of making the video:

> 'Video' was a picture like a little screen play which we tried to illustrate with the music. We wanted the album to have that precise clinical feel – it's all part of the concept of the plastic age. But rather than totally rely on machines we took different musicians and made them play like machines. (Pike 1980)

MTV heralded a new era, symbolised by a spaceman stepping onto the moon and holding an MTV flag. Its first music videos were conceived as promotional clips for both artist and channel: saturation play and cross-promotional synergy (airing songs that plugged MTV in their lyrics) guaranteed that aired songs would become hits, in turn granting commercial success to band and channel alike.[1] MTV founder Bob Pittmann realised the advantage of marketing this radical medium to a naïve and rebellious youth culture, who became their target consumers. He once remarked that 'the strongest appeal you can make is emotionally. If you can get their emotions going, make them forget their logic, you've got them. At MTV, we don't shoot for the 14-year olds, we own them!'[2] Pittmann's revolution was, in fact, a marketing farce; as testimony to Ballard's and Horn's prophecies, music diminished in favour of manmade stage presence – the song and musicians became subordinate to the eye candy. These 'self-contained packages of sight and sound' eliminated the need for listeners to embellish songs with their own interpretation. Music videos were stigmatised as a simple 'electric fix' (Saltzman 2000:17).

Who would have surmised that two decades later youth culture would 'hand MTV's ass back to it on a silver plate', by announcing the death of video by Internet?[3] In 2000 eStudio created a music video titled 'Internet Killed the Video Star', which, producers Mark Cohn and Ken Martin explain, 'chronicles the explosive growth of a whole new medium . . . and leaves a lot of road kill in its wake – MTV, AOL, Bill Gates, and others'.[4] The music in the video is performed by a fictional group, the 'Broad Band', comprised of three animated girls performing with 'Internet' instruments – a computer keyboard as piano, mouse guitars, and Apple laptops as drums. The plot? A disgruntled, fat man is about to blow his head off while watching redundant MTV videos when a computer magically appears to provide an alternative: home-generated, quality music videos. The marketing ploy? Freely shared music and video files over the Internet and affordable editing software allow people to customise listening and viewing experiences for themselves. eStudio was broadcasting an already nascent, bastardised art form: the 'unofficial' music video.

Unofficial Music Videos (UMVs): A Parody of Status Quo Production

Unofficial music videos (UMVs) are created by 'ultimate fans'. They collate (mash up) footage from televised series, movies and traditional music videos with music they have sampled and possibly mixed at home. Although distributing their videos is considered copyright infringement, the unauthorised video is generally created under the premise that the music and video industries are drowning in a sea of greed and corporate politics that rarely promotes true talent or gives artists their monetary due for the intellectual property they create. Some groups, like Eclectic Method, argue that ignoring copyright is the essence of UMVs, not merely as a sign of rebellion, but with the aim of changing existing laws.[5] Others use them to promote political propaganda: one well-known example is Franklin Lopez's 'George Bush Don't Like Black People' (2005), which combines news footage from the Katrina disaster with a remix of Kanye West's song 'Gold Digger', subversively broadcasting a side-comment made by West that 'George Bush don't like black people'. In addition to news footage of black people stuck on their rooftops or children asking for food, the rewritten lyrics (set on top of West's original music) criticise Bush for his tardiness in visiting New Orleans after the Katrina aftermath, and the reappropriation of Katrina funds to the war in Iraq: 'Bush ain't a gold digger, but he ain't fuckin' with no broke niggas' and 'Come down Bush, come down come down' replace the original lyrics, which had criticised women for valuing wealth and manipulating their men for it.[6]

One universally shared ideology amongst creators of unofficial videos (UMVers) is that the sum of spliced parts remains greater than the originals from which those parts hailed. This process mirrors the traditional music-video technique of *commutation*, in which an object's 'cultural parameters' are jarred. A polar bear appearing in a Madonna video, for example, seems nonsensical – its appearance forces the viewer to question how a polar bear relates to the quintessential pop icon.[7] Danger Mouse's 'Grey Video' (directed by Ramon and Pedro, 2004) combined rapper Jay-Z's *Black Album* with the Beatles' *White Album* to emphasise the kindred relation between music and video of different genres and eras. The video mashes clips from the Beatles' *Hard Day's Night* with footage from a Jay-Z live performance, and features a computer-generated scene of John Lennon break-dancing and Ringo Starr scratching. Inadvertently, the album sparked an electronic civil disobedience protest known as Grey Tuesday (24 February 2004), during which participating websites allowed 24 hours to download Danger Mouse's album freely. They permitted this in defiance of current laws that limit sampling and using unlicensed music, and to promote copyright reform. Producers Ramon and Pedro offer little commentary on their 'Internet cult video', other than a disclaimer that it was made for experimental purposes, under the influence of drugs, and in homage to the Fab Four and Jay-Z. Brian Burton (Danger Mouse) also never intended his mixing and matching CD to spark legal controversy; he simply referred to his album as an exercise in 'deconstruction and reconstruction' (Paoletta 2004). Contrary to Eclectic Method's work, Burton did not want to delineate the problems with current music/videos. His focus remained on experimentation, on producing an avant garde collation for its own sake. When asked why the album stimulated such demand, he offered an even simpler response: 'I'm surprised that this many people like the CD. What I made was a f***ed-up recording. It confirms that people want that which they cannot have' (ibid.).

What do UMVers want that they cannot have? Certainly they no longer want their MTV! Rather, they crave the time, talent and freedom to re-envision music and video – to play, blur genres, contradict 'pop' meanings, and revitalise what has become a slowly dying, ever greedy, talent-lacking industry. Thus, the Internet has become home to many types of UMVers. Some use spliced clips to enhance music with poignant imagery (and vice versa). Others jumble or mock traditional associations in ways that result in funny, political or nonsensical videos. Still others focus exclusively on showcasing their technical prowess. Regardless of motivation or ability, the underlying intent is to form a community in which everyone and anyone can participate and contribute.

Anime Music Videos (AMVs): A Self-Referential Genre of UMVs

One unique faction of UMVers is the anime music video collective. While their talents and intent can be categorised among the broad range described above, AMVers must – in order to fit the AMV genre – limit their footage to anime-related media. Although they are more restricted in materials, AMVers hold the distinct advantage of industry ambivalence towards the 'pirating' and rendering of video footage in music video form. Most industry Anime Expos feature a panel on AMVs, and host a variety of fan contests including an 'AMV Iron Chef', which – on the model of the world-renowned cooking show – allots AMVers a set time limit to create and 'serve' their AMV to the audience for judgement in several categories. The anime industry only recently gained a foothold in the Western world, so AMVs are essentially free marketing: they not only promote awareness of anime products beyond the small base of hardcore fans, but also allow companies to recruit editors for making trailers and DVD extras.[8]

Vlad G. Pohnert's 'Orange Road' (September 1993) marked the first notable appearance of an AMV. Pohnert bridged Samantha Fox's remake hit 'I Only Wanna' Be with You' (1993) with clips from Matsumoto Izumi's *Orange Road* (1988) to create an AMV that represented a plot both works shared: intellectual boy falls in love with wilful girl and must overcome external hindrances (i.e. social class, distance, other boys and girls) to be together. Fox had debuted in the UK as the ultimate Page 3 girl – she was a topless model converted into pop star overnight. Her music video promo 'I Only' featured the singer in lingerie and leather, trying to tempt 'good boys' into giving her attention. *Orange Road* also appealed to 'young love' tastes and was among the most popular romantic comedy *shōnen* manga, often targeted at young male readers. Thus, Pohnert did not reinterpret the song or anime; ironically, his underground bootleg promoted the pop aspect of both. This video, while a pioneer in the UMV and AMV scenes, nevertheless mimics MTV's first phase of videos: it is a mood-enhancing narrative that *typifies* adolescent experience.[9] But – unlike Fox's and Izumi's work – this AMV was not created to *appeal* to teen sensibility for commercial gain; it was shown only in local clubs, as one fan's devotion to anime, as an exercise in the then uncommon art of making a video using the VCR-to-VCR method.

First-generation AMVers like Otaku Vengeance and Dark Rose Studios also produced works that merely took obscure, rebellious songs and perverted the original anime's intent. Otaku's 'Bitches', for example, features Mindless Self Indulgence amalgamated with the children's anime *Pokemon*, in which cute and fuzzy Pikachu lip-synchs the lyrics 'Bitches love me' cause they know that I can rock, and bitches love me 'cause they know that I can rhyme, and bitches love me' cause they know that I can fuck, and bitches love me 'cause they know that I'm on time.' Dark Rose Studios lodged Relient K's 'Pirates who Don't Do Anything' in *Cowboy Bebop* (1998), emphasising that the main protagonists as bounty hunters did little but 'lie around, and if you ask [them] to do anything, [they'll] just tell you, [they] don't do anything'.

Today's AMV producers are less interested in blanket reiterations and mockery of themes and generally fall into two camps: those interested in using effects to further the video's meaning, and those who use the video to further the appearance created by effects. Popular effects include color shifts, freeze-frames, cross-fades and inversions, and serve the purpose of synchronising music with video. Trickier, more impressive effects such as compositing allow the editor to fabricate a scene that doesn't exist in the source, by using bits and pieces from various anime. AMVs are typically categorised by one of the following approaches:

1 Storytelling: combines audio and video to tell a story, whether true to the original sources, or an entirely new story.
2 Exploratory: focuses on the message, not the character or narrative, to convey the editor's feeling about war, innocence, love, etc.
3 Examination: character development videos that examine an individual's personality, biography or relationships. Sometimes groups of characters are examined in terms of some commonality.[10]

From the viewer's perspective, AMVs are judged similarly to traditional music videos. Expressiveness, originality, sensory appeal and reviewability affect a viewer's appreciation of the work. Among these elements, reviewability – the desire to watch a music video more than once – is the most critical, because it reinforces the viewer's interest in the media being promoted (in the case of traditional videos, the music; in the case of AMVs, the anime).

Reviewability sounds easy enough to accomplish: simply make a video fun and visually appealing enough so that viewers will remain captivated. But the methods are more complicated and diverse. Traditional music-video-makers such as Nigel Dick, Michel Gondry, Mark Romanek and Spike Jonze use a variety of techniques to ensure reviewability. Dick promotes 'cool stuff' videos, 'crammed full of accessories and visual aids to disguise the lack of substance' (Saltzman 2000: 37); Gondry has been compared to Georges Méliès and labelled a special-effects wizard (he was among the first to use the 'bullet time' effect, and is well known for his manipulations of mise en scène), and uses these effects to emphasise 'how stories become created, amplified and distorted', because 'our lives are shaped by these stories' (Thrill 2006); Romanek – whose 'Closer' (Nine Inch Nails) and 'Bedtime Stories' (Madonna) videos are in New York's Museum of Modern Art permanent collection – builds music videos around the 'charisma machine' embodied in the musician; they do not so much define performance as provide a context that parallels the artist's intent (Rainer 2005). Jonze, a master of commutation and offbeat videos, underscores the improvisational aspect of video-making: 'The first third is the ideas you bring to it, the second third is what other people, like the DP, the FX guys or the actors bring to it, and the final third is what ends up happening by chance or via spontaneity on the set, which you don't plan for but what is often the best stuff' (Hunter 2000). Contained within these statements is a kernel idea: reviewability is essentially grounded in the viewer seeing something unexpected and overwhelming (whether by content or by sensory overload).

Unfortunately, perhaps because they tend to be younger and exempt from 'selling' their products, AMVers rarely articulate a personal vision or provide ready formulas for reviewability. The majority of AMVs seem to lean toward retelling the anime's narrative or character profiling, while a few others focus on one-upping their own technical feats. Reviewability stems from three main approaches. Some AMVers create technical effects so original and breathtaking that it requires several viewings to absorb them; at times, a select few even kick off new genres by playing with the relationship between effects and theme. XOST Productions, for example, recently developed 'Recursive' videos, in which the source footage for the AMV is derived from the AMV itself. The first editor's segment uses anime footage, and all subsequent editors use the previous editor's footage, so that the 'theme' of the AMV is created from a random chain. Decoy Ops Studio describes an 'Educational' genre, which has a two-fold purpose: anime's elite characters' fighting techniques are portrayed while simultaneously revealing the AMVers' technical weaponry. The second approach to reviewability relies on using lesser-known anime and/or music, or from twisting well-known anime with a new story or set of associations. Suberunker Studeosh, for example, is known for its parodies of pop culture, in which segments from an anime are matched to pop iconography in music. Premonition Studios, by contrast, is like the Spike Jonze of anime; it offers quirky videos that promote lesser-known bands, and relies on commutation to create interesting parodies ('Elvis vs. Anime'). Finally, reviewability can be accomplished by inventing a new scenario that is completely unrelated to the original footage or song. Istiv Studios calls this 'Scenaristic' videos, and comments upon the technique in the making of 'The Race': 'I search[ed] for a story that can motivate the characters to participate in the race. I had the idea of a mysterious Great Prize that no one knows what it is. So the participants are imagining their own anime story.' [11] One might argue, then, that traditional music-video-makers (TMVers) generally use effects that cater to the viewer, while AMVs rely upon self-referentiality: they are created more for the producer's personal gratification and in homage to anime than to elicit a response from their audience. AMVs that perfectly match a song and anime (as with Pohnert's video) get less reviewability than AMVs that define new themes and trademark the producer.

Consider, for example, the translation of AC/DC's 'Back in Black' (1980) into the Evolution Control Committee's political parody of Dan Rathers and the CBS news, and then Aquiline Studio's audio sampling from this parody to parody the foremost (and most corrupt) informant in the anime *Neon Genesis Evangelion* (1995). AC/DC's song appeared on an album of the same title, and delved into themes of mortality and hedonism. It was composed in tribute to the band's former lead singer, Bon Scott, who had died of mysterious causes earlier that year. In 2000, the Evolution Control Committee created a UMV titled 'Rocked by Rape': they took the background music from AC/DC's song and mingled it with sampled words from Dan Rathers's newscasts, then mingled both with footage from wars, government officials and Hollywood icons to criticise the manner in which television bombards us with depraved situations.

> As we watched Rathers convey the news each night, we were struck at the brutal violence that was delivered, day in, day out. Unfailingly, the good news ALWAYS appeared as the very last segment of each broadcast. You may call it dessert, but we call it empty calories – a meaningless gesture; an insincere smile to follow 25 minutes of carnage. How can we sit idly by, watching that insincere smile on Dan Rathers's face? When you offer a daily parade like that, you must expect that some people will wonder just what the emperor is wearing.[12]

Rathers had used the phrase 'rocked by rape' to cover a story about a girl's abduction and murder. Evolution Control's UMV mocked Rathers's words, implying that the innocent public is being raped by sensationalist media – a media more interested in delivering shocking news that gathers viewer ratings than in focusing on positive current events.

In 2003 Aquiline Studios sampled the entire audio from the ECC's UMV, and created an AMV that mocked the ever-popular apocalyptic anime *Evangelion*. Dan Rathers becomes a voiceover for Gendo Ikari, the leader of NERV – an organisation that fights aliens that are trying to wipe out humanity using bio-engineered weapons. Ikari, like Rathers, should be the most trusted man in the news; the AMV presents him not only as the trustworthy 'teleprompt spokesperson' for NERV, but also as a news story. Ikari does have his own agenda in NERV – to resurrect his dead wife – and he commits heinous crimes to achieve it. Arrows point to Ikari's head when the words 'liar' and 'unremorseful killer' appear as if he is reporting on himself, whereas Rathers's use of these words reported nothing about his character. The AMV also takes scenes from the original anime and alters their meaning so that they refer to 'real' fan culture. When the words 'economic collapse' are voiced by Ikari-Rathers, an image of Asuka Langley's notebook appears with a false subtitle: 'Asuka Langley Soryu Photo Application, Only 30 Yen Per Picture'. Asuka is a temperamental, redheaded teenager desired not only by the main protagonist, but also by a host of real-life fans who render her in explicit outfits and poses in their fan art. The implication here is that obsession with a fictional character has created a real-life economic disaster. One would have to be part of anime culture to get the joke; otherwise, one would assume the subtitle to be an exact translation of what was happening in the anime.

FROM TMV TO AMV

Aquiline's video attained high reviewability and excellent overall ratings on the central website for AMVs, AMV.org. The website hosts an annual competition for 'Best Video' in several categories. MTV also hosts an annual video awards show (VMA). Their 'Best Breakthrough Videos' corresponds to AMV.org's 'Most Original Video', and it is interesting to compare the quality and intent of the videos in both competitions.

The MTV music video awards allow for only one 'winner' per category each year. Surprisingly, I found on average 40–80 AMVs for each MTV winner from 1998–2005. The MTV 'Best Breakthrough' award list is as follows:

    1998: Prodigy, 'Smack My Bitch Up'
    1999: Fat Boy Slim, 'Praise You'
    2000: Björk, 'All is Full of Love'

Figure 1 Image of Asuka Langley

2001: Fat Boy Slim, 'Weapon of Choice'
2002: White Stripes, 'Fell in Love'
2003: Coldplay, 'The Scientist'
2004: Franz Ferdinand, 'Take Me Out'
2005: Gorillaz, 'Feel Good Inc.'

Generally, the concept behind each of these songs was as groundbreaking as the video. Sadly, their AMV counterparts rarely deliver more than a stale, regurgitated impression. Prodigy's 'Smack My Bitch Up', for example, encountered censorship and criticism for its seeming references to rape and violence towards women. Prodigy member Howlett, however, explained that the song referred to 'doing anything intensely, like being on stage – going for extreme manic energy'.[13] The few lyrics in the song, 'Change my Pitch Up, Smack my Bitch up', were actually sampled from rap group Ultramagnetic MC's 'Give the Drummer Some', which itself used samples from James Brown's 'Funky Drummer' and others. The TMV, directed by Jonas Åkerlund, was filmed as though through the eyes of the protagonist and features a drunk, coked-up vandal who smacks and fondles women; the shocking twist is that what seems to be a man is revealed in the closing seconds as a lesbian. Unfortunately, the AMV variants add nothing to the originals. They are all action videos that feature heroes and their nemeses beating each other.

Fat Boy Slim's 'Praise You' samples the lyric 'praise you' from the opening of 'Take Yo' Praise' by Camille Yarbrough; Slim says of his music that his interest rests with sampling from 'crap records' to create mainstream dance tunes rather than developing meaningful themes. Spike Jonze directed the TMV, which was groundbreaking not only for its cameos of Jonze and Slim, but mainly because it was filmed *guerilla style*: outside a movie theater without permission to film on the premises (the theater manager actually attempts to turn off the portable boom box in the video). More arbitrarily, Jonze had originally filmed the video for a different Slim song, 'Rockafeller Skank', using random people named as the fictional Torrance Dance Community Group, and spending a mere $800 – most of which was used to replace the portable stereo and feed crew and cast. Again, the AMVs leave much to be desired, and little to the imagination: they focus on praising the impressive feats of anime heroes. To Jonze's credit, a degree of self-referentiality exists in this work. His cameo as one of the untrained, aloof dancers relates to his spontaneous, untraditional and isolated personality in real life.

Slim's 'Weapon of Choice' sampled Sly & the Family Stone's 1968 recording 'Into My Own Thing'. The video – also directed by Jonze – became legendary overnight because celebrity Christopher Walken starred in the video as a flying, savvy dancer in a hotel lobby. Again Jonze attained a degree of self-referentiality not only for his own quirkiness, but also for depicting Walken as a suave if odd man, not unlike his personality in real life. Among the AMVs one parody appears: the 'Ode to Perversion'. Producer Der Kommissar decided it would be funny to splice perverted dialogue from various anime – *Cowboy Bebop* (1998), *Last Exile* (2003), *Neon Genesis* (1995), *Trigun* (1998), *FLCL* (2000), *Love Hina* (tv) (2000) and *Outlaw Star* (1998). 'Weapon' was not the first song he intended to use, but he decided upon it because out of several upbeat instrumentals it was one that would complement rather than drown out the dialogue. Kommissar realised the song would work when, in a visit to the mall, it played in the food court; the producer instantly felt like 'jumping on top of my table and dancing' as Walken had in the original, and chose the song for its 'fun' element. Some of the snippets, which comprise only a fragment of the entire anime, are 'Hey you're not looking up my dress are you?', 'Mind if I hang out and watch?' and 'I lost my room can I share yours?' Kommissar's AMV does not always parallel the original anime's themes (most being serious in tone), but does complement the comical, if infrequent, perversion in their dialogues.[14]

Björk's 'All is Full of Love' comes off the album *Homogenic*, which the artist describes as being 'about inventing your own paradise, but underneath your kitchen table, so it's very secretive'.[15] The album proceeds chronologically and this song – the last track – culminates in a formerly trapped woman overcoming her oppression not through battle but through love. The highly controversial video, directed by Chris Cunningham, features a passionate embrace and kissing between two very human-looking robots (the female robot looking uncannily like Björk); Cunningham brainstormed the video when first hearing the track, at which time he 'wrote down the words "sexual," "milk," "white porcelain," "surgery." [The video]'s a combination of several fetishes: industrial robotics, female anatomy, and fluorescent light in that order.'[16] Again, like Jonze, Cunningham managed to produce a video that was self-referential (to Björk's physical appearance and native culture). This was the one award-winning TMV that had an equally impressive trail of AMVs. Ingress Production's 'All Full of Geist' revisits the TMV's main theme using the anime *Key the Metal Idol* (1994). The anime is Pinocchio retold – Key is a dying android with an irreplaceable battery, and can rejuvenate only by befriending 30,000 friends before she flickers out. The anime's theme recalls the song's story of a girl who can escape her sterile life only through love. Ingress's AMV takes the TMV and anime a step further in several aspects:

> The style of the technology in the anime, and particularly the vision of the white-shelled robot Key emerging from the water in the OP sequence, also fits very well with the 'lesbian robots' in the real music video for 'All Is Full of Love.' In his video, Cunningham uses the sound of the strumming *koto* to go into a close up of the machinery around the robots, and I tried to imitate this here with shots of Ajo Heavy Industries' robotics technology. The clip of water dripping off Key's face played backwards at 0:50 is a homage to the backwards-dripping milk that appears in Cunningham's video.[17]

Embryonic Productions 'All is Full' is also a technical masterpiece, although the producer emphasises that, unlike her previously shallow 'special-effects' videos, this one strongly accentuates the source anime's plot. *Lain* (1998) traces a girl's rite of passage from lost adolescence in the dead, real world to omnipresent being via Wired, an international computer network. The final scene involves Lain shedding this metaphysical protective 'shell' and speaking with a father-figure/god who mentions madeleines (a classic metaphor for memory) after his attempts at comforting her with regard to the transformative and dramatic events that have unfolded.[18] The AMV pays homage to Lain and the TMV's character development and plot; however, the music and effects also imitate the anime's theme: Björk's song combined Icelandic tones with machine sounds to blend her childhood nostalgia with synthesised techno music, just as Lain's youth merges with her computerised state. In addition to Lain lip-synching the lyrics, the producer creates a 37-layer overlay, each with its own motion effect, that slowly disappears to reveal a full-screen facial of Lain.[19] Perhaps most impressively, though used only to mask the repetitive aspect of Björk's song, the producer removed the closing parts of 'All is Full' and ended the AMV with Olive's 'You're Not Alone' (1995). The subdued trip-hop song forms a triplet with 'All is Full' and *Lain*; its lyrics perfectly compliment the theme of a girl's split personality, separated between the real and virtual worlds and trying to find serenity: 'Two minds that once were close, Now so many miles apart I will not falter though, I'll hold on till you're home. Safely back where you belong, And see how our love has grown.'

While 'All is Full of Love' remains the only 'Best Breakthrough' MTV video that is outdone by its respective AMVs, the same cannot be said of award-winning AMVs and their complementary TMVs. In fact the Top 4 in the run-off/final vote for 'Most Original AMV' for 2005 received awards in several categories:

- Yann J., 'Jihaku': Best Drama, Sentimental, Most Artistic, Video of the Year;
- Decoy Ops, 'Naruto's Technique Beat': Best Instrumental, Visual Effects;
- Kevin Chiou, 'Still Preoccupied with 1985': Best Character Profile, Comedy, Fun, Parody Video;
- Kevin Chiou, 'The Wizard of Ozakasuberunker': Most Original Video, Creator.

Yann J.'s 'Jihaku' remains impressive for the sheer magnitude of anime featured – about 120 joined as a montage using the Foo Fighters' song 'Best of You'. The Foo Fighters' lyrics and video depict one person (lead singer Grohl, perhaps) vying to stop his escapist tendencies, and encouraging his listener to abandon his defeatist attitude and block out the person 'getting the best of you'. The TMV focuses mainly on Grohl's open mouth singing into the microphone, then shifts to various, seemingly unrelated images of fighting children, sex, a wall graffitied with words like 'They all died in the fire I started' and 'Resist', and animals attacking each other in the wild. The Fantasy Studios producer intended to mimic the theme and appearance of its TMV:

> It's a video about life in general, a confession about life, full of passion, rage, deception, determination, desire to fight, desire to give up. . . . Some people said to me this video is really pessimistic, others said the message is very hopeful. I'm glad this video brings this ambiguity. Like in the real music video, I have put neutral scenes and elements, without explanation or reason . . . I love it. I have inset also real scenes of the Foo Fighters' singer to keep the side of a real music video.[20]

Interestingly, Yann J. titled his AMV *jihaku*, which means 'confession', and while critics have made biographical speculations about Grohl's life via the lyrics and TMV, both Grohl and his AMV counterpart remain silent on the intentions behind their work, stating that it is based on an inexplicable feeling. This may be the quintessential example in which TMV and AMV exhibit self-referential qualities based on the artists' observations of, and experiences in, the 'real' world.

Decoy Ops, mentioned earlier in this chapter, created 'Naruto's Technique Beat' as an 'Educational' video. The chosen song, 'Seizure of Power', was an instrumental work borrowed from industrial icon Marilyn Manson; it was created for the *Resident Evil* (2002) movie score, and therefore has no TMV. Interestingly, the movie has anime-esque offshoots: it was based on a Japanese video game titled *Biohazard* (2000) and created by Shinji Mikami (who, in turn, had borrowed the basic story from the Japanese horror film *Sweet Home* (1989)).[21] As Decoy Ops explains, the AMV is a character development from *Naruto* (1999), in which 'A ninja delivers the complete study on the Five created by Decoy Drone. As the ANBU members watch the tape, they witness the incomprehensible power of the chosen five subjects.'[22] Viewers likewise watch the character study from the Drone's perspective, while witnessing the 'incomprehensible power' of the producer's talent. In addition to altering the original anime's colors, the AMV features its own plot, a series of stunning overlays, fabricated subtitles, and semblances of how a drone would see things. The AMV is self-referential not only in highlighting the producer's technical prowess, but also in representing his character. Like the anime's main character Uzumaki Naruto, Decoy Ops' commentary typecasts him as a prankster – a loud, hyperactive adolescent who 'ninjas' (pirates) footage and searches for approval and recognition from the AMV community.

Kevin Chiou of Suberunker Studeosh won a host of awards in 2005 for two AMVs. Chiou's penchant for comical and parodied work parallels his self-image: his live virtual journal is titled 'Suberunker's Superbly Santastic, Sufficient (Sometimes Stupid) SiveJournal', and the weekly entries reveal a self-absorbed, energetic college student who makes deprecating or quirky comments not only about his own work, but about Disneyland, movies and friends/project associates. Briefly mentioned earlier in this chapter, Chiou's jokes stem from finding anime footage that matches his selected song's iconography (or is manipulated to do so). The music is drunk-punk-pop band Bowling for Soup's '1985', which describes a suburban mother's confusion about contemporary pop culture, her shattered dreams of being a libidinous actress, and her nostalgia for 1985 – the time when she was still cool and music was 'still on MTV'. The TMV parodies the band more than the woman. When her husband leaves, the voyeuristic lead singer pulls his mates indoors, and they perform as an amateur garage band, dressed up as Robert Palmer's sexy women, break-dancers who can't break-dance, George Michael, and a Motley Crew/Whitesnake heavy metal hair band. They do this in order to attract the 'M.I.L.F.' (mother I'd like to fuck), and she delivers her goods by jumping onto their car, partially stripping, and gyrating to their performance. When asked why they titled the song '1985' when the references were about 1984, lead singer Reddick offered a droll excuse: '1985 rhymes better with "preoccupied".' [23] Lyrics as nursery rhymes mattered more than historical accuracy, and this lack of regard for truth is a frequent accusation made about the 1990s generation. Chiou's video, likewise, is faithful to the original anime's history. It is based on *Azumanga Daioh* (2002), which aired 5-minute episodes and a 6-minute movie, itself representative of the theory that today's youth suffer from attention deficit disorder (ADD) and a lack of interest in anything serious. The anime's title has little meaning either, being a play on the creator's name 'Azuma' and the magazine in which the story (as manga) was first published, *Daioh*. Only two males appear in the anime (one being a teacher obsessed with teenage girls), and the story revolves around the absurd behaviour and experiences of six high school girls, a few of whom exhibit ADD behaviour. Like '1985', the anime's theme song refers to themes of teenagers' nonsensical behaviour and disconnection from reality. Titled 'The Cake of Mishearing', the chorus lyrics read 'CAKE FOR YOU! A simple happiness TEA FOR YOU! With a big smile the chorus of angels at the window is to you, just your ear playing tricks? The voice saying "I love you, I love you".' [24] Chiou takes the AMV one step further than the TMV, parodying both '1985''s iconography and popular anime by creating perversions of the original album covers: Nirvana translates into *Evangelion*'s 'Nerv'ana with the evil Angel replacing the original – a beautiful, naked angel with internal organs exposed; U2's 'Wide Awake in America' translates into 'Wide Awake in Japan' with the archetypal, evil Pokemon replacing Bono, the quintessential rock icon; Blondie's 'No Exit' features *Full Metal Alchemist* characters instead of the original band members; and *Moulin Rouge*'s movie poster features Ozzy Osbourne as an absinthe Green Fairy. What distinguishes the AMV above Bowling for Soup's TMV is that the former intentionally mocks anime and music classics, while the latter only parodies the youth culture of 1985. Perhaps most ironically, the award-winning AMV was categorised as a 'tiny project' by its producer.

Last but not least, Chiou's 'Wizard of Ozaka' was meant to parody the classic *Wizard of Oz*. The title has a double meaning: first, it pokes fun at the American mispronunciation of Osaka – the third largest city in Japan, known in Tokyo for its comedians, which in turn becomes the land of 'Oz'aka. Chiou's anime uses *Azumanga Daioh* for the main footage (the protagonist Osaka takes Dorothy's role), and splices in characters from *Full Metal Alchemist* (Alphonse Elric – a boy whose soul is trapped in a suit of armour – as the Tin Man), *One Piece* (loyal protagonist Luffy in a straw hat becomes the Scarecrow), *Bleach* (plushy sap

Kon embodies the Lion), and *Evangelion* (evil mastermind Gendo is the Wizard). The anime is set to the instrumental on the *Chicken Run* soundtrack (2000); while no TMV exists for the song, the animated film plot is reminiscent of Orwell's *Animal Farm*, and the protagonists (the chickens), like Dorothy and her travelling companions fleeing the Wicked Witch of the West, desire to escape the grasp of egg farmers who intend to make them into chicken pot pies. Chiou describes the evolution of the AMV from a simple parody of the film into a criticism of real-life role-playing games (RPGs), in which people assume the role of fictional characters. Theorist Tracy Hickman notes of RPGs that

> In role-playing, the *characters* must constantly be confronted with problems and situations strongly based on their morality, so that they face the ethical dilemma of being faithful to their beliefs or betraying them, and *players* must be aware of the consequences of their decisions, within the conscience of the role the player chose to play at the beginning of the game. (Hickman 1996)

Chiou's self-referentiality here rests with a theme shared between anime, film and RPGs: the plots trace character development based on moral issues. In *Oz*, the characters must realise they have the resources to overcome evil and develop self-confidence; in *Azumanga Daioh*, the immature girls learn to take life, knowledge and etiquette seriously; in *Full Metal*, *Evangelion* and *Bleach*, characters learn to accept the inevitable death of loved ones and allow closure; in *One Piece*, they learn the value of unity and fighting for one's dreams; and in RPGs, they learn to take responsibility for their decisions and use their conscience.

CONCLUSION: IT'S A MAD MAD WORLD

Members of anime culture express their devotion to the art in several ways: 'Cosplay', in which fans dress in the fashion of anime characters; 'fan sub', in which Japanese anime are subtitled for foreigners; fan art, in which drawings and manga reinvent the characters and plot lines of the original; and finally, AMVs. In Japan AMVs are labelled MADs, 'Videos of Madness', perhaps because of an obsession so extreme that the creator defines himself or herself via the anime. Among Japanese creators of MADs are Kanzuki Yasiro, Otone Tamu, S2H and Nodoame. Piano is a Japanese AMV editor who distinguishes between two forms of MADS: *Douga* MADS based on anime, and *Bishojo* MADs based on game footage. In an interview with Alan Clontz for the AMV.org site (30 August 2004), Piano disagrees when Alan states that Japanese MADs 'seem to have better design and graphic style' than Western AMVs. He feels, instead, that the technique is similar, but argues in favour of Western

AMVs because technology – more accessible to Westerners than youth in Japan – has made the content of Japanese MADs 'thin'.[25]

The AMV may be a nascent and unaffordable art for Japanese fans, but music from and as an offshoot of anime remains quite popular. Japan's MTV introduced anime VJ Lilli in 1992. The virtual VJ calls herself 'cyberbabe' in a live interview with CNN (25 May 2001), and mentions that she is currently recording her own CD and is in talks to produce her first music video.[26] Additionally, anime-related music has its own Top 25 chart in Japan. Currently the top three songs are Younha's 'Houki Boshi' from the *Bleach* original soundtrack (OST), Origa's 'Inner Universe' from *Ghost in the Shell*'s OST, and Lia's 'Tor No Uta' from *Air*'s OST. Various kinds of soundtrack are written and released in conjunction with anime: image albums, which have songs that develop the anime character but are not included in the anime; CDs released in the character's name rather than the actor's own; BGM – the background music from the show; OSTs; and music box instruments. Image albums are rather interesting because they supplement the anime and often 'explain' confusing or underdeveloped elements. For example, a 24-track CD was released in 1997 for *Key the Metal Idol* with monologues from Key's perspective, whereas in the original anime Key rarely expresses her thoughts, feelings, or why she made certain decisions. *Seiyu*, or voice actors, often later become musicians and release their own records. Seiyu develop their own fan base to the extent that shows are watched for the sake of hearing the seiyu's voice. Among the more popular seiyu are Kikuko Inoue, Megumi Hayashibara, Aya Hisakawa and Mari Iijima. Frequently the seiyu will sing the opening or closing themes for the show in which their character stars. Kikuko Inoue was part of the groups DoCo and Goddess Family Club, and is perhaps best known for her roles in *Ah! My Goddess* (2005) (for which she sings 'Anata no Birthday' as Belldandy on the soundtrack) and *Chobits* (2001), and for her voice acting in several video games such as *Metal Gear*. Megumi Hayashibara, though little known outside Japan, is popular for her roles as Faye Valentine in *Cowboy Bebop* and Rei in *Evangelion*; her voice featured in several video games including *Ranma 1/2* and *Slayers*, and she produced several solo albums for King Records including *Half and Half* (1991) and *Center Color* (2004). Aya Hisakawa is a J-pop singer and member of the Peach Hips, the name for five voice actors from the anime *Sailor Moon* (1992), who produced several *Sailor Moon* albums and performed the themes 'Tuxedo Mirage' and 'Moon Revenge'. Mari Iijima, for example, was the voice actor for teen idol superstar Lynn Minmei in the hit television series *Macross* (1982), and later sang the number one single 'Do you remember love?' over the closing credits to the anime's film (1984).

Perhaps the opening and closing trailers for the above named anime count as AMVs, although most television shows begin and end with a song and show clips/character profiles. It is possible, though, that some anime intentionally use music videos. Mima Kirigoe, for example, plays the heroine and leader singer for the J-pop group CHAM! in *Perfect Blue* (1998); they give a live music performance in the opening sequences. The film features Mima as a pop idol whose reputation becomes soured after a diminishing music career and a questionable role in a soap opera. Its plot focuses on the impact of fame and fortune on pop icons, including pleasure, paranoia and depression during the rise and fall of their careers.

AMV subculture continues to spread to the extent that Iron Chef competitions are held at almost every Anime Expo internationally. Many AMVers are avid gamers as well. Because anime is produced and translated at a slower rate than that at which video games appear, AMVers are looking to video games for more footage. This has extended into the music scene as well: in 2006 the Norwegian band Rektor developed *Princess*, the world's first playable music video game, which can be played at www.rektor.no. Rektor describes the game as '[the player] being a hero making your way through various missions, [such as] beating up the Beatles, steal[ing] Elvis's moon burgers, and dancing in the shiny yellow Rektor hero suit'.[27] Last but not least, there is the band Osaka Popstar and their *American Legends of Punk*. The album was released in May 2006; its punk-based songs are named after famous anime including the tracks 'Sailor Moon', 'Astro Boy' and 'Shaolin Monkeys' as a play upon the recent show *Shaolin Showdown*. Included with the CD are a booklet featuring the band in anime form and a bonus DVD of the songs 'Insects' and 'Wicked World' as AMVs.

Creators of AMVs, by producing self-referential works, become the ultimate fanime (fan + anime) champions. Like the Ultimate Fighting Champion, AMV culture is 'an exciting alternative to [an entertainment] climate controlled by idiot-savants and overpaid wannabes' (Syken et al. 2005: 30). Technological means have become accessible, allowing individuals to create an artificial world in which natural 'sound' is transformed into something more pleasing, more 'silent' (underground), more based upon reaching a utopian world in which there is no ownership of the means of production and private property is non-existent. In deferential perversion of Madonna's famous lyrics, AMVers do not live in a Ballardian world, nor are they Ballardian girls (boys).

Notes

1. For example, Dire Straits' song 'Money for Nothing' (in which Sting sings 'I want my MTV' repeatedly in the background), was the first video aired on MTV Europe, 1 August 1987. The video features an animation-rendered man who enters the television to take part in a 'real-life' Straits concert.
2. 'MTV is Rock Around the Clock', *Philadelphia Inquirer*, 3 November 1982. Retrieved from the Inquirer's Internet Archive Database, no page numbers: http://www.philly.com/mld/philly/archives.
3. Random comment made during a group interview at the AMV contest, Anime Expo 2006.

4. Introduction preceding the video by eStudio: http://www.poptix.net/funny/videostar.swf.
5. *DJ Mag*, November 2005, retrieved from www.eclecticmethod.net. Eclectic Method also disdains the traditional music video's favoritism of visuals over music.
6. Other examples of mashups include LMC's 'Take me to the Clouds Above', which mashes U2's 'With or Without You' with Whitney Houston's 'How Will I Know' and depicts the band as angels with a Houston impersonator; Josh Wolf's 'The Hand that Feeds', in which a Nine Inch Nails video is spliced with protest footage of the government blowing up mosques; and Fatalshade's 'My Little Pony' with 'I'm too Sexy'.
7. This example and definition are borrowed from Vernallis (2004).
8. This is not to imply that AMVs are immune to legal disputes over copyright infringement. In 2005 the main hub for AMVs – AnimeMusicVideos.org, which is a small-scale server with peer-to-peer sharing – was served a cease-and-desist order by Wind-Up Records. As a result, 2000 music videos were removed from the website. Posted on the Anime News Network (November 2005), http://www.animenewsnetwork.com/article.php?id=7837.
9. Pittman referred to MTV as a 'mood enhancer to create a televisual form that was nonlinear, using mood and emotion to create an atmosphere' (Vernallis 2004: xiv).
10. This section on AMV is largely borrowed from the general AMV theory section found on http://www.amvwiki.org.
11. Taken from Istiv Studio commentary on the Amv.org website: https://www.animemusicvideos.org/members/members_videoinfo.php?v=78914.
12. http://evolution-control.com/press/cbs/ecc.html.
13. http://theprodigy.info/discography/official/Smack_My_Bitch_Up/index.shtml.
14. Cowboy Bebop, Trigun and Outlaw Star are 'Space Westerns'; Evangelion and FLCL are apocalyptic surrealistic shows that explore dysfunctional relations; Last Exile explores four philosophical questions in a Victorian war setting; and Love Hina explores an unrequited adolescent love.
15. http://unit.bjork.com/specials/albums/homogenic. Taken originally from *MTV News*, March 2001.
16. http://www.director-file.com/cunningham/bjork.html. Included on the site are files about Gondry, Joseph Kahn and Johan Renck.
17. Commentary provided by Ingress Productions on the AMV.org website: https://www.animemusicvideos.org/members/members_videoinfo.php?vid_id=15933.
18. Summary taken from http://en.wikipedia.org/wiki/Serial_Experiments_Lain.
19. From Embryonic's commentary on AMV.org: https://www.animemusicvideos.org/members/members_videoinfo.php?vid_id=51652.
20. Commentary by Yann J. (Fantasy Studios) on AMV.org: https://www.animemusicvideos.org/members/members_videoinfo.php?vid_id=90488.
21. Interestingly, both films also promoted video games named after them in the same years.
22. Commentary by Decoy Ops on AMV.org: https://www.animemusicvideos.org/members/members_videoinfo.php?v=74029.
23. Comment made on the band's website: http://www.bowlingforsoup.com/bio.html.
24. Lyrics translated on http://www.animelyrics.com/anime/azumangadaioh/ soramimi cake.htm.
25. https://www.animemusicvideos.org/members/interview.php?interview_id=11.
26. http://edition.cnn.com/COMMUNITY/transcripts/2001/05/31/lili.
27. Retrieved from Rektor's website: http://www.rektor.no/index.php.

REFERENCES

Ballard, J. G. (2006), 'The Sound Sweep', in J. G. Ballard, *The Complete Short Stories: Volume 1* (London: Harper Perennial).

Hickman, T. (1996), 'The Moral Imperative of Fantasy', *Ethics in Fantasy*, part III, http://www.trhickman.com/Intel/Essays/Ethic3.html (accessed September 2006).

Hunter, S. (2000), 'He's Jonzin' for Films', *A Boards Online Interview*, February, http://www.boardsmag.com/articles/online/20000224/jonze.html?print=yes (accessed September 2006).

Paoletta, M. (2004), 'Danger Mouse Speaks Out on "Grey Album"', *Billboard*, 8 March, http://www.billboard.com/bbcom/news/article_display.jsp?vnu_content_id=1000455930 (accessed September 2006).

Pike, A. (1980), 'The Age of Buggles', *Beat Instrumental*, http://thebuggles.4t.com/articles/beatmay1980.htm (accessed September 2006).

Rainer, P. (2005), 'Mark Romanek', Spotlight section, *New York Magazine*, May, p. 17.

Saltzman, J. (2000), 'Predigested Dreams', in S. Reiss (ed.), *Thirty Frames per Second* (New York: Harry Abrams).

Syken, B., Bechtel, M., and Cannella, S. (2005), 'All the Rage', *Sports Illustrated*, Vol. 103, Issue 17, p. 30.

Thill, S. (2006), ' "How My Brain Works": An Interview with Michel Gondry', *Morphizm*, 15 March, http://www.morphizm.com/recommends/interviews/gondry_block.html (accessed September 2006).

Vernallis, C. (2004), *Experiencing the Music Video* (New York: Columbia University Press).

WEBSITES

AMV-wiki (an information and theory website), http://www.amvwiki.org/index.php/Main_Page.

The AMV.org site, http://www.animemusicvideos.org/members/members_videoinfo.php?v=44948.

Anime Music Video Creators Webring, http://a.webring.com/hub?ring=animemvs.

Directory of International Producers (by Dark Moon Studios), http://www.members.shaw.ca/darkmoonstudios/links.html.

The Anime News Network, http://www.animenewsnetwork.com/index.php.

SECTION TWO:

VIDEO-GAME MUSIC

3. MUSIC IN VIDEO GAMES

Rod Munday

The first and perhaps most important observation one can make about contemporary video-game music is that there is no longer any such thing as video-game music. This was not always the case and whether it will be the case in the future is open to question. A few years ago the genre known as 'Bitcore' (Collins 2005: 2) or 'Chiptune' (Wikipedia) defined, to all intents and purposes, the phenomenon known as video-game music. This genre, usually characterised in negative terms by its rudimentary electronic timbres and restricted number of voices, nevertheless produced some extremely innovative and memorable tunes. Since the mid-1990s, the improved memory capacity and increased processor speeds of game consoles have freed video-game composers from the technological constraints which gave the work of their predecessors such an identifiable aesthetic. Today, video-game music inhabits every style imaginable, from baroque to bluegrass, rockabilly to symphonic (Belinkie 1999). It is for this reason that I claim it no longer exists. Today's video-game music is more accurately described as music that has been written for, or adapted to, video-games. Therefore the analytical focus must shift away from form and towards function.

While video-games have become 'the hottest and most volatile field of study within new media theory' (Perron and Wolf 2003: 1), academic articles on video-game music are few and far between. The majority of them are more descriptive than analytical, and tend to be organised around a timeline structure.[1] Partly as a reaction against this, but mainly because I think a theoretical understanding of this area cries out to be elaborated, I will be examining video-game music from a more analytical perspective, focusing primarily on contemporary games, which I define as played on platforms that have the capacity to reproduce CD-quality audio.

In this investigation, my approach will be primarily text-based. The video game as a text can be defined in the Barthesian sense as something which is produced as a result of actions or discursive operations, rather than existing as a material thing in itself (Barthes 1977: 156–7). The danger of this approach is that it can lead to a conception of the subject that is too pristine and ahistorical and ignores the situated interpretations of gamers. This is clearly inappropriate for a new-media form like video-games, the academic understanding of which is continually being outdistanced by the changing technology of gaming itself. It would be useful to be able to draw on other research, but at present sufficient data is simply not available to offer anything more than anecdotal or speculative observations on such important areas as the institutional context of video game music production, the economic reasons for its success, or the social context of its reception. This is why I am introducing a note of caution into the proceedings at this early stage, because the aim of this chapter is not so much to supply a definitive explanation of how video-game music functions as to communicate enough of a theoretical understanding to make the case for future research as compellingly as I can.

The analysis is divided under three broad headings:

1. Environmental: how music supports the perception of a gameworld.
2. Immersion: how music supports the player's involvement in the game.
3. Diegetic: how music supports a game narrative.

Environmental

As Trevor Wishart observes, a person's sensory experience of the environment is always a multimedia one (Wishart 1986: 49). While vision is generally regarded as the most important sense for apprehending an environment, sound has certain advantages over sight. Sound surrounds the listener, blending and combining in ways that visual information cannot emulate. In the context of mediated communication, a virtual doorbell sounds exactly like a real one, because waves of recorded sound are perceived in exactly the same way as waves of real-world sound. In contrast, the visual representation of a doorbell does not have the same equality of experience (Kaltenbrunner and Huxor 2002). Visual representations are hampered by imaging technologies which render obsolete the advantages of human binocular vision. Visual images are usually two-dimensional and the viewer's gaze is concentrated in only one place. In contrast, stereo sound takes advantage of the fact that humans have two ears. Stereo recordings arguably constituted the first electronically generated 'virtual reality', because, as Wishart observes, loudspeakers create an immersive acoustic space, in which a sonic representation of any real or imaginary environment can be projected (Wishart 1986: 43). Sue Morris claims the main purpose of a sound-track in video games is to imply space through sound. In first-person shooters like *Doom* and *Halo*, Morris argues that successful players always perceive the gameworld in 360 degrees, with most of the information outside of the visual frame being provided by the soundtrack (Whalen 2004).

Michel Chion conceives of sound as not merely duplicating visual informa-tion, but also enriching it. Thus he claims the meaning of images is actually determined by sound, rather than the other way around (Chion 1994: 5). This is born out by Annabel Cohen's observation that the less realistic an image is, the more music and sound effects are needed in order to fix its meaning (Cohen 2000: 367). In video games, it is worth remembering that computer-generated environments make no natural sounds: hence the importance of music and sound effects to give them meaning.

While the above arguments make the case for sound representing environ-ments, the question can also be approached from the opposite direction – in terms of representing environments in sound. Historically, composers have responded to the environment by painting nature in musical images. Beethoven's *Pastoral Symphony* is perhaps the most famous example of what is called 'pictorial music' (Komar 1980: 1). As an art form, music is not frozen in time like painting, nor does it speak in the monophonic voice of literature. Hence the nineteenth-century essayist Walter Pater's famous dictum, 'All art aspires towards the condition of music' (Pater 1925: 135). A contemporary appreciation of Mendelssohn's *Fingal's Cave Overture* from the 1830s describes the work as a continuous 'sea picture', with the 'restless Atlantic sometimes fierce, then suddenly docile . . . its playful waves glittering in the bright sunlight' (Komar 1980: 13). This illustrates how a purely auditory work can be interpreted in strikingly visual terms. This is why, before the advent of film or sound recording, music was considered to be the only artistic medium able to communicate a dynamic sense of being in a different place.

Early video games made extensive use of music's ability to represent envir-onments. Zach Whalen notes, in his analysis of *Super Mario Brothers*, how Koji Kondo's melodies serve to characterise the different levels of the game: a happy 'overworld theme', contrasting with a sinister 'underworld theme (Whalen 2004). However, wall-to-wall music is no longer a prominent feature of many contemporary video games, and consequently it can be argued that sound effects have begun to supplant the environmental function hitherto assigned to music. For example, *Grand Theft Auto San Andreas*, *Spiderman 2* and *Tom Clancy's Ghost Recon* all use music sparingly. While this argument is correct, it can be contested because it is premised on a musicological definition of music which, as Joseph Kerman points out, focuses narrowly on tonal music, or more precisely, the history of Western tonal music in the high-art tradition (Kerman 1985: 24).

This definition can be challenged if one examines how music functions in the context of other audiovisual media. Here it becomes apparent that music in this context is actually a very different music to that heard in the concert hall, or on personal music players. For instance, many film music researchers go so far as to argue that a major function of film music is paradoxically not to be heard at all (Gorbman 1987: 76; Donnelly 2005: 7). Cohen likens film music to a typeface in a book: something which is always read but seldom noticed (Cohen 2000: 366). If this analogy holds, hiring a musicologist to critique a film or video game would be like hiring a typographer to critique a work of literature. This remark is obviously not intended to be taken seriously, but it does highlight the shortcomings of an exclusively musicological definition of music when one tries to apply it in all contexts and circumstances. What is needed for audiovisual media is a definition of music that takes into account the specificity of the medium (Lipscomb and Tolchinsky 2004: 2). For video games this would include taking account of ambient sounds, sound effects, silences and even certain speech sounds (known to video-gamers as 'barks') as being part of 'the score.' My attempt to fulfil this criterion results in the following definition: video-game music is a discrete patterns of sounds and silences generated by the game software which, in combination with other visual, kinaesthetic and tactile sensory stimuli, contribute to creating the phenomenon of the gameworld.

The advantage of this definition is that it permits the contemplation of a more profound connection between sound, music and the environment suggested by Gilles Deleuze and Felix Guattari in their book *A Thousand Plateaus*.[2] Deleuze and Guattari define the content of music as *the refrain*. The refrain designates a collection of characteristic sounds (not necessarily tonal) that function to mark out a territory. In other words, the refrain is a sign that says, 'here I am' and 'this place is mine' (Deleuze and Guattari 2004: 331). Any sound can be interpreted as a refrain; for instance, bird song and animal cries are refrains, as is the sound of a motorcycle screaming past an open window with its silencer removed. When people are assaulted by such sounds they may remark, 'I can't even hear myself think.' In other words, according to Deleuze and Guattari's reasoning, they have been so successfully territorialised by the motorcycle's refrain that even their minds belong to it.

The function of music on the other hand is to repel this invasion by a process of deterritorialisation. Music does not preserve the refrain but expresses it. This involves taking the refrain up and challenging it; lifting it out of its territory and changing it into something else (Deleuze and Guattari 2004: 331). Conversely, the function of the refrain is to prevent music. This may seem contradictory, but Deleuze and Guattari are at pains to point out that these categories are neither stable nor monolithic. Rather, they liken music and the refrain to a couple of wrestlers who can no longer break free from each other's grasp (p. 341). The refrain therefore acts as a kind of magic circle that people draw around themselves to prevent the 'music' of the outside from invading (p. 343), or, vice versa, music can act as the magic circle that prevents the refrain. Hence, the popularity of personal music players is their ability to define a fortified personal space around the listener by blocking out sounds from outside. Video-game music arguably performs a similar function, cocooning players in a sonic zone of protection, where they can forget about interruptions and lose themselves in the game.

The above arguments contend that a musicological definition of music fails to illuminate its meaning, both in the context of audiovisual media and arguably also in real-world environments. It fails because it is primarily concerned with tonality and instrumentation and treats as secondary music's ability to communicate a mood or emotion to the listener. The power of music is such that it can turn an ostensibly non-threatening environment into a sinister place (Whalen 2004): sombre music can darken a sunny picture, whereas no end of sunny pictures can ever lighten sombre music. However, this effect is not symmetrical since sombre pictures are not lightened by sunny music either, so much as made comic by its ironising sense of defiance. This lack of symmetry suggests a sombre mood takes interpretative precedence over any particular qualities a medium possesses, presumably because it makes good evolutionary sense for human beings to be more responsive to danger signals than benign ones. Of course, this reasoning is speculative and therefore the contrary proposition can be asserted just as convincingly – namely that the power of music derives not from instincts but from conventional associations which have been naturalised over time. And the fact that such debates between semioticians and musicologists continue to enliven music theory (Donnelly 2001: 2–3) is a testament to music's resistance to being reduced to a mere category.

However, in the light of this debate, it is interesting to note that Deleuze and Guattari's theory does not refute the assertion that the power of music might stem from a conventional source. Rather, they suggest that these conventions are formed in a more primordial semiosis. The aggregate of refrains in a given environment is already music, and human beings are therefore already part of an orchestra as both listeners and players. In fact, this is the conceptual ground upon which our notions of 'what music is' rests. Viewed from this perspective, the musicological definition of music is overly narrow. However, the real problem here is not exclusivity, but that the musicological definition abstracts music away from its environmental referent, which means that, rather than clarifying the mysterious power of music, it leads instead to its further mystification.

IMMERSION

Music is important in video games because it contributes to the player's sense of immersion. Generally speaking, immersion has two meanings. The first describes the literal sensation of being totally submerged in water, as in the baptism ceremony, where the Latin word *immergere* or 'dip' first came into common usage (*SOED* 1973: 1025). The second meaning is a metaphorical application of the first. Here, immersion describes either the heightened sense of a particular aspect of a person's immediate surroundings, or the sensation of being transported into a mediated alternate reality. The activity of threading a needle or hammering a nail can be immersive in the former first of these latter senses, while reading a book or watching a film can be immersive in the second of them. For immersion to occur, the activity or stimulus has to be sufficiently engaging to block out the normal sense impressions of one's surroundings. This implies that immersion has a privative aspect as well as a stimulating one, and in the context of immersive media, it means that the real world must be dimmed in order for the mediated one to be illuminated.

There is little doubt that playing video games can be immersive. One study found that UK children aged nine to sixteen play them for an average of forty-four minutes a day. Another noted that the duration of play often tends to last longer than intended, with 14 per cent of subjects playing for over two hours a day (Newman 2004: 59). The feeling of being immersed in a video game can come from any number of factors, including the activity of play, involvement with the task, or the feeling of being transported by the story. The subjective nature of these experiences and the different contexts in which they operate illustrate that immersion cannot be defined with any conceptual precision. Nevertheless, it is a useful term, because the enjoyment of a video game is, to a great extent, premised on a player's deep involvement. In this respect, video-game music plays an important contributory role. There are two main processes that account for this, which I call *cognitive immersion* and *mythic immersion*.

Cognitive Immersion

Cognitive immersion focuses on the way certain neuropsychological aspects of the brain are stimulated by video-game music to promote the player's involvement in the game. One thing that distinguishes audio perception from visual perception is the ability of the brain to perceive any number of sounds simultaneously, and yet still focus on a particular sound to the exclusion of others. This phenomenon is known as the *cocktail party effect* (Altman 1992: 29). Music exploits the ability of human beings to appreciate polyphonous sound in a particularly rarefied and complex way. However, in the context of video games, music is but one of a multitude of information sources, simultaneously occupying a number of sensory channels.

Cognitive immersion is premised on the idea that the human brain is divided into many different areas, whose job is to perform specific perceptual and cognitive tasks. At an early stage of perception, these areas operate independently of each other, and only at a later stage are they cognised as an integrated whole (Cohen 2000: 364). It is generally thought that music contributes to video-game immersion by occupying the area of the brain dedicated to dealing with non-linguistic sounds. In this way, music prevents this area from hunting around for stimuli outside of the game. Music also functions as a 'wall of sound' which serves to prevent potentially distracting sounds from entering into the gaming situation. In the context of normal gaming, these cognitive operations are performed in the background, the player's conscious attention being focused on the graphics and the gameplay itself.

This 'modular theory' of the brain, first proposed by Jerry Fodor in 1983, has yet to be proved (Cohen 2000: 368), but results from experiments suggest that certain tasks are localised to certain areas of the brain. For instance, it has long been known that a part known as Wernicke's area handles the cognition of speech (p. 364). Experiments conducted on patients who had only one cerebral hemisphere intact found that right-handed patients who had retained their right hemisphere performed much better in musical memory tasks than right-handed patients who had retained their left hemisphere. Separate research also suggests different parts of the brain 'light up' when certain kinds of listening occur.

If cognitive immersion is correct, it would suggest the choice of music played in a video-gaming situation is immaterial to the immersion it provides. This hypothesis is anecdotally supported by a study commissioned by the BBC in 2005. Researchers surveyed just under three and a half thousand gamers across the UK. They found that at least 70 per cent of them had other media on in the background, either the television, radio or personal music (Pratchett 2005: 5).

I imagine this finding will make uncomfortable reading for those who study video-game music exclusively within an aesthetic tradition of film music, because it suggests that aesthetic considerations are secondary to music's ability as an aid to concentration. Of course the survey data needs to be qualified further before such an assertion can be made. For instance, it utilised a very broad definition of 'video game', which included the solitaire game bundled with the 'Windows' operating system and mobile phone games. Also, it did not provide information about whether the players' familiarity or unfamiliarity with a game affected their listening behaviour. These variables obviously have a bearing on how the claim of the BBC survey is qualified and addressed. However, it is equally obvious that a finding as important as this cannot be dismissed. More implications of this will be discussed in the conclusion of this chapter.

Mythic Immersion

Many video games, especially the role-playing type, tell mythic stories. Roger Callois claims the pleasure of these games comes from the player pretending to be someone else (Callois 2000: 19). This act of pretence is not intended to deceive, but takes advantage of the game's licence for the players to transcend their everyday selves and act as heroes or villains (p. 21). Royal Brown defines the extent to which something becomes 'mythical' as the degree to which a character, object or event escapes its causal or historical determination (Brown 1994: 9). In this sense, if we accept Callois's reasoning, the more mythic the game scenario, the fewer inhibitions the players have in exploring certain aspects of their personalities that are normally constrained.

Many if not all of the mythical themes found in video games are propagated in popular culture by the cinema. A film like *Star Wars* (1977) is a good mythic template for role-playing games, because it is an archetypal story of good against evil and because it provides a common currency of characters, settings and situations readily adaptable to imaginative play. Role-playing games in the real world typically employ props to deepen the immersion of the player. In *Star Wars* games, two sticks can stand in as lightsabres, or commercially manufactured toy lightsabres can be used; the effect is the same, although the demand on the player's imagination is different in each case. Video games take this notion a stage further, since the fantasy setting no longer has to be imagined. This leaves the players free to concentrate on exploring those normally constrained aspects of their personalities that are freed by the mythical scenario of the game.

However, this does not explain the importance of music to these games, since traditional role-playing games have never required a musical accompaniment. Contrastingly, many role-playing video games, such as the *Final Fantasy* series, are especially noted for their epic cinematic scores. The reason for this is that video games have aligned themselves with an aesthetic tradition of 'mythic drama' found in both opera and film.

Music, taken by itself, is often accorded a powerful mythical function. Kevin Donnelly argues that the abstract nature of music bypasses human rational defence mechanisms (Donnelly 2005: 9), whilst Claudia Gorbman points out that lushly scored, late Romantic music creates an 'epic feeling' (Gorbman 1987: 81). These ideas are most developed in the theories of the composer Richard Wagner, who explicitly likens the function of music to myth:

> The orchestra is so to speak the loam of endless universal feeling, from which the individual feeling of the separate actor draws power . . . In a

sense, [music] dissolves the hard immobile ground of the actual science into a fluent, elastic, impressionable ether, whose unmeasured bottom is the great sea of feeling itself. (Wagner 1895: 190–1)

Wagner's compositional technique was to associate people, objects and ideas with musical phrases known as *leitmotifs*. By creating these leitmotifs and intertwining them, Wagner attempted to weave a dynamic musical tapestry, unconstrained by the spatial and temporal limitations of more denotative representations (Wishart 1986: 52).

Film music borrows the basic idea of the leitmotif from Wagner, but has been criticised for reducing its mythic signifying function to that of a mere signpost (Donnelly 2005: 58). However, as James Buhler argues: 'the demythifying impulse of film music leads not away from myth but back towards it. Thus, even in a wholly demythologized state, the function of the leitmotif remains mythic' (Buhler 2000: 43). Buhler's theory offers an explanation for the paradoxical transformation of cinema, from an industrial technology whose only use was in scientifically documenting reality, into the dominant storytelling medium of the twentieth century (Brown 1994: 17). In cinema, the abstract nature of music, when combined with the objective nature of photography, produces a powerful tension: music seemingly mythologises the photographic image, while the photographic image realises the mythical aspects of the music. When these devices are used in the service of a narrative by a skilled filmmaker, a powerful effect occurs. I call this the aesthetic of cinematic realism.

The aesthetic of cinematic realism has powerfully influenced the aesthetic of video games to the extent that it can be argued contemporary video-game designers do not attempt to represent an unmediated sense of reality, but rather the heightened reality of a cinematic experience. Those working in video-game music often cite film music as a model: 'We want to take the experience that everybody has at the movies and make it into something that you control' (Liam Byrne quoted in Belinkie 1999); 'every game audio designer will tell you that the ultimate goal is movie-quality game soundtracks' (Carl n.d.). In this respect, the aim of the makers of video-game versions of films like *Star Wars* or *Lord of the Rings* seems to be to place the player not in the world of the films' *stories*, but in the world of the *films* themselves.

However, in striving to recreate the aesthetic of cinematic realism, video-game designers face a different set of formal problems to those of filmmakers. The video-game image is arguably already mythic, because it is computer generated and as such is abstracted away from reality. The mythical quality of computer-generated imagery is exemplified by some of the imagery in a game like *Gran Turismo 4*, which is uncanny in its verisimilitude and therefore already possesses a mythical power without the need for a Wagnerian-sounding score. In fact an epic-sounding score would actually detract from the power of the images, turning the spectacle into kitsch.

Cinematic music can be criticised when it is used in video games because it acts merely as a kind of quotation of the epic music found in cinema, connoting all the epic associations of the aesthetic of cinematic realism, but without actually performing any of its functions. Thus, it can be argued that the cinematic aspirations of game designers have led to a further collapse of the Wagnerian model of mythic music, reducing the leitmotif to the lowly status of a looping underscore.[3] In this respect, Jean Baudrillard might be considered a better theorist for video-game designers than Wagner, because the mythical power of the video-game image is that of the *simulacrum*, which Baudrillard defines as 'a real without origin, or reality: a hyperreal' (Baudrillard 2004: 1). However, the problem here is that this concept would not be able to account for the aesthetic of cinematic realism because it cannot be used to distinguish between levels of realism found in indexical media like film, and levels of myth found in non-indexical media like computer-generated imagery, since Baudrillard's theory denies reality to both.

In examining the concept of mythic immersion, it is clear that music in video games cannot function in exactly the same way as it functions in cinema, because there are not the same tensions between myth and reality. If this tension is to be maintained, it becomes necessary to anchor the spectacle in some other referent of reality. The most obvious candidate is to use real-world sound effects instead of music. In this way the mythical video-game images are realised in sound. Of course, if game designers choose to go down this road (and many are already doing so) then their games will inevitably end up being less cinematic, but then the question that needs to be asked is 'Is that a problem?', since video games are not cinema. In this case perhaps this whole debate is merely symptomatic of the challenges video-game designers face in attempting to define their own unique aesthetic.

DIEGETIC

The third of my video-game music categories is diegetic, or the ability of games to tell stories. It is a discernible tendency of human beings to ascribe narrative meaning to the most inert or abstract phenomena. In cognition studies, test subjects anthropomorphise even the most rudimentary animated shapes such as circles and triangles and make up stories to 'explain' their behaviour (Cohen 2000: 362–3). Music adds meaning to these stories, either by confirming the visual message, or by resolving the ambiguities in an unclear message (pp. 363–4).

A video game's 'story' manifests most conspicuously in its cut scenes – which, as Whalen points out, can be best understood using the techniques of traditional film analysis (Whalen 2004). However, this is not to imply that video games are devoid of narrative content when they are played. For while game stories might not resemble traditional literary or cinematic narratives, as Espen Aarseth contends, the struggles (aporias) and triumphs (epiphanies) of the player actually reach deeper into 'a fundamental layer of human experience from which narratives are spun' (Aarseth 1997: 92).

In terms of narrative, video games are more schematic than either film or literature. A game may present a player with a set of goals to aim for, and a corresponding set of obstacles to overcome. But video games do not micro-manage their narratives in the way that films, plays or novels do (in fact, bad video-games are criticised for doing this). Steven Poole notes that video-game soundtracks fall into two main classes: either pop compilations or specially composed scores (Poole 2000: 81). The choice of music tends to be determined by the game's narrative content. Games with simple narratives (like *Gran Turismo 4*, *WipEout* and *SXX Tricky*) use pop music soundtracks while games with more complex narratives (like *Halo*, *Metal Gear Solid 2* and *Goldeneye*) use specially composed scores. It is often the case that music is used so conventionally in these contexts that it is possible to guess the narrative content of a game merely by glancing at the music credits.[4]

In the case of games with simple narratives, the primary function of music is to motivate the player. Tonal and rhythmic music has long been thought of as an aid to motivation. During the Cold War, for example, music was played to military personnel who watched the radar screens for signs of incoming missiles, precisely because it helped them to concentrate for longer periods of time. But worryingly, this policy was only instigated after a series of experiments conducted by the psychologist William Wokoun showed that, even in this pressurised environment, a person could only concentrate for a maximum period of half an hour (Lanza 1994: 150).

Zach Whalen argues that the application of what he calls a *safety/danger binary* drives the motivational function of music in game narratives (Whalen 2004). In early video games like *Space Invaders* or *Pac Man*, music signalled a danger state simply by altering its tempo or pitch (Newman 2004: 78). Today, more sophisticated methods are used. In *Enter the Matrix*, for example, the game's action is accompanied mostly by sound effects, with music only coming in when a mission reaches its climax, and this has the effect of heightening the tension. Here, in addition to energising the player, motivation consists of providing emotional cues that reinforce the meaning of the various rewards and setbacks a player faces.

Music can also be used to reflect the player's psychological state. For example, horror games employ dissonant music to rack up the tension and put the player on edge, for, as Whalen points out, these games lack a safety state where the player can relax (Whalen 2004). A novel variation of this device is found in the Gamecube title *Eternal Darkness: Sanity's Requiem*. The game has a 'sanity meter' to monitor the player's psychological state. At scary points, the meter drops and the player hears all sorts of odd noises, like wind chimes, babies crying, and the sound of a woman being violently beaten (Majaski 2002). These sounds have no obvious connection to the story, and so appear to be happening outside of the game, an effect also enhanced by the designers' clever use of the Gamecube's spatial-audio capabilities. Thus the audio transgresses the imaginary boundary separating the game and the player, creating a powerfully disturbing effect.[5]

As discussed earlier, video-game music also borrows from many cinematic conventions. However, in this context the music functions not to mythologise but to structure the game's narrative elements on the basis of familiar dramatic conventions. Games, like films, have opening and closing title sequences where music is used as a formal device to ease the transition between the real world and the storyworld (Buhler et al. 2000: 35). Furthermore, they both employ the notion of the leitmotif, although in this context it is the particularly cinematic interpretation of the leitmotif that Wagner would have disparaged and Kevin Donnelly referred to as a 'signpost' (Donnelly 2005: 58). Cinematic leitmotifs are used primarily as storytelling signposts that tell the player a certain environment is dangerous, or that a character is not to be trusted. Finally, both film and video games use music to provide stylistic cues to aid the comprehension of their particular setting and narrative genre. For example, stealth games use suspense music, games set in jungles may employ stereotypically 'jungly' musical motifs such as tribal drums and chanting, while fantasy games typically opt for epic-sounding orchestral scores.

However, despite sharing many functions with film music, diegetic video-game music differs in a fundamental respect. Theodore Adorno defines serious music as structured around a specific part–whole relationship, dealing chronologically with causes and effects (Lastra 1992: 71). This definition could very well describe the structure of narrative also. Tonal music complements a film narrative, because both are causally predetermined[6] and, as Michel Chion observes, 'each audio element enters into a simultaneous vertical relationship with a narrative element contained in an image' (Chion 1994: 40). However, a significant amount of the video-game narrative is not causally predetermined, because it is generated 'on the fly' by the actions of the player. This creates a conflict with tonal music, because sudden changes in music produce a very jarring musical effect. Consequently, video games are unable to recreate the same vertical correspondence between their musical themes and narrative events (Bessel 2002: 141).[7] Tonal game music therefore flounders in its attempts to imitate cinema, because, as the game composer Mike Pummel succinctly puts it, 'the game doesn't know where the music is, and the music doesn't know where the game is' (Belinkie 1999).

Nevertheless, some attempts have been made to develop game music along interactive lines. This technique, known as *adaptive audio*, is defined as music modulated in real time by the actions of the player (Wilde 2004: 1). While adaptive audio is successful at altering the volume of the music, or dynamically applying effects like reverb, it is less successful when it comes to 'adapting' the rules of tonal composition. The problem here is a musicological one and therefore not amenable to a technological quick-fix solution. The challenge facing composers of adaptive music is to write tonal-sounding music that somehow manages to overcome these prohibitions. Not surprisingly, many composers choose not to (Bessell 2002).

CONCLUDING REMARKS

I have divided this examination into three distinct areas, although it must be borne in mind that the division is only analytic and therefore arbitrary. In reality there is much cross-talk: for instance, the claim that music has a mythic power, which I critiqued in the immersive section, can be further contended by considering the conclusion of the environmental section, suggesting that the so-called mythical power of music, rather than having no real-world referent, is rooted in the everyday struggles of different animals in the environment. Similarly, the reasons given in the mythic immersion section for cinematic music's lack of power in video games can be further justified in the diegetic section by the lack of correspondence between linear tonal music and non-linear game narratives. However, there are also contradictions. For example, the claim advanced in the environmental section that music is a powerful signifier of meaning is contradicted in the immersive section when I suggest that many gamers have other audio playing in the background. The contradictions show that while this chapter has been quite ambitious in attempting to map out the theoretical groundwork for the study of music in video games, its reach has often been greater than its grasp.

Of the three areas of video-game music, I consider the immersive function to be the most important. Music acts both as a territorial zone of protection (Deleuze and Guatarri 2004) and as a means of occupying the brain (Cohen 2000). These two theoretical explanations, although supported by quite different lines of reasoning, actually lead to the same conclusion, namely that the primary function of music in mediated gaming situations is to keep the outside world at bay so that the player can focus exclusively on the game. If this theory is correct, it would suggest the choice of music is immaterial to its immersive function. This is a conjecture supported by the findings of the BBC study cited above, which reveals 70 per cent of gamers choose to have other audio playing in the background (Pratchett 2005). While this does not imply that music *per se* is becoming less important to the video-game experience, it does suggest that video games (along with television, radio, music players etc.) constitute a potentially rich multimedia environment – its individual sensory components being orchestrated by the player rather than authored by any one provider. What general aesthetic or social implications this particular finding discloses have yet to be properly recognised, let alone theorised about.

For this reason alone, more research needs to be undertaken in order to understand how players are using music in video games. The results from the BBC survey threaten to undermine confidence in aesthetic theories of game music, which have borrowed from film, and which have up until now dominated the academic study of this phenomenon. Yet to conclude that video-game music serves no aesthetic function beyond blocking out the sounds of the real world would be a mistake. The questions left open here need to be delineated more clearly by further study before they can be answered. In this respect I hope this chapter is seen as a challenge for those seeking to elaborate an aesthetic for video-game music, rather than an argument that forecloses the possibility of one.

Acknowledgement

I am indebted to Kevin Donnelly for his advice on this chapter.

Notes

1. Some of these 'descriptive' articles are very good, I would particularly recommend Matthew Belinkie (1999) and Karen Collins (2005). And there are a few honourable exceptions where the analysis of video-game music is concerned. Zach Whalen's (2004) excellent online article 'Play Along – An Approach to Videogame Music' and David Bessel's (2002) chapter 'What's that Funny Noise?' are ones that immediately come to mind, but there are others. This chapter builds on complementing this work, but I feel it would be a wasted opportunity, given the scarcity of scholarly material available, merely to summarise their findings without trying to contribute something of my own.
2. Deleuze and Guattari's theory cannot be adequately summarised here, because it is deeply interwoven with the wider themes of their book. However, I think certain aspects of it can be lifted out of their proper context and usefully applied to the study of video-game music.
3. This argument surveys the problem from a particularly narrow perspective and ignores the fact that cinematically styled video-game music is both hugely popular and widely admired. For example, Nobuo Uematsu's sweepingly cinematic scores for the *Final Fantasy* series of games made him the most commercially successful video-game composer ever (Belinkie 1999).
4. There are a few exceptions to this rule, most notably the *Grand Theft Auto* series, which uses no tonal music until a player steals a vehicle. Then music plays via the vehicle's radio. The use of sound in these games is so innovative that it deserves a whole chapter of its own, as it is the best example of the kind of dedicated video-game aesthetic I refer to at the end of the section on immersion. Suffice it to say that the radio in GTA presents a reflexive commentary on the world of the game, and

presents a satirical commentary on American culture, specifically its consumerism and its attitudes to violence. For more information see IGN, 'The Pet Sounds of *Grand Theft Auto III*', http://uk.ps2.ign.com/articles/098/098444p1.html, and Wikipedia's entry on *Grand Theft Auto III*'s audio, http://en.wikipedia.org/wiki/Grand_Theft_Auto_III_soundtrack.

5. Thanks to Richard at Games Park, Aberystwyth, for this observation.
6. The term 'causally predetermined' is not to be confused with 'linear', and neither is 'non-causally predetermined' the equivalent of 'non-linear'. The so called non-linear narratives of films like Kubrick's *The Killing* and Tarrantino's *Pulp Fiction* tell their stories out of chronological order, and Nolan's *Memento* adopts the novel device of telling its story in reverse. However, these non-conventional uses of narrative are still causally predetermined, because their non-linearity only applies at a stylistic level, while the cinema text itself is what Aarseth calls 'transient' (Aarseth 1997: 63), a term which means that the actual perception of a film as it runs through the projector is temporally inflexible, in the sense that users cannot influence the way the narrative is presented to them.
7. This may be a way of clarifying the infamous dispute in game studies as to whether games are primarily 'ludic' or 'diegetic' (Frasca, in Perron and Wolf 2003: 222–3). The intimate connection between tonal music and narrative could be used by researchers as a measure to determine how much a game did or did not conform to the conventions of classic narrative, simply by noting the presence or absence of tonal music at any point in the game.

Bibliography

Aarseth, E. J. (1997), *Cybertext: Perspectives on Egodic Literature* (Baltimore, MD: Johns Hopkins University Press).
Altman, R. (1992), 'The Material Heterogeneity of Recorded Sound', in R. Altman (ed.), *Sound Theory, Sound Practice* (London: Routledge).
Barthes, R. (1977), *Image Music Text*, trans. S. Heath (London: Fontana Press).
Baudrillard, J. (2004), *Simulacra and Simulation*, trans. S. F. Glaser (Ann Arbor: University of Michigan Press).
Belinkie, M. (1999), 'Videogame Music: Not Just Kid Stuff', http://www.vgmusic.com/vgpaper.shtml (accessed August 2006).
Bessell, D. (2002), 'What's that Funny Noise? An Examination of The Role of Music in *Cool Borders 2*, *Alien Trilogy* and *Medieval 2*', in G. King and T. Krzywinska (eds), *Screenplay: Cinema/Videogames/Interfaces* (London: Wallflower Press).
Brown, R. S. (1994), *Overtones and Undertones: Reading Film Music* (Berkeley, CA, and London: University of California Press).
Buhler, J. (2000), '*Star Wars*, Music and Myth', in J. Buhler, C. Flinn and D. Neumeyer (eds), *Music and Cinema* (Hanover, NH, and London: Wesleyan University Press).
Buhler, J., Flinn, C., and Neumeyer, D. (2000), *Music and Cinema* (Hanover, NH and London: Wesleyan University Press).
Callois, R. (2000), *Man Play and Games*, trans. M. Barash (Chicago: University of Illinois Press).
Carl, J. (n.d.), 'Sound & Fury, Part 1', http://www.xbox.com/en-us/fable/behindthegame3.htm (accessed August 2006).
Chion, M. (1994), *Audio-Vision Sound on Screen*, ed. and trans. C. Gorbman (New York: Columbia University Press).
Cohen, A. J. (2000), 'Film Music: Perspectives from Cognitive Psychology', in J. Buhler, C. Flinn and D. Neumeyer (eds), *Music and Cinema* (Hanover, NH, and London: Wesleyan University Press).

Collins, K. (2005), 'From Bits To Hits: Videogames Music Changes its Tune', *Film International*, Vol. 3, Issue 13, http://www.dullien-inc.com/collins/texts/bits2hits.pdf (accessed August 2006).

Deleuze, G., and Guattari, F. (2004), *A Thousand Plateaus*, trans. B. Massumi (London: Continuum).

Donnelly, K. J. (2001), 'The Hidden Heritage of Film Music: History and Scholarship', in K. J. Donnelly (ed.), *Film Music: Critical Approaches* (Edinburgh: Edinburgh University Press).

—— (2005), *The Spectre of Sound: Music in Film and Television* (London: BFI).

Gorbman, C. (1987), *Unheard Melodies: Narrative Film Music* (London: BFI).

Harland, K. (2000), 'Composing for Interactive Music', http://www.gamasutra.com/features/20000217/harland_01.htm (accessed August 2006).

Johnson, S. (2005), *Everything Bad is Good For You* (London: Penguin).

Kaltenbrunner, M., and Huxor, A. (2002), 'Multiple Presence through Auditory Bots in Virtual Environments', http://yuri.at/marvin/delft (accessed August 2006).

Kerman, J. (1985), *Musicology* (London: Fontana).

Komar, A. (1980), *Music and Human Experience* (New York: Macmillian).

Lanza, J. (1994), *Elevator Music* (London: Quartet).

Lastra, J. (1992), 'Reading, Writing and Representing Sound', in R. Altman (ed.), *Sound Theory, Sound Practice* (London: Routledge).

Lipscomb, S. D., and Tolchinsky, D. E. (2004), 'The Role of Music Communication in Cinema', http://lipscomb.umn.edu/docs/FilmMusic_LipscombTolchinsky_final_asPublished.pdf (accessed August 2006).

Majaski, C. (2002), '*Eternal Darkness*', *Gaming* Age, http://www.gaming-age.com/ cgi-bin/reviews/review.pl?sys=gamecube&game=ed (accessed August 2006).

Newman, J. (2004), *Videogames* (London: Routledge).

Pair, J. (n.d.), 'Virtual Environment Sound Design Primer', http://www.jarrellpair.com/primer.html (accessed August 2006).

Pater, W. (1925), *The Renaissance: Studies in Art and Poetry* (London: Macmillan).

Perron, B., and Wolf, M. J. P. (2003), *The Videogame Theory Reader* (London: Routledge).

Poole, S. (2000), *Trigger Happy: The Inner Life of Videogames* (London: Fourth Estate).

Pratchett, R. (2005), 'Gamers in the UK: Digital Play Digital Lifestyles', http://crystaltips.typepad.com/wonderland/files/bbc_uk_games_research_2005.pdf (accessed August 2006).

SOED (*Shorter Oxford English Dictionary*) (1973), third edn, vols 1 and 2 (Oxford: Oxford University Press).

Wagner, R. (1875), *Richard Wagner's Prose Works. Vol. 1: The Art-Work of the Future* (2nd edn), trans. W. A. Ellis (London: Kegan Paul, Trench, Trübner).

Whalen, Z. (2004), 'Play Along – An Approach to Videogame Music', *Game Studies, The International Journal of Computer Game Research*, http://www.gamestudies.org/0401/whalen (accessed August 2006).

Wikipedia (n.d.), 'Chiptune', http://en.wikipedia.org/wiki/Chiptune (accessed August 2006).

Wilde, M. D. (2004), *Audio Programming for Interactive Games* (Oxford: Focal Press).

Wishart, T. (1986), 'Sound Symbols and Landscapes', in S. Emmerson (ed.), *The Language of Electroacoustic Music* (Basingstoke: Macmillan).

Game References

Enter the Matrix (2003) Atari.
Eternal Darkness: Sanity's Requiem (2002) Silicon Knights.

Goldeneye (1997) Nintendo.
Gran Turismo 4 (2004) Sony Computer Entertainment.
Grand Theft Auto San Andreas (2004) Rockstar North.
Halo (2001) Microsoft Game Studios.
Metal Gear Solid 2: Sons of Liberty (2001) Konami.
Pac Man (1980) Namco.
Perfect Dark (2000) Rare.
Silent Hill (1999) Konami.
Space Invaders (1978) Taito.
Spiderman 2 (2004) Activision.
Super Mario Brothers (1985) Nintendo.
SXX Tricky (2001) Electronic Arts.
Tom Clancy's Ghost Recon: Jungle Storm (2004) Ubisoft.
WipEout (1995) Psygnosis.

4. CASE STUDY: FILM MUSIC VS. VIDEO-GAME MUSIC: THE CASE OF *SILENT HILL*

Zach Whalen

The central question of this chapter can be stated simply: how do we as critics and students of media understand the relationship between sound and image as it occurs in the video-game environment? A well-established body of litera-ture exists analysing the role film music plays in cinematic storytelling, but the problem of game music – as well as, for that matter, the ontology of the game image itself – presents a surprising number of challenges for the would-be analyst. At first glance, the crucial problem seems to centre on the fact that a game is *played* rather than viewed, and the difference that interactivity makes in the player's relationship to the work in question would seem to provide a logical starting point for analysis. The problem, however, is that interactivity as such is notoriously difficult to define, and drawing conclusions about the expressive content of a work based on this approach rapidly advances towards the tautological. In cinema, the equivalent approach might hold that studying film music must begin with understanding the audience as opposed to situating music within the semiotic apparatus of the film itself, and it is not clear which approach is the most productive. In any case, applying either an audience-oriented or film-oriented approach requires certain ontological assumptions about the relationship between the constituent parts of the media event. Specifically, creating predictive or general rules about how music in film can express meaning or emotion requires a stable configuration of the components being analysed, and in turning the same analysis to video games where this con-figuration is constantly changing, it becomes clear that new strategies must be adopted.

In this study, I want to examine the *Silent Hill* (1999) series of games to consider ways in which its use of music highlights the critical differences between film and video-game music. Understanding such differences is important not only as a way of developing a better understanding of these games, but also towards leveraging the unique development in communication that video games provide. In particular, I argue that, through the example of *Silent Hill* series of games, we can identify different critical assumptions made in analysing either film music or game music, and by seeking new formulations, we can arrive at a more robust approach to the ways in which music contributes to cross-medial storytelling. I do not want to claim, however, that through the following examination I can develop or generalise an approach which can be applied as a template to other examples of video-game music. In fact, I hope to demonstrate that earlier studies which seek to generalise video-game music, including my own earlier work on the subject, produce arbitrary and inappropriately rigid taxonomies which fail to account for the full expressive potential of the genre. Still, K. J. Donnelly notes of horror film music that 'in its extremity and direct aim at effect, [horror film music] exemplifies the way that film music works more generally' (Donnelly 2005: 14), and as *Silent Hill* is a Survival Horror game, a genre notable for its rigid framework and close relationship to cinematic horror,[1] it provides a logical common ground for comparing film and game music. Ironically, it is because Survival Horror games are in many ways exceptions to more general patterns of games that *Silent Hill* becomes a useful subject for this study. In other words, because Survival Horror as a genre is more self-consciously cinematic in its presentation, at least to the extent that its games can be said to mimic horror film music specifically in some regards, the musical features uniquely available to the game environment of *Silent Hill* provide a convenient counterpoint for exploring game music techniques.

Film Music

An entire discipline has risen around studying film for its artistic and cultural qualities, and a perennial conversation within that field deals with music and the impact it has on the experience or exposition of cinema. It is difficult to survey the total discourse on this subject, but a few dominant themes emerge. In particular, one approach construes filmic sound as an element in a semiotic system that comprises the total film experience. In other words, 'sound' refers to a subset of basically linguistic signs – one of which can be music – that together comprise the film itself, which can then be interpreted. Donnelly observes the weakness of this approach for its failure to account for the emotional complexity evident in film music, and both structural and poststructural thought employ these semiologic assumptions at the expense of the work itself.[2] While it is beyond the scope of this chapter to explore each of these approaches and how they might bear upon a study of video-game music, a few core ideas from film-music analysis prove to be useful in making comparisons across both media and are, therefore, worth looking at briefly.

In its broadest sense, the study of film music attempts to understand the ways music influences or participates in the narration of the film. At least in mainstream film, the visual element of the film's story dominates its reception while the sonic elements are understood only in the sense in which they enhance, contrast or detract from the visual elements. Along these lines, composer Aaron Copland famously describes five purposes of film music:

1. Creating a convincing atmosphere of time and place;
2. Underlining psychological refinements – the unspoken thoughts of a character;
3. Serving as a kind of neutral background filler;
4. Building a sense of continuity;
5. Underpinning the theatrical build-up of a scene, and rounding it off with a sense of finality. (Copland 1957: 154–5)

What each of these purposes has in common is an orientation to the rules of narrative. Even though terms like 'continuity', 'background', 'tension' and 'finality' can be used to describe music, the root of their meaning applies to functions or phenomena of narrative. Indeed, the extent to which these terms do effectively describe music may reflect the influence of a narrative turn in music theory, which uses the grammars of narratology for characteristics of music that are otherwise notoriously difficult to describe. Not surprisingly, semiotic approaches have taken hold, as exemplified in the work of Eero Tarasti, who argues that, taking a minimal condition for narrativity, 'we may argue that music constitutes a fundamentally narrative art. It unfolds in time, and very often we feel that something happens in a musical piece – even if we are completely unable to verbalise our experience' (Tarasti 2004: 283). In the passage this citation comes from, Tarasti then proceeds through several different music theoretical models based on Levi-Straussian and Greimasian systems, demonstrating the applicability of narrativist terminology within the study of music. However, Marie-Laure Ryan reminds us that without semantic or diegetic content, speaking of the narrative function in music is primarily metaphorical (Ryan 2004: 267). So within that gap film, and perhaps video games, may supply the remainder of the equation, defining a multifaceted form of narrative exposition that includes both image and sound.

Some approaches to film music unpack this relationship and use the logic of semiotics, like that of Michel Chion, who argues that film music is either 'empathetic' – that is, working with the other elements of the scene – or 'a-empathetic' – working independently or otherwise neutral in relation to the scene (Chion 1994: 8). By adding diegesis as an additional configurative, Stam, Burgoyne and Flitterman-Lewis catalogue twenty-four different possible positions for film music (Stam et al. 1992: 59–62). Whether the diegetic space of the film serves or is served by the interplay of sound and image, these three elements work together to create the phenomenal experience of film, and dominant film theory has proceeded on the assumption that the viewer's role is to interpret the interplay of these signs in a way that produces meaning.

There are, of course, alternative models for approaching film music. Donnelly, for example, argues that the dry conjectures of the semioticians are based on a logic rooted in linguistics, a field not unrelated but perhaps inappropriate for encompassing the rich emotional and physiological effects of music. Instead, horror music in particular can be considered primarily affective in the sense that its impact on the viewer is pre-cognitive and has as much to do with a physiological response to the sound (as in, say, an orchestral stinger, or startling burst of music, at a frightening moment in a horror film) as it does with any cultural associations of particular sounds with situations of terror or fear (Donnelly 2005: 97). In a different vein, Nicholas Cook develops an interpretative framework for discussing meaning-making in music as the result of a mutual interaction of semantic elements potentially including critical interpretation, text or images (Cook 1998: 23). In other words, this logic sees music as one component in a system which generates meaning through the co-involvement of its parts, and this direction proves to be far more fruitful in discussing video-game music.

Creating a sense of atmosphere is an important role for film music, as Copland has duly noted, and in this sense it is closely tied to the unfolding of the film's diegesis. The diegesis, or 'storyworld', of a film includes the entire imagined space in which the events of the film occur, so it provides vital semantic content as well as implying a phenomenological relationship between the audience and the film world. This includes elements that appear on the screen as well as events, objects or sounds which the film's characters interact with or refer to that may be off-screen or temporally removed. A common use of non-diegetic music in film is for it to underscore events or emotions experienced by the characters even though the characters themselves do not actually hear the music. In other words, it is a kind of mediation between the space of the film and the audience, and in this way, music can accomplish some of the most dramatic emotional aspects of the immersive experience of film, all the while acting for the most part without the viewer's being conscious of it. The fact that this subtle effect can be described in terms derived from semiotics, furthermore, suggests a particular ontological status to the film space in how it relates to the viewer, and distinguishing this status from that of the gameworld provides an important point of departure when approaching game music.

VIDEO-GAME MUSIC

At first glance, video-game music seems quite similar to music in film. Game scores are often arranged by professional, well-respected composers. Soundtracks frequently feature lush, orchestral compositions or collages of pop music, which are often available as standalone albums. Ultimately, whilst the two have a good deal in common, there are clearly unique uses of music in video games, which I outline below. As a starting point, however, I will outline some structural similarities. To begin with, game music can be diegetic or non-diegetic (though it is often impossible or irrelevant to tell the difference), and it can reinforce the visual elements of the game in much the same way that film music helps describe a scene. In some games, the music is nearly all diegetic – the *Grand Theft Auto* games, for example, include very brief non-diegetic music to signify the completion of missions, but most of the music projects from user-selected radio stations within the gameworld. In *Katamari Damacy*, on the other hand, presumably non-diegetic music saturates each environment that the player explores. Many games feature both, and often a game will include an array of discrete diegetic stances within which music and image appear together. In the same vein as Mark J. P. Wolf's (2002) taxonomies of game elements, one could potentially compile an exhaustive list of such uses. Briefly, this list could include start screens, loading screens and cut scenes in addition to actual gameplay. For the purpose of this discussion, though, I should clarify that I'm exclusively interested in music that accompanies gameplay, since cut scenes are essentially miniature films and as such respond to the theoretical models afforded by film. Loading and start menu screens, by contrast, are generally still images with narrowly constrained narrative weight, so their analysis would require special contextualisation.[3] Overall, gameplay accompanied by music exemplifies the best potential for games to innovate in terms of interactivity and demonstrates the best opportunity to examine what I think are unique contributions to the practice of music and media.

Video-game music is relatively new (video games themselves having only been around since the 1960s), but it is still surprising how few studies endeavour to apply the same rigour to its analysis as is the case with film music. In an earlier project, I attempted to outline general uses of game music and how it configures the actions of the player in relation to the game. Adopting a structural model derived from Chion and linguist Roman Jakobson, I argued that whereas the film score proceeds by encouraging a viewer to be emotionally involved, a game score additionally demands the player's concentration and action (Whalen 2004).[4]

A number of writers have also looked to the history of game music for insight into modern game music. In a presentation at the 2004 Princeton Video Game Conference, for example, Robert Bowen argued that the limitations of early game systems encouraged early composers like Nobuo Uematsu (*Final Fantasy*) and Koji Kondo (*Super Mario Brothers*, *Legend of Zelda*) to develop innovative techniques that resulted in what might be called the 'bleeps and bloops' musical style. The disarming simplicity of the sound belies the complex sonic illusions taking place to produce rich tonalities that are surprising given the obvious limitations of the systems. As Bowen argued, the resulting compositional practice has more in common with the serialism of Schoenberg than the programme music generally associated with narrative features. Other writers have taken this problem in different directions by focusing on the unique challenges of the game composer. While modern game systems have advanced to include high-quality recorded music, a significant challenge still exists in applying the narrative-enhancing features of film music to a game environment.

If one role of film music is to heighten the drama of key events in the narrative, free-form gameplay prevents a technical challenge whereby it becomes rather difficult to cue music in relation to significant game events. For example, a game like *Grand Theft Auto* defines a world which creates an illusion of being autonomous, and a player wanders through the environment seeking out goals to accomplish. Non-diegetic 'reward music' occurs to signal the completion of such a mission, but there are smaller, non-discrete mission states which go unadorned by musical signifiers. This is because by opting for a high degree of spatial granularity, the game's designers have made it difficult to tie music in to significant events like, say, stealing a particularly fast car. One option that is available to three-dimensional games seeking finer musical granularity is for the programming that cues the music to be attached to objects in the game environment. One form of this practice would be for 'battle music' to be tied in to the object code of enemy units. Approaching the enemies within the 3D space would cause the volume of the threatening music they 'emit' to increase. Defeating the enemy ends the battle music, and the return of the dominant 'safe music' signals the kind of closure Copland listed as a role film music can play. Dozens of games exhibit this kind of structure, but the challenge for the would-be critic is in determining whether the apparent success of this formula depends on preconceptions supplied from familiarity with film music or, rather derives from the emergent properties of the situation within which the player is performing.

That is, if one considers the player's experience of the music as it accompanies play to be its semiotic content, then certainly a structural approach could, with some minor adjustment, adapt film-theoretical models for understanding game music. On the other hand, proceeding from this essentially linguistic base would have to assume that the sequence of the interaction and not the rules of the interaction itself constituted the content of gameplay. In fact, Bowen has argued that the sequential production of sounds during gameplay can be considered a kind of aleatory composition such that playing a game generates a musical product. This is a fascinating argument, but the problem I see with the result is that music need not have any contact with the player. One could imagine a player 'performing' by playing the game while an 'audience' listens in on headphones. By considering the musical content of a game as a kind of output, the critic has pre-empted analysis of the game itself. In other words, taking literally the implications of applying narrative structure to video-game music, one closes off the gameness of the game by making an arbitrary determination of its expressive content. Furthermore, if music can be described as only metaphorically narrativistic and film images complete a cumulative narrative situation by supplying the experience with semantic and diegetic content, one must ask whether video games exhibit the same semantic and diegetic qualities that film does. In the growing field of game studies, this is a somewhat controversial question, but the consensus seems to be that it does not.[5] In any case, an alternative model that takes more seriously the underlying logic of video-game technology might offer a more practicable theory that accounts for the history and complexity of video-game music as well as addressing its expressive qualities. To this end, Ian Bogost's *Unit Operations* provides an instructive example for analysing *Silent Hill*, and it is this model that I want to use to approach the musical features of this game.

In order to forge new ground in the analysis of game music, it seems that the terms of the interpretation of video games must be renegotiated. To the extent that both film-music analysis and video-game studies exhibit a degree of controversy over semiotic methods, it is interesting to note a similarity between K. J. Donnelly's objection to semiotics-based musical analysis and Bogost's response to the ludology vs. narratology 'debate' within game studies. Donnelly contends that '[m]ost semiotic approaches would consider music simply to be a selection of signs that are decoded by the listener, translated into words, ideas and narrative' (2005: 97). Instead, he argues, a theory of film music should be able to appreciate the expressive and emotional effects of music within the aesthetic context of film. Bogost lays out his case for unit analysis similarly by observing that both ludology and narratology (or narrativism) are 'haunted by a functionalist ideology' in which the structure or system proposed by each viewpoint has the ability to override expressive meaning (Bogost 2006: 70). For Bogost, this is the trap of analytical schemas derived from semiotics: the tendency of these schools of thought to collapse into self-contained systems belies or ignores the actual programmatic basis of digital games. The result in terms of game studies is that the systems-based approaches threaten to exist for their own sake. A more faithful method for thinking about video games exposes the operations of units acting within their systems, which together generate the net experience of the work. Rather than assuming the totality of the system and then 'filling in the blanks' to assign meaning-making roles to its constituents, unit operations proceed from the immanent qualities of the units themselves and their co-operation with the larger system. This approach is uniquely appropriate for video games in the sense that many exhibit system behaviour of this kind, whilst the underlying programming of video-game software can generally be described as object-oriented, where semi-autonomous units of code are used and reused in a number of different contexts and the output of the system depends on the local interdependencies of these objects.

To understand this logic it is helpful to think of a video-game character – say, Harry, the protagonist of the first *Silent Hill* game – as a programming object. He can interact with other objects in different contexts and has rules for doing so (rules like gravity), but his appearance and character remain constant throughout the game. Better yet, what we identify as Harry in the game environment is really an assembly of different units of code such as rules for physics, bitmap graphics for depicting the surfaces of Harry's body, and libraries of rules governing how the gameworld responds to Harry. All of these components working in congress constitute the apparent totality we can identify as Harry. Unit analysis is particularly appropriate for approaching video games because it works by exposing the dominant forces at work in the process that generates apparent totality. As Bogost demonstrates unit operations functioning within a variety of other works, it becomes apparent that this model also applies particularly well to musical analysis in that successful musical performance, say in an ensemble, requires musicians to be aware of their own performance in the context of the group. As *Silent Hill* demonstrates, analysing the interaction of musical and programmatic objects within the same system allows for an approach which simultaneously embraces the fundamental logic of both.

'HUH, RADIO . . . WHAT'S GOING ON WITH THAT RADIO?'

The original *Silent Hill* game was released in 1999 by Konami for the Playstation console. It was well received by the gaming public, and early reviews noted its more cerebral approach to the Survival Horror genre, including an emphasis on story and character development as well as artfully crafted atmospheres, that distinguished it from its main predecessor in the genre, *Resident Evil*.[6] The game has since led to three major sequels for the Playstation 2 and Xbox consoles as well as a number of ports to handheld systems and PC. The franchise also spawned a graphic novel series, which met with limited success, and a 2006 film adaptation directed by Christophe Gans. While each of the games follows the same themes and many of the same gameplay elements, I intend to focus primarily on the original game for this analysis because it most clearly demonstrates the features which define the signature feel or atmosphere of the series.[7] Furthermore, approaching this sense of atmosphere with a unit analytical logic leads to the conclusion that, through the innovative sound design of Akira Yamaoka, *Silent Hill* is above all a meditation on the meaning of silence.

The plot of *Silent Hill* deals with supernatural horror and centres on the town of Silent Hill being infested with demonic or nightmarish forces. As presented in the game, the spaces of the town manifest two distinct versions: a relatively normal world that is saturated with white fog, and a dark world version of the same space. Monsters pervade both spaces, and the major difference between the two is conveyed visually in that in the dark world, surfaces are frequently transformed into blood-soaked rusty metal populated with images of incredible torture and violence. Throughout, the player's view is often sharply limited, either by the limitations of a third-person, trailing-camera position or by the fog, darkness, and the narrowness of corridors within buildings. In order to succeed and keep Harry alive, players must learn to rely on auditory clues which can alert them to the presence, type and proximity of monsters. The key to this ability is an object Harry carries with him but which is usually not visible: a broken radio, which emits static as a monster approaches. The sounds this radio produces are specific to the type of monster it is detecting, and can modulate in response to the number of monsters within its range. In effect, the monsters are broadcasting white noise through their bodies, and as the static levels increase or decrease, the player can isolate the direction the monster is approaching from and choose either to confront or to avoid it. This key element forms a link between the player and the diegesis, and complicates the diegetic formulas received from film studies to the extent that such models quickly become too cumbersome to accommodate the necessary adjustments. Whereas the signifying status of the radio could perhaps be called 'acousmatic', after Chion's term for sounds which lack an on-screen source, it is difficult to say whether the monster or the radio itself is the source of the sound, and in either case the detail of whether the source is on or off the screen depends on the player's path through the environment. As such, a categorical determination of its signifying practice would have to be ambiguous or at least multivalent.

Also, while the static itself is definitely atonal, it does demonstrate musical properties such as pitch modulation, rhythm and repetition, and it would be possible – though, I think, inadequate – to think of the static sound as parallel to the horror film music formula wherein a sustained ostinato that increases in tempo or volume builds tension towards a stinger, signifying an attack.[8] Below the static sound, the dominant base sound in *Silent Hill* is a chilling ambient wash which throbs with the sounds of machinery and sirens. The volume level of this ambient sound is low, but its ubiquitous presence keeps the player on edge and sets the ominous tone for the visual environments of both worlds of *Silent Hill*. Its mechanical tone also blends smoothly with the machine-produced static of the radio such that the sonic texture of the atmosphere remains consistent. And that consistency maintains the contiguity of the visual environments through the sound's correlation to *Silent Hill*'s virtual space, and in this sense constructs the game's diegesis from two distinct channels of code. In other words, if one had access to the underlying programming of *Silent Hill*, one would find graphics libraries and code for generating the three-dimensional environments of the town. One would also find instructions for attaching specific audio tracks to areas within that space. Similarly, the code for the monsters likely contains instructions for broadcasting their position to the environment and Harry, as well as for adjusting the appropriate audio track accordingly. In this case, it is certainly possible to think of the game's sound as declarative to the extent that it corresponds to pre-programmed features of the game experience and behaves predictably according to its instructions. But instead of constraining that seeming signification to a single one-to-one correspondence of meaning, for example, it is more valuable to recognise that the presence or absence of the static sound indicates a particular state of the relationship between the player, Harry, the environment, the monster(s), and the radio itself. Each of these constituents is, moreover, composed of interacting parts which call their local totality into existence as the situation dictates, and, taken together, the situation that produces the static sound composes the full diegesis of the game. Note that this diegesis includes the player within its boundaries; its contents are immanently unstable as they project the chaos of the narrative and move between silence and noise.

Furthermore, the background music in *Silent Hill* addresses a pair of challenges video-game composers routinely face: avoiding monotony and minimising audible traces of looping. The fact that a player will spend an unpredictable amount of time exploring any given area means that background music must be just interesting enough to avoid tedium, whilst for it to appear seamless it must not have sharp start-over points when the music reaches the end of a loop. Even having a clear melodic structure that proceeds conventionally towards a resolution and then starts over can be distracting, so one approach to solving this problem which *Silent Hill* demonstrates is to create ambient music which lacks melodic structure. Yamaoka's ambient sound is still musical in the sense that it exhibits pitch variation and rhythmical features, but its progression is so gradual and its cohesion so atonal that the only observable repetitive structure is to employ short loops of similar sounds lasting maybe two to four seconds but repeating indefinitely. The result is a soft but unsettling blend of wind, air-raid sirens, machine-like chugging, indeterminate groaning and infrequent instrumentation such as strings or organ, and what little dynamic change occurs within the music is cued to specific locations which seem to blend into one another gradually. Also, because separate audio tracks can be played simultaneously, this blending effect is produced by the progressive addition of sonic layers. This practice is most apparent in an opening scene in which Harry first encounters the dark Silent Hill. As Harry follows what he thinks is his daughter down an alleyway, the space becomes tighter and the trailing camera is forced into fixed positions above discrete sections of the alley. Progressing from one section to another produces the visual effect of a jump-cut, and these are paired with extra audio layers adding on to the base ambience. This causes the general volume, as well as the harmonic and rhythmic chaos, to increase, so that the music is behaving somewhat like film music to the extent that it increases dramatic tension as events progress towards a climactic event and the visual space becomes more tense and horrific. It must be noted, however, that this observable progression is only possible because of the compression of the space and the audio that corresponds to the increasingly horrific and constrained alley segments. In other words, the emotional potential of the scene (that is, the degree to which it is frightening) is bound up in the deployment of units which co-operatively render the sequence.

Although Harry observes as he enters Silent Hill for the first time that it is 'too quiet', actual silence is rare in the game, and the constant blanket of noise, which varies dramatically in volume and complexity, drives the anxiety of the game experience. Silence generally only occurs in interior spaces where a save point is possible, and even those cases are brief and spatially constrained. Even in these instances, the echoes of Harry's footsteps reverberate through the empty space, highlighting his isolation as he proceeds on his solitary quest to save his daughter. In one of the final areas of the game, for example, the background music consists of a single blast of white noise lasting about two seconds, with about five seconds of silence in the interval between repetitions. This alternation keeps the player off-balance and compresses the dialectic between silence and sound into an encapsulation of the game's overarching rhythm of silence and noise. In this way, the innovation of *Silent Hill* is that within its environment, silence expresses the loneliness and exhaustion shared by Harry and the player. More specifically, the presence or absence of silence communicates the configuration of the gameworld in relation to the player-character and the player herself or himself, and the movement between silence and sound generates the emotional contents of the game experience. In a finer sense, situations or patterns that exhibit narrative-like structure, in building and resolving tension through musical elements like volume or dissonance, operate through the same logic of adding or subtracting layers to or from the soundtrack. Thus, neither extreme of silence or noise is at rest, but rather, the dynamics of *Silent Hill* work through the fluid exchange between these two extremes and the corresponding programmatic units which produce these effects through their configuration relative to one another. Though silence corresponds occasionally to safety, its presence is always threatened by the encroachment of sound, and the presence of monsters within *Silent Hill* guarantees its dissolution. This dissolving constitutes a form of expression through silence, and the game demonstrates a meditation on the forms and sounds of fear. Even the orchestrated accompaniments to cut scenes and the game's opening video reflect a deliberately low-fi sound (distinctly reminiscent of the group Portishead), which reinforces the themes of claustrophobia and constraint that characterise the game as well as the genre.[9] This effect is accomplished through adding a fair amount of signal noise or static to the piece, so the point seems to be that the darkness is pervasive and that monsters lurk in the silence.

CONCLUSION

Video-game music is clearly capable of many kinds of complex expression, but significantly that complexity does not arise as the output of a codified or even a predictable system of signifiers. Rather, video-game music demonstrates the way in which video games express meaning through the interplay of their compositional units. Expression is, as it were, rendered in real time as one of several units operating within the total structure. Furthermore, this approach can in turn be applied to cinema or other media, and in fact Donnelly's discussion of horror film music and Cook's approach to musical multimedia use some of the same logic. In short, considering film music as a signifier actually has the same problems as applying narrative terminology to describe musical effects. By approaching film music as a signifying practice within the semiotic system of a film, critics risk making metaphoric elements literal and limiting analysis to the rigidly linguistic. Similarly, though it is tempting to assign signifier status to elements of game music for the allegedly scientific conclusions one can draw, it does a discredit to the fundamental structure of a game and implies the illusion of an essential or correct reading. Within the spaces of *Silent Hill*, such a reading is impossible, and any narrativising energy we might ascribe to the game's music is more accurately a result of the dissonance that obtains in the configuration of relationships between the player and the game objects. Through this dissonance and by way of its logic of unit operations, *Silent Hill* as a game meditates on loneliness, fear and love through the expressiveness of silence.

NOTES

1. Though the term 'genre' is used to distinguish among types and categories of video games, the generic distinctions available for game categories are often quite different from the normal sense of the term. For example, game genres include labels like 'Action', 'First-Person Shooter' and 'Graphical Adventure', which describe the mechanism or circumstances of play more than any narrative content. One could have a Western-themed First-Person Shooter, for example, but its fundamental genre would still be First-Person Shooter. Survival Horror is somewhat different in that its label does depend on the horror milieu. The 'Survival' modifier reflects the fact that the players' goal is often not simply to destroy everything in their paths but often to avoid combat so as to make it out of the environment alive; thus, this label includes both a semantic and syntactic element related to the game. Prominent examples of Survival Horror games like the *Resident Evil* and *Silent Hill* series develop other conventions

(or clichés), some of which include a use of constrained third-person 'camera' views and puzzle-solving.

2. A number of different scholars explore this general trajectory, but I am thinking in particular of those influenced by Christian Metz as well as the studies of film music by Michel Chion. Also, while there are certainly many valuable approaches which are not strictly semiotic in their logic, the influence of structuralism and poststructuralism is undeniable, especially as structuralism gained critical currency roughly in parallel to the proliferation of film.

3. This is, of course, not to say that loading screens and menu screens are insignificant in terms of narrative. In fact, they provide a crucial element in any rigorous narrativity in video games. For example, Laurie Taylor has discussed the function of loading screens in *Resident Evil: Code Veronica* as a crucial syntactic element segmenting the visual space of the diegesis (Taylor 2004).

4. In the original *Super Mario Brothers*, for example, when the time remaining to complete a level begins to run out, the music increases in tempo. This not only increases the perceived excitement of the scene taking place, it also directs the player with interaction-specific information. The music instructs the player to hurry up and finish the level. I want to move beyond my original argument, but in May 2004 paper I discuss two separate axes within which game music operates: a 'vertical' or metaphoric axis that defines the space or diegesis of the gameworld and that operates through a logic of substitution, and a 'horizontal' or metonymic axis along which game sequences are made to be coherent by musical sequences that progress the experience of the game further along.

5. The so-called 'ludology vs. narratology' debate is one in which scholars studying video games allegedly take one of two positions, and argue either that games are unique systems that should not be studied with critical tools derived from other media (ludologists), or that games are simply a new form of narrative (narratologists). For more on both sides of the discussion, see the various essays in Wardrip-Fruin and Harrigan (2006).

6. See, for example, Reyes (1999).

7. *Silent Hill 4: The Room* (2006) is the major exception. Even though the game itself is innovative and interesting, many *Silent Hill* fans found it disappointing and do not consider it to be a 'true' *Silent Hill* game.

8. See Donnelly (2005: 90–4) for an insightful discussion of this formula.

9. See Taylor (2006: 86) for a thorough discussion of this theme.

REFERENCES

Bogost, I. (2006), *Unit Operations: An Approach to Videogame Criticism* (Cambridge, MA: MIT Press).

Chion, M. (1994), *Audio-Vision: Sound on Screen*, ed. and trans. C. Gorbman (New York: Columbia University Press).

Cook, N. (1998), *Analysing Musical Multimedia* (Oxford: Clarendon Press).

Copland, A. (1957), *What to Listen for in Music*, rev. edn (New York: McGraw-Hill).

Donnelly, K. J. (2005), *The Spectre of Sound: Music in Film and Television* (London: BFI).

Reyes, F. (1999), '*Silent Hill*: Konami's answer to Capcom's Resident Evil Takes the Horror Genre into Uncharted Territory', *IGN*, 24 February, http://psx.ign.com/articles/153/153982p1.html (accessed August 2006).

Ryan, M-L. (2004), 'Music', in M-L. Ryan (ed.), *Narrative across Media: The Languages of Storytelling* (Lincoln, NE: University of Nebraska Press).

Stam, R., Burgoyne, R., and Flitterman-Lewis, S. (1992), *New Vocabularies in Film Semiotics: Structuralism, Post-Structuralism and Beyond* (New York: Routledge).

Tarasti, E. (2004), 'Music as a Narrative Art', in M-L. Ryan (ed.), *Narrative across Media: The Languages of Storytelling* (Lincoln, NE: University of Nebraska Press).

Taylor, L. (2004), 'Compromised Divisions: Thresholds in Comic Books and Video Games', *ImageTexT: Interdisciplinary Comics Studies*, Vol. 1, No. 1, http://www.english.ufl.edu/imagetext/archives/v1_1/taylor (accessed August 2006).

—— (2006), 'Not of Woman Born: Monstrous Interfaces and Monstrosity in Video Games' dissertation, University of Florida.

Wardrip-Fruinn N., and Harrigan, P. (eds) (2006), *First Person: New Media as Story, Performance, and Game* (Cambridge, MA: MIT Press).

Whalen, Z. (2004), 'Play Along: An Approach to Videogame Music', *Game Studies: The International Journal of Computer Game Research*, Vol. 4, No. 1, http://www.gamestudies.org/0401/whalen (accessed August 2006).

Wolf, M. J. P. (ed.) (2002), *The Medium of the Video Game* (Austin, TX: University of Texas Press).

SECTION THREE:

PERFORMANCE AND PRESENTATION

5. REFLECTIONS ON SOUND ART

Jamie Sexton

This chapter is concerned with sound (or sonic) art, as opposed to the art form known as music. This is, nevertheless, a quite difficult artistic category to describe straightforwardly. There are, for example, no boundaries that divide 'sound art' and 'music' in any total manner. Rather, the differences emerge through the ways in which the works are defined and presented within a nexus of – to name a few examples – creators, promoters, critics and audiences; how a work travels within particular institutional segments. There are, however, always points where such distinctions collapse, overlap or blur, because a work straddles borders that previously may have policed categorical tidiness.

David Toop argues that, at its most basic level, sound art is 'sound combined with visual practices' (Toop 2000: 107), organised in a manner that differentiates it from more traditional practices associated with 'music'. Such a definition points to the ways in which sound art is a largely multimedia form: a context-specific work that exists within the gallery space (generally perceived as a visual area) or as a site-specific installation. Nevertheless, such a basic definition could be questioned in the sense that there are pieces which often get designated as sound art that are not combined with visual practices, at least not in the conventional sense. For example, Jonty Semper's *Kenotaphion* (2001) is generally considered to be sound art, though it is a conventional CD release, not an installation: the double CD compiles two-minute silences that have been observed on Armistice Day (Poole 2001: 9). Why is it considered sound art? It is possibly because it falls outside of most people's definition of music and is presented within an artistic context (as a CD, presented by an 'artist'). In this sense, whilst broad definitions are never entirely satisfactory, I would still rather follow Brendon LaBelle's general notion of sound art as a conceptual practice in which music/sound 'is both the thing *and* a reflection on the thing' (LaBelle 2006: 4). Thus, whilst in this chapter I will mainly give an overview of sound art that does contain visual as well as aural components (to differing degrees), I will not confine myself to such work. I will begin by tracing the roots of sound art within particular reflections on sound and music.

Organised Sound

One important theoretical line underpinning the practice of sound art is the questioning of the boundary separating noise from music. As Douglas Kahn has detailed, noise has often been perceived as music's 'other', as sound that does not easily fit into the dominant conceptions of musical practice. Western musical traditions, for example, have often distinguished *music* from *sound* in terms of the former's structural organisation into a series of harmonic sequences, whilst sound itself is differentiated from *noise* in terms of stability and uniformity (Kahn 2001: 72–83). Such views were modified drastically in the twentieth century, with a number of avant garde artists interested in the incorporation of less 'regular' sounds into 'musical' compositions. One of the most infamous of such interventions was by the Futurists, in particular Luigi Russolo, who insisted on the importance of noise and debated the tendency to block its presence from musical composition. For Russolo, reacting against the classical tradition, a new form of composition was needed in order to capture the spirit of the modern world, which he called *noise-sound* (Russolo 1913). Whilst he wrote that such 'noise-sounds' should ultimately be incorporated within a harmonic and rhythmic composition, Russolo nevertheless was a key figure in expanding the source sounds of musical construction.[1] Other inter-war avant garde artists were also experimenting with the presentation of noise in live performances: Hugo Ball, founder of the Dada movement, used grunts, coughs, screams and whistles in his 'simultaneous poetry', whilst Russian artist Arseni Avraamov directed a number of 'sound spectacles' which incorporated choirs, foghorns, artillery guns and factory sirens (Heon 2005: 91).

For Russolo the proliferation of machinery within society had profoundly altered the soundscape of everyday life, and he thought machines should be built to reflect this soundscape more suitably in musical form. Yet, ironically, whilst he aggressively praised technological progress, hopes for the commercialisation of his machines were dashed by such progress: just when there was hope of his Noise Harmonium going into production to accompany silent movies, the era of the 'talkies' consigned his machines to oblivion (Toop 2000: 110–11; Kahn 2001: 128). One of the next major events in organised sound, *musique concrète*, was very much influenced by recording technology developments, particularly the commercial availability of magnetic tape recording (though it was first practised using phonograph recording technologies). Combined with the existing possibilities of microphone recording, practitioners associated with *musique concrète* – in particular Pierre Schaeffer, who began experimenting in 1948 – edited together the concrete sounds of everyday life into sonic montages. This was once again an organisation of sound that questioned the existing boundaries separating music from noise. It was an invitation to listen to a succession of sounds that had been recontextualised, ruptured from the flux of everyday life, and inserted within a deliberate series of sound events, often having undergone further manipulation.

Another important figure who questioned existing distinctions between noise and music was Edgar Varèse, who incorporated the dissonant sounds of sirens in compositions such as 'Ionisation' and claimed that he was an 'organiser of sound' rather than a musician. His 1958 composition for the Brussels Word Trade Fair, *Poème électronique*, stands as a landmark of sound art. Not only did this piece radically employ synthesised electronic sounds, but it was produced for a specially designed installation by Le Corbusier in the Phillips Radio Corporation Pavilion. It was therefore part of a multimedia installation, utilising 400 speakers in a series of rooms – creating a sense of sound travelling with participants as they moved from room to room – and also a series of projected images. Crucially, then, this piece, in conjunction with architectural space, drew people's attention to the materiality of sound, a concern that has preoccupied a number of subsequent sound artists (a point I will return to).

Nevertheless, at this historical juncture the term 'sound art' was not in itself an accepted designation for a particular approach towards sonic composition. Even now, whilst it is a term that is gaining increasing cultural currency, it is still rather inchoate, dispersed amongst, and informed by, different institutional contexts, and not even accepted by some artists; Max Neuhaus – often described as a sound artist – rejects the term because it is too loose (Neuhaus 2000). Whilst the main emphasis in this chapter is on sound art within gallery exhibits or site-specific installations, the very porosity of the practice sometimes calls into question such straightforward categories. For example, was John Cage's seminal performance of 4' 33" in 1952 a live performance or was it something more akin to a sound installation? In terms of audience expectation it was contextualised as a live performance of music, but there was no 'music' present, in a traditional sense, thus challenging the very notion of live performance. Whilst, once again, the notion of sound art was not in general currency when this piece was 'performed', it has become a key event in terms of tracing the many influences and concerns of contemporary sound artists. This is because it was going against the institutionalised conceptions of music, attempting to draw attention to sound in a different way from the conventional (in this sense, through extending the boundaries of the composition beyond what was issuing from the musicians on a stage).

Following on from Cage's use of performance space to challenge listening habits, sound art has tended to manifest itself as a type of practice that invites people to pay attention to sound in new ways, beyond habitual processing. Commonly, sound is experienced in everyday life as non-artistic, except with the case of music. Sound art often attempts to challenge these demarcations through artistically arranging non-musical sounds, sometimes reconceptualising 'music' into contexts where its modes of consumption are reconfigured. It is manifested in a number of ways: objects, sound sculptures, and installations both inside and outside of galleries; live performances (both inside and outside of buildings); and more recently new avenues have been opened up through the development of digital technologies, particularly network technologies, which have led to the extension of sound artworks into platforms such as CD-ROMS and websites.

MATERIALITY AND SPACE

A recurrent preoccupation of a number of sound artists has been an interest in sound as a *material* presence within everyday life, which overlaps with interest in how different spaces can shape the behaviour of sound. It has often been assumed that sound is immaterial and temporal – absorbed by the ears, processed, but then lost in the midst of time. Of course, this is not true: sound is the product of material vibrations whose acoustic properties arise from their interaction with other physical properties. None the less, the lack of attention paid to the material aspects of sound is an area of research that many sound artists seek to address. In this sense, the sound artist can cross over into the terrain of physics, but does not follow standard scientific conventions; instead she or he creates an artistic piece that demonstrates a concept in action. Alvin Lucier, for example, states that he often uses scientific principles experientially rather than theoretically, in the process attempting to uncover the 'poetic beauty of nature' (quoted in Buck 2004: 44).

Lucier himself is a concert performer *and* sound artist, creating works for live performance as well as sound installations (sometimes it is difficult to place such work in either category, as it straddles both). His seminal piece *I Am Sitting in a Room* (1970) consists of text read out in a room, recorded upon a tape recorder, then played back and recorded on a second tape recorder. This process is then repeated a number of times, so that the resonant frequencies of the room increasingly impact upon the recording, eventually drowning out the clarity of the words themselves and producing amorphous, drone-like textures. It is a demonstration of how recording technology can 'capture' the characteristics of a space, and how that space itself can impact upon sounds in a particular manner (thus the piece will change according to the environment it is performed in). As Paul Morley has written, 'You can in fact begin to make out the shape and size of the room if you listen to the music, from the way the music begins to develop in sonic reaction to its surroundings. The sound as it progresses creates a kind of aural diagram of the room' (Morley 2003: 33). Lucier has also constructed a number of sound installations, such as *Music on a Long Thin Wire* (1977), in which a long piece of wire is attached to a tuned oscillator and left to sound by itself. The sound can vary in terms of the length of the wire and the space within which it is placed, thus interacting in a kind of 'organic' manner with nature and the vibrations produced by human visitors.

A number of sound artists have interrogated the relations between sound and environment, thus drawing attention to the physicality of sound and its context-specific properties. These include (amongst many others) Michael Brewster, and Annea Lockwood, and Bill Fontana. Fontana, who has been creating sound sculptures since 1976, has described all sound as 'really a description of the space you put it in' (Cowley 2004: 82) and has attempted to map and explore a variety of sound spaces. For example, his installation at Leeds City Art Gallery, *Primal Soundings* (2004), uses recording devices such as acceleromoters (material sensors) and hydrophones (underwater sensors) to map a number of different sounds within the Yorkshire environment, including water in underground tunnels, wind farms, and recordings picked up from far beneath the earth's surface. These sounds are then transmitted within different spaces of the gallery, so the listener encounters a constantly changing sonic landscape as she or he moves through different rooms. Fontana's most recent project is the *Harmonic Bridge* (2006) at Tate Modern in London, which places a number of acceleromoters under the capital's Millennium Bridge. The various sounds of natural elements, as well as the movement of people and traffic over the bridge, combine with the architecture of the bridge itself, the sounds of which can be heard both in Tate Modern's Turbine Hall and at Southwark Underground station. In a sense, the everyday landscape here becomes transformed, in that architecture (the bridge) is turned into a musical instrument that is 'played' by its surrounding environment, resulting in a continuous 'improvised composition'. The result is an ever-shifting soundscape of scrapes, clangs and hums, not unlike a number of 'dark ambient' compositions produced by artists such as Lull and Zoviet France.[2]

Fontana's sound art also probes into the sound of the environment: partly, in a manner that can be linked to Cage as well as composer/sound theorist R. Murray Schafer, to encourage us to listen to our everyday environment more attentively; partly to zoom in on the environment and to magnify sounds that we may not otherwise be able to hear. In the latter respect, technology and nature – which have frequently been placed in opposition – grow in symbiotic tandem with one another. That is, expanding developments in technology enable us to hear more and more sounds, thus expanding the environmental soundscape. Sounds that were previously beyond the hearing range of humans have now loomed into focus through the prosthetic augmentation of our sensory apparatus. In addition, as Fontana himself has pointed out, these works can play around with perception, particularly through their potential to rupture sight-sound expectations. For example, the usual sounds heard outside of Southwark tube station are overlaid by the amplified sounds of the Millennium Bridge, which can create a strange tension between what the eye leads the ear to expect. This foregrounds how our senses are intricately linked and how our brains hardwire associations through experience and memory.

TECHNOLOGY AND MODERNITY

Whilst recording technologies have enabled us to listen to nature more carefully, such technologies developed in tandem with a shift towards urbanism, when the sonic ambience of many humans was undergoing considerable transformation. The late nineteenth and early twentieth centuries brought forth a new host of sounds, amplifying the variety and degree of sonic information: trains, cars, factories, aeroplanes and an ever expanding network of mechanical devices, as well as the noise of densely packed crowds of people, were amongst the contributors. This alarmed many and led to the development of a number of noise abatement campaigns such as the Anti-Noise League, which was founded in Britain in 1933 (Bijsterveld 2003: 172). The composer and sound theorist R. Murray Schafer, however, took a different line, arguing for a more detailed understanding of our sonic environment. He argued in 1973 that the world was becoming more low-definition than previously: with so many sounds now vying for our attention and overlapping with one another, it was difficult for us to hear any single sound with clarity, compared to ancient times when, because sounds were scarcer, we could hear them in higher definition. Thus, for Schafer, the advent of 'hi-fi' recording and playback technologies was, contradictorily, appearing as the world was turning 'lo-fi' (Schafer 2004: 32). Nevertheless, whilst countering noise abatement campaigns, there was a vestige of noise aversion within Schafer's thesis: it was clear that he bemoaned the proliferation of 'hi-fi' technologies, believing that they contributed to our inability to hear properly.

Whilst Schafer's tendency to rail against certain noises has been criticised on many occasions, he has nevertheless proven an influential figure within the world of sound art, particularly through the establishment of the World Soundscape Project, which was an attempt to map the changing sound environment and engage in 'acoustic ecology'. German sound artist Christina Kubisch sums up the ambivalent respect that many sound artists feel towards Schafer in her claim that 'I don't belong to the eco-faction like Schafer . . . But I think his approach is tremendously important. He was one of the first to place importance on simply listening' (quoted in Toop 2004: 78). Despite

Schafer's aversion to certain industrialised sounds, he and his Soundscape cohorts nevertheless recorded many such sounds in their documents of aural life. They therefore utilised 'hi-fi' technologies to sample the sounds of every-day life, to rip aural moments from their everyday contexts and to isolate them for scrutiny. Such audio 'snapshots' recalled the techniques of Pierre Schaeffer and other *musique concrète* practitioners, who also edited the sounds of the everyday, albeit for different – more avowedly 'artistic' – pur-poses (and were more interested in modifying such sounds). Likewise, there are a number of subsequent sound artists who have explored the urban sound-scape in different ways, and also many who have reflected upon the very nature of sound technologies.

One particularly striking manifestation of sound art within urban space focuses upon mobility through one's external environment and a transforma-tion of sonic ambience via certain technological processes. Kubisch herself has been involved in this line of work through her 'electromagnetic induction' works. These began in the early 1980s as interactive gallery installations, whereby people could experience different sounds according to their move-ments via a pair of magnetic headphones that responded to electrical wires placed around the room. This work was then extended into a series of 'elec-trical walks', as the headphones picked up signals from a range of electrical fields within the environment, emanating from technologies such as surveil-lance cameras, mobile phones, computers and ATMs. A person's lived envir-onment is thus transformed into a type of virtual installation, enabling him or her to hear a unique pattern of sounds and also to perceive a very real, but usually imperceptible, aural dimension permeating living space. These walks thus tap into an alternative sonic realm and create a schism between percep-tual modes: only the sense of hearing is technologically transformed, but the other senses are nevertheless affected through the rerouting of sensual co-ordinates.

In a sense, Kubisch's work can be compared, though certainly not reduced, to the ways in which many people's cultural lives were undergoing such schis-matic transformations from the early 1980s onwards, with the advent of the Walkman. A major difference is that the Walkman feeds the ear with the per-sonal selections of its individual users; the 'electrical walks' were not designed to fit into pre-existing aural tastes, but rather to introduce participants to a new phonic experience. Nevertheless, there is a comparison to be made in that the Walkman also allows its users to enter a mobile, secret listening event (Thibaud 2003: 330). Such listening is also part of Janet Cardiff's *The Missing Voice (Case Study B)* (1999). In this walk, the participant is handed a Discman and headphones at a library in Whitechapel, London, and proceeds to walk around the area whilst, sonically, a narrative unfolds so that the spaces walked through become part of the fiction unfolding in the listener's head.

Figure 2   Participants using magnetic headphones in one of Christina Kubisch's *Electrical Walks* – Magnetic Forest, Kyoto, 1991 (courtesy Christina Kubisch)

Kubisch's and Cardiff's mobile pieces draw attention to accustomed ways in which we often hear in public space. By layering new sonic information upon our movement through familiar space, they reconfigure expected sight-sound connections. As a result, we may well become aware of how we often process and filter everyday sounds, but rarely pay them thorough attention. Such a concern is certainly a component of a number of Max Neuhaus's sound works. His *Listen* (1976), for example, consisted of stamping people's hands with the word 'listen' and then directing them through an urban walk in New York. Participants were thus encouraged to focus more attentively on their surrounding aural fabric, to pay attention to the nuances of sounds they often took for granted. Neuhaus also constructs public sound installations, such as *Times Square* (1977), in which he installed sound-generating devices in a subway ventilator underneath a small triangular patch in Times Square. The result is a subtle transformation of phonic ambience within this small area, which changes in relation to the surrounding city sounds: thus the electronic sound is more noticeable late at night, when the traffic becomes less frantic.

Music Technologies

Many of the preceding examples of sound art make use of recording technologies in order to open up new ways of hearing, but there is also a line of sound work that incorporates musical technologies and foregrounds them within the actual work itself. At the 'Sonic Boom' exhibition at the Hayward Gallery, 2000, there were a number of works that employed music technologies within their remit, thus drawing attention to the material machines that produce and process sound in different ways. These included Pan Sonic's *2 × 50 Hz Thru Leslie Speaker*, a work in progress that produced two similar pitches to create a beat frequency, the sound rising and falling as the speaker rotated; and Lee Ranaldo's *HWY SONG*, which displayed a TV monitor within the sound-hole of a 1920s Stella guitar, presenting a loop of a stretch of highway. Whilst the former primarily focused upon the materiality of the sound-producing objects, the latter seemed to display the object in order to reveal, via the film loop, its mythological connotations. Both of these concerns were woven into another exhibit, Christian Marclay's *Guitar Drag*, a video installation that featured an amplified Fender guitar tied to the back of a truck and dragged across various surfaces. The work addresses not only the texture of sound that the guitar is capable of producing in unlikely contexts (which is incredibly noisy), but also addresses the mythology of the guitar (guitar songs about the road, guitar abuse by performers), as well as the subject of racial lynching in the rural south, the location in which the drag takes place.

All of the above artists are also musicians, though Ranaldo and Pan Sonic are more associated with their musical work than Marclay, who crosses over into the sound art world on a more frequent basis, often creating works that blur the line between sound art and music. Having exhibited his work in a number of galleries throughout the world, Marclay frequently addresses the materiality of sound in relation to the various media through which it is transmitted. In his DJ work in the 1980s, Marclay began to incorporate a number of scratched and modified records into his work (including broken and melted records), which he termed *Recycled Records* (1980–6). These pieces, which became the basis for his first standalone artwork, created collages constructed from such pieces, delving into the sheer physicality of vinyl as a medium: not only foregrounding the manner by which vinyl's encounters with the physical world through time often affect the noise signals it produces (through the accumulation of dust and scratches), but also seeking out the possibilities of new sound signals within objects conventionally regarded as damaged and thus useless. These concerns were also strikingly addressed in Marclay's *Record Without a Cover* (1985), which was a limited edition record (50 copies) sold without a cover, so that it would deliberately degrade in its unprotected state (on the side of the record without grooves, there is an instruction not to store the record in a protective package). This, once again, addresses issues of time and degradation: this is a 'functional' artwork that exists in the lives of the individuals who purchase it, and which will change according to the manner in which they store it in their particular surroundings. If, as instructed, it isn't placed in a protective cover then it will be subject to a continual process of change, so that the piece of music inscribed upon the vinyl will undergo a continual, entropic transformation. The piece is also, as David Toop has pointed out, a sly comment on record collecting, a subtle subversion of the compulsive respect and shielding from harm that serious collectors accord their prized possessions (Toop 2004: 169–70).

Philip Jeck and Janek Schaefer are two other artists who address the materiality of vinyl and how it can be manipulated beyond the remit of conventional usage. Like Marclay, Jeck and Schaefer create gallery installations as well as taking part in live performances and releasing audio recordings; like Marclay, they also partake in an experimental type of 'turntablism'.[3] Jeck's most recognised work is his 1993 piece *Vinyl Requiem* (1993, with Lol Sargaent), which was a performance for 180 Dansette record players, twelve slide projections and two movie projectors. Jeck's work, which also includes the piece *Off the Record* (1996, included in the Sonic Boom exhibition), resurrects old media hardware and brings it alive, though at the same time reflecting on the antiquated status of such media. By using old records on multiple old turntables, and looping segments to play in tandem, Jeck creates a dense noise-scape that is like a requiem for these objects, an 'exploration of the ghost world created by vinyl's gradual dissolution' (Shapiro 2002: 171). Schaefer, meanwhile, specialises – amongst many other pursuits – in constructing his own custom-made turntables. Inspired by Jeck's *Vinyl Requiem*, Schaefer constructed one record player that could play three different records simultaneously, which he calls the 'Tri-Phonic Turntable' (Schaefer 2001: 73). The player can be played at a number of different speeds, as well as backwards, and plays records that Schaefer specifically cuts for incorporating into these pieces (featuring, for example, locked grooves and found sounds). Schaefer has developed an improvisatory approach to performing on this turntable, which has developed through chance, and has also developed a simpler twin turntable for easier portability. His approach mixes indeterminism and environmental sampling with a creative bypassing of predictable consumptive patterns. He is a kind of exploratory, semi-scientific sound artist, modifying hardware and software in an attempt to explore the untapped potential sounds of everyday objects.

If I have focused upon the presence of vinyl at length within this brief overview, it is not to suggest that other recording and playback technologies are rarely addressed within the world of sound art. It is to suggest, however, that vinyl does seem to generate a particular fascination: as a form of media that is becoming outmoded it is suggestive of memory, nostalgia, preservation and decay, yet it has also enjoyed a longer life and tended to engender a more vocif-erous collecting culture than other related media. Additionally, as Toop has highlighted (2004: 181), there is a real physicality about vinyl which makes it ripe for incorporation into sound art practice: unlike a cassette, for example, or newer digital playback formats such as the CD and MP3 files, we can actu-ally see the information traces in the vinyl grooves, can see the stylus make its way across the surface of the vinyl during playback, and can detect the physi-cal reasons as to why a record may not be playing the way we want it to (such as when the stylus cannot continue past a scratched area). It may be the case, however, that other media formats will grow in interest as their own particular properties are uncovered and celebrated. This appears to be occurring, to an extent, with the case of the audio cassette: in particular, its enabling of home taping and the construction of personalised compilation tapes has been seen as important, and it is increasingly perceived as playing a crucial part within the development of 'DIY culture'.[4]

Interactivity

As a visitor to the 'Sonic Boom' exhibition in 2000 I found two particular things seemed to be lacking: an ability to become fully immersed within many of these works (a problem I often experience within gallery spaces), but also – perhaps more specifically related to the exhibition – opportunities to interact with the pieces. I don't believe that interactivity is always a positive dimension within a piece of art, but there were certain pieces here that I thought could have bene-fited from a more interactive dimension, particularly the works by Brian Eno and Pan Sonic. One of the few pieces that did allow for interaction was Christina Kubisch's *Oasis 2000: Music for a Concrete Jungle*, which allowed visitors to don headphones, walk onto the Hayward Gallery's Sculpture Court, and move around a changing sonic landscape, via the installation of magnetic induction cables. The piece demonstrated how interactivity could be built into sound artworks in a positive manner, opening up a singular space of immersion within the rigid environs of the public gallery.

In line with the increasing spread of networking technologies across the globe, interactivity within artworks has become a growing concern. This interest in network art has precedents, such as the Fluxus group and its international, co-operative nature, which itself was an outgrowth of the spread of global telecom-munications. Nevertheless, newer forms of communications technologies – in particular the Internet, but also mobile phones – have altered the ways in which artists utilise and address technologies and their social implications. The growth of digital technologies has often been linked with increasing interactivity, because of the ways in which networked technologies allow users to take part in instan-taneous feedback with the media that they are engaging with.[5] One particularly striking example of an attempt to create an interactive sound artwork in relation to digital networking is Henrik Frisk's *etherSound* (2003), which was a specially designed instrument that could be played by anybody who sent an SMS from their mobile phone. The information within the SMS was converted into control signals that were then sent to a sound synthesis engine (Frisk and Yoshida 2005: 122). In this, Frisk was aiming to raise the level of public interest in sound art by engaging people in the actual process of sound production, through the use of an extremely widespread piece of communications technology. Though people did not know how the technology was converting their text messages into sounds, they were aware that they were contributing to the sonic emissions, and were thus centrally involved within the creative process.

Frisk has written about this piece and its aims, amongst which were:

- opening up sound art to people often excluded from the 'class hierarchies' linked to arts consumption;
- engaging participants in the art work and breaking down the roles between engineer, composer, audience;
- stimulating, through interactive processes, the participants into a reflective consideration of sound;
- creating a sound work that links to the wider growth of communications within everyday life, through the production of a collaborative art work that exploited the potential of communication networks. (Frisk and Yoshida 2005: 127)

In terms of the networking aspect of the work, it does reflect a broader sociological trend in terms of how sounds are generated through a collaborative, interactive process, but in a way that is not entirely predictable. Of course, the design of the software means that the resultant sounds are circumscribed to an extent, but the fact that they are produced by the types of text messages sent by participants instils in the work an unpredictable dimension. The process by which individual elements contribute to a greater, complex whole is in line with theories about 'complexity' and 'emergence' that have been observed not only within the physical sciences, but also within the social sciences (a good example is Urry 2003). Certainly, then, this piece does to an extent confuse any simple attribution of authorship: it is the result of continual contributions from a number of individuals. Yet there is still a hierarchy at work here that places doubt upon the claims made by Frisk and Yoshida that there is 'no obvious author to credit' (2005: 126). Frisk created the sound installation and is credited with doing so, whilst Yoshida commissioned it (for part of a project entitled *Invisible Landscapes*); the people who merely contributed to the overall sound within a specific context only had a fleeting moment of authorship, in comparison to the sustained credits that the creator/commissioner will enjoy.

This is not, however, to detract from the fact that this does create an interactive piece that involves participants in the creation of an ongoing sonic composition, and also relates to networks and communication technologies in a relevant manner.

etherSound can, in some respects, be linked to another form of interactive aural form with a growing tradition: generative music, another mode of sound practice that has been linked to notions such as emergence. Generative music is not a new phenomenon, but it has become more prevalent within the digital age. A key theorist and practitioner of generative music is Brian Eno, who states that: 'the idea of generative music is to think of the role of the composer differently: not as someone who specifies and builds a whole piece of music but as someone who designs a few seeds that flower and fruit in different ways, including ways that the composer couldn't have anticipated' (quoted in Gray 2006: 18). Eno sees 1960s avant garde composers such as Terry Riley and Steve Reich as playing key roles within the development of generative music. Riley's *In C* (1964), for example, specifies a set of rules out of which a composition will emerge, as opposed to a more rigid score that musicians must adhere to. The piece consists of fifty-three bars of music in the key of C, which the musicians can proceed through at any speed they choose. This piece thus contains within it a sense of indeterminacy, as the ways in which the musicians interlock is left open for each performance. Reich's *It's Gonna Rain* (1965), meanwhile, is a piece generated by two tape machines playing the same loop. Whilst they start off in synchronisation, the inconsistency of the machines leads them to slip out of synch and, in the process, generate a shifting and complex set of sound relations. It demonstrates how an extremely simple beginning can, from a set of basic rules, form into intricate yet unpredictable shapes.

Eno himself developed these ideas as crucial components within his composition process, using Koan software to create pieces that developed complex, unpredictable results from simple instructions. With these generative pieces, the same simple instructions will result in different pieces each time, which are also endless (though, of course, they have to be edited if released on CD). Thus, to some extent, control of the composition is relinquished by the artist and given over to chance procedures. Whilst much of Eno's work in this area – which has also extended to image-based work – has tended to be limited in terms of user interaction, generative music has been developed further by others in such directions. For example, the German collective Oval developed a generative project entitled *Ovalprocess* (2001), which encompassed a software application, audio CDs, and three interactive sound installations. Continuing the act's attempt to question the production and consumption of music in contemporary society (they are well known for damaging CDs and producing music out of the resultant glitches), this project is an attempt to engage users in a fuller understanding of the work processes involved in digital music production. It also lets them intervene in such production, thus further opening up the process of music production. This tends to extend Eno's comments about the artist relinquishing control: here, the sounds are not only moving away from the artist's starting point, but are doing so through the intervention of many others. Thus, whilst the authorship of the piece is still very much related to Oval (it would be erroneous to claim that there is no hierarchy here), they act as the facilitators of a project which is then modified in unanticipated directions, continuing for an indefinite period.

SOUND ART AND THE INTERNET

Interactivity is, of course, a key concept associated with the Internet, with its ability to connect people from spatially distinct locations so they can write to, speak to, and view others from afar. The Internet opens up fresh opportunities for sound art praxis, some examples of which I will survey in this final section. Whilst the capability of accessing sound artworks on the Internet is far from universal, the ability to encounter such work is nevertheless far greater than it is for a site-specific installation. In this way, the net contains the potential to open up access to works such as *ethernet* to a broader audience, though issues such as class hierarchies cannot be thought of as being magically resolved in this way, as is implied in the comments made by Frisk: potential opening up is not the same as actual opening up, and it is likely that class, as well as other factors, will still play a part in issues such as who has knowledge about the existence of such sites, as well as who will actually be drawn to them.

There are a number of different types of sound art projects on the web, which can vary in type and kind. I shall survey a few basic examples: pieces that do not allow users to modify the sound work in any way; pieces which allow an individual user to interact with the sound work; and pieces that open up active intervention by more than one person (so that the sound work is inscribed by a virtual community that extends beyond a single instance). The first example is the most basic, and does not utilise the interactive capabilities of the Internet. It is perhaps because the net is so commonly connected to the concept of interactivity that this mode is the rarest of the three upon the Internet. Such examples may perhaps therefore be criticised for not actually exploiting the inherent possibilities of the net. Yet this view is rather ungenerous and also rather restrictive in that it implies that the Internet is comprised of ontological essentials, and that artwork designed for it should therefore fall in line with this prescriptive essentialism. The problem with this is two-fold: first, essentialist descriptions of any media platform generally tend to fall down in the light of further scrutiny, particularly regarding the fact that media platforms generally are in a constant state of technological flux; secondly, and more pertinently in this case, there is the fact that certain media often transmit content that has been designed for other media, or that some media are actually designed with the knowledge that they are going to cross platforms.

Jem Finer's *Longplayer* (2000) is a piece that exemplifies the difficulties inherent with arguments based on ontological suppositions. It is a sound installation designed to play for a thousand years (before it will start again from the place where it began); it takes an existing piece of music and chops it into six sections, then combines these sections into further permutations, a process that takes a thousand years to complete before it repeats the same combination. Finer designed this to be played in concrete spaces and it was first installed (as a computer program) in the lighthouse at Trinity Buoy Wharf in East London. It has since been installed in locations within Alexandria, Egypt; Brisbane, Australia; and Rufford Park, near Nottingham. The placing of a live stream on the Internet (which began in 2004) simply allows Finer to extend the reach of this sound work, which is suited to transmission in both concrete and virtual spaces because it runs on a computer program. Even, however, in cases where the physical dimensions of the sound piece may be an important factor in actually 'being there' (at the physical place where the installation exists), the reproduction of such sounds on the web, or (as is more common) on a CD, does not invalidate this alternative means of transmission. Like, perhaps, watching a widescreen film on a modestly sized television, the experience may not live up to encountering it in a cinema (or, in this case, at the site of installation) but it is not thereby rendered worthless. By arguing in favour of the above types of work being displayed upon the Internet, I am not dismissing attempts to exploit what have been seen as some of the unique strengths of the medium (though we must be aware that these may be transitory rather than ontologically fixed). Rather, I am adopting a flexible view of the status of art on the Internet, which can take a variety of guises and can exploit different strengths of the medium's multifaceted properties.

If interactivity is seen as a crucial strength of the net then this is also reflected in the amount of sound art there that integrates an interactive dimension. Singular interaction, in all its forms, is far more common than actually interacting with an interface *and* with other distant users at the same time. Creating a sound art piece that allows for synchronous (or nearly synchronous) interaction amongst different people at the same time is far more difficult to design. Nevertheless, there are works that allow for such interaction, and these are pieces that Álvaro Barbosa has termed 'shared sonic environments', which are 'openly shared spaces' where members of an 'on-line community can participate in a public event by manipulating or transforming sounds and musical structures or by simply listening to music created collectively' (Barbosa 2003: 57). These shared environments harness the strengths of the Internet by connecting a network of spatially dispersed users and uniting them in virtual space, so that new forms of sonic collaboration are possible. Such synchronous (or virtually synchronous) networking, which allows people to respond to the inputs and outputs of others almost instantaneously, has been enabled by the exponential growth of computing power and network speed, as well as increasing access to such technologies.

An example, as noted by Barbosa, is Phil Burk's *Webdrum* (2000, now in its second version), a virtual drum machine that allows up to eight people to play at one time in order to 'jam' with each other. The software is simple to use and has the advantage of enabling people with little technical or musical skill to be able to play. The problem with this is that the simplicity results in a general lack of parameters to explore; thus for people who have even had a fleeting experience with music software programs such as *Rebirth*, the results feel somewhat flat. And whilst the interactive jamming with unknown others in real time is undoubtedly *the* main point of such a program, there are problems with actually finding a person to jam with. A similar problem exists with Chris Brown and John Bischoff's *Crossfade*, two separate, yet related, interactive soundworks (*Eternal Music* from Brown and *Aperture* by Bischoff) that allow up to four separate users to interact. Again, these pieces are relatively simple, yet sonically more interesting than *Webdrum* in that they allow users to drag their mouse over an area in order to create rich, shifting noise patterns. These pieces, because they are capable of creating denser sound textures than *Webdrum*, are perhaps closer to more 'traditional' examples of sound art than Burk's piece, which is closer to a more simplified, yet network-capable, piece of audio software. Yet all of these pieces, because they blur the lines between audio software and sound art, could be seen as continuing the lineage of sound art in a broader sense, as hybrid sonic pieces that defy easy categorisation and thus draw our attention to the ways in which we classify sound objects.

Another line of interactive sound work on the net is non-synchronous interaction between spatially distinct people. One particularly interesting example of this is an educational project aimed at children aged between nine and fourteen, entitled *Sonic Postcards* (2005), which is run by the Sonic Arts Network. This project is aimed at encouraging children to become more aware of their sonic environment. Through the help of workshop leaders they are introduced to their sound environment, take recordings of it and then edit these sounds on audio editing software. They then convert these sonic compositions into MP3 format and email them to other schools involved in the project (as well as vice versa), thus gradually building up a network of sonic environments. The results are then available for anyone with Internet access to view on the sonic postcards website, which enables people to select various schools, to listen to a number of MP3s of the surrounding area, and also to view photographic images taken by members. A less 'educational', more international, but similarly collaborative work is the *Sonda* project (2005), originating in Barcelona. A found piece of sound was posted on the Internet and people were invited to modify the sound in any way that they wished as long as they did not add add-itional instrumentation. The results were once again posted onto a website for everyone to experience. Unlike the sonic postcards project – which creatively engaged with specific environments – this work was concerned with reimagin-ing the same sound. Site-specificity as such did not play a role in the way that the sound became modified, though global location was important in that each person taking part in the finished project is placed on a world map. This not only visually emphasises the global nature of the project but also invites visi-tors, if they wish, to speculate upon whether any patterns exist between the location of the modifiers and sound that they produce.

Perhaps the most prevalent type of sound artworks on the net, though, are those pieces that allow for some kind of interaction between a single user and the virtual piece itself. Within this category there is a real growth of a certain type of such work known as soundtoys. Whilst there is no rigid definition of soundtoys, the term broadly refers to any audiovisual work that uses new tech-nologies on the web. Generally, soundtoys tend to be interactive and for single users (in that they are generally not co-ordinating the interface with a number of spatially distant online visitors). They can vary in type, but most prominently include online music instruments, audiovisual installations, and generative audio tools. The amount of work that has been classified within this admittedly broad category is testified by the fact that there now exists a specific website devoted to soundtoys, which lists a number of artists working in this area and also some of the works that they have produced. There is actually far too much work here to give any kind of adequate overview, so I will merely end this section by pointing out a couple of interesting works that exist here.

Michael Szpakowski's *Work* (2002) lies somewhere between an online instal-lation and a generative work, and is an attempt to create a visual shockwave piece that is closely tied to the audio content. The visuals consist of seven Muybridge-inspired dancers, whilst the sound is a looped piano piece. The user can then, at any point, click on a highlighted figure, which adds another loop on top of the existing one, and also alters the movements of the dancer. Whilst the basic material is always the same, there is an indeterminate element built in which depends on the precise point at which the user clicks on, so that different rhythmic combinations can exist each time the user visits. Whilst the piece is relatively simple, it takes advantage of the complexity-through-simplicity pieces that stand as key moments within generative music: as the piano lines accumu-late and overlap, there is in particular an echo of Steve Reich's *Piano Phase* (1967), though there is more layering at work here, and there is also a visual dimension added to the mix. Neil Jenkins's *Tag Navigator* (2006), on the other hand, is a piece that is more concerned with digital sounds and images. In a sense, it could be seen as a meta-work, as it is a sound object that links to other soundtoys in existence. It is thus an interface that animates a series of words that float in to, out of and around the screen (movements influenced by your mouse), accompanied by bouncing digital sounds. If you click on a word, you will be given details of a sound work linked with that word and be able to click into that work and explore it, whilst the digital sounds of the *Tag Navigator* continue at the same time.

CONCLUSION

Whilst 'sound art' is still a relatively hazy concept, there is nevertheless a growing awareness of this mode of artistic practice. This is testified not only by the increasing mentions of 'sound art' in articles, in books and on the web, but also by the increase in academic courses devoted to sound art and the increase of sound art exhibitions within galleries over the past decade or so. It is clear that this has become a demarcated field, with a growing institutional respectability. Such points should not be overstated, though: whilst this is an expanding field, it is still fairly marginal, and there still exist ocular prejudices within the gallery. The architectural spaces of galleries are often designed with a concentration upon visual phenomena, though the growth of sound art exhibitions will probably lead to the future gallery space becoming more aurally focused. Of course, sound art cannot be limited to the gallery, but neither can other forms of art practice, and it is – as LaBelle has argued (2006) – the case that visual art's breakaway from gallery confinements in the 1950s and 1960s (with site-specific art and happenings) was a key context for the emergence of sound art. In this sense, it could be argued that only now is sound art being recuperated by institutional space, tamed by the very forces that once repelled it. Less pessimistically it may be argued that the art world is finally waking up to a dimension that it criminally overlooked for much of the twentieth century.

Whilst defining sonic art remains problematic, creative practice focusing on the nature of sound will inevitably continue to grow. After all, it is not as though sound is going to disappear: as technologies mutate and proliferate, new sounds will be emitted, heard, categorised and manipulated. Sound art's strength resides in its exploration of our aural worlds, worlds which we perhaps too often take for granted, unless of course our ears feel as though they are under assault from unwanted noise. Sonic art is often designed so that we may reflect upon the sounds we filter out of our immediate perception, attuning aural sensation, encouraging speculation or perhaps a more active exploration of the sonorous flow that continually surrounds us.

NOTES

1. His practical attempts to realise these ambitions were made possible through his creation of noise machines (*intonorumori*). Public performances, however, were met with general hostility.

2. 'Dark ambient' is a form of music that moved away from the 'New Age-y' associations that ambient music had accrued by the late 1980s and early 1990s, in order to express a sense of unease. A key compilation of dark ambient tracks is the 1994 release *Isolationism*, compiled by Kevin Martin.
3. Turntablism is the manipulation of records in order to create new sounds. It is most commonly associated with hip-hop, and includes techniques such as scratching and beat matching.
4. In fact, there was a recent art project which celebrated the cassette for these very reasons: *Blank Tape Spillage Fete* was a project set up by Matt Hunt and Mat Fowler in which they sent out blank cassettes to a number of different people to fill up in any way they wish, and asked them to produce accompanying artwork for these cassettes. 'Fetes' were then set up to preview artwork and cassettes (in London), which also featured live bands. The contents of the cassettes were also accessible through the project's website at http://www.blanktapespillagefete.com.
5. Actually defining interactivity is a difficult task, particularly as there are different *types* of interactivity. I will use the term here to refer to a particular form of interactive engagement, a *functional* mode that refers to users/audiences/participants being able actually to modify in some way the media/artwork that they are engaging with (Lister et al. 2003: 20).

REFERENCES

Barbosa, Á. (2003), 'Displaced Soundscapes: A Survey of Network Systems for Music and Sonic Art Creation', *Leonardo Music Journal*, Vol. 13, pp. 53–9.

Bijsterveld, K. (2003), 'The Diabolical Symphony of the Mechanical Age: Technology and Symbolism of Sound in European and North American Noise Abatement Campaigns, 1900–40', in M. Bull and L. Back (eds), *The Auditory Cultures Reader* (London and New York: Berg).

Buck, C. (2004), 'Positive Feedback', *Wire*, Issue 245, July, pp. 40–5.

Cowley, J. (2004), 'Cross Platform', *Wire*, Issue 242, April, pp. 82–3.

Eno, B. (1996), 'Generative Music', (lecture presented at the Imagination Conference, San Francisco, 8 June), *Motion Magazine*, 7 July, http://www.inmotionmagazine.com/eno1.html (accessed October 2006).

Frisk, H., and Yoshida, M. (2005), 'New Communications Technologies in the Context of Interactive Sound Art: An Empirical Analysis', *Organised Sound*, Vol. 10, No. 2, pp. 121–7.

Gray, L. (2006), 'Cross Platform', *Wire*, Issue 270, August, pp. 18–19.

Heon, L. (2005), 'In Your Ear: Hearing Art in the Twenty-First Century', *Organised Sound*, Vol. 10, No. 1, pp. 91–6.

Kahn, D. (2001), *Noise, Water, Meat: A History of Sound in the Arts* (Cambridge, MA, and London: MIT Press).

LaBelle, B. (2006), *Background Noise: Perspectives on Sound Art* (London and New York: Continuum).

Lister, M., Dovey, J., Giddings, S., Grant, I, and Kelly, K. (2003), *New Media: A Critical Introduction* (London: Routledge).

Morley, P. (2003), *Words and Music* (London: Bloomsbury).

Neuhaus, M. (2000), 'Sound Art?', http://www.max-neuhaus.info/soundworks/soundart (accessed September 2006).

Poole, S. (2001), 'Prick Up Your Ears', *Guardian: Saturday Review*, 17 November, p. 9.

Russolo, L. (1913), 'The Art of Noises', http://www.unknown.nu/futurism/noises.html (accessed October 2006).

Schaefer, J. (2001), 'AudiOh!: Appropriation, Accident and Alteration', *Leonardo Musical Journal*, Vol. 11, pp. 71–6.

Schafer, R. M. (1994), *The Soundscape: Our Sonic Environment and the Tuning of the World* (Rochester: Destiny Books).

—— (2004), 'The Music of the Environment', in C. Cox and D. Warner (eds), *Audio Culture: Readings in Modern Music* (London and New York: Continuum).

Shapiro, P. (2002), 'Deck Wreckers: The Turntable as Instrument', in R. Young (ed.), *Undercurrents: The Hidden Wiring of Modern Music* (London and New York: Continuum).

Thibaud, J-P. (2003), 'The Sonic Composition of the City', in M. Bull and L. Black (eds), *The Auditory Cultures Reader* (London and New York: Berg).

Toop, D. (2000), *Sonic Boom: The Art of Sound* (London: Hayward Gallery Exhibition Catalogue).

—— (2002), 'Humans, Are They Really Necessary?', in R. Young (ed.), *Undercurrents: The Hidden Wiring of Modern Music* (London and New York: Continuum).

—— (2004) *Haunted Weather: Music, Silence and Memory* (London: Serpent's Tail).

Urry, J. (2003), *Global Complexity* (London: Polity).

WEBSITES

Chris Brown and John Bischoff's *Crossfade*, http://crossfade.walkerart.org/brownbischoff2.

Phil Burke's *Webdrum*, http://www.transjam.com/webdrum.

Jem Finer's *Longplayer*, http://longplayer.org.

The *Sonda* Project, http://www.totts.org/web_sonda/sonda.htm.

Sonic Postcards, http://www.sonicpostcards.org/index_f.html.

Soundtoys, http://www.soundtoys.net.

6. POP MUSIC, MULTIMEDIA AND LIVE PERFORMANCE

Jem Kelly

A key convention of the popular music concert is the co-presence of spectator and performer, with both sharing a physical proximity, a spatial being-together in the event. This chapter interrogates inter-medial pop concerts in which the presence of performers is intersected with, or replaced by, virtual representations, or animated avatars, producing new interactions of image projection, sound reproduction and perceptual conditions. I explore modes of performer embodiment in an emergent genre – the virtually animated pop performance – and ask how new relations between space, body and sound address the spectator in new ways. I examine features of this genre in the context of debates centred on inter-mediality, examining issues of representation and reception, actual and virtual presence, authenticity and identity, liveness and affective sound. I delineate examples of past music/sound-driven performances by the Velvet Underground and Madonna to illustrate generic conventions of the inter-medial pop concert, and analyse new techniques and intermedialities employed by the animated pop group Gorillaz.

BEING THERE: PRESENCE, LIVENESS AND INTER-MEDIALITY IN POP-MUSIC PERFORMANCE

It is not possible to define exhaustively the parameters of artistic performance, as the term has accrued multiple meanings for different contexts, genres and modes of expression including theatre, dance and live art, but aspects of the concept require investigation in the light of musical mediated expression.

Musical performance implies that something, usually a systematised musical work, is presented by performers during a live event before an audience. David Horn defines popular music performance as:

> The sum of a number of smaller occurrences, which might include . . . the origination or the borrowing of a musical idea; the development of the idea; the conversion or arrangement of the idea into a performable piece; the participation of those (musicians, producers, technicians) whose task is to produce musical sound; the execution or performance of this task; the transmission of the resulting sounds; the hearing of those sounds. (Horn 2000: 28)

This process of summation confers upon the pop-music performance a commonality with theatrical stagings, in that both activities are reiterations of past practices, or rehearsals. Musical works can be based on extemporisation or improvisation, but in pop-music performances, even those not using playback technologies, the work performed tends to be a re-presentation of that which has been composed, arranged and rehearsed in advance. This apparent limitation is conventionalised as the audience has come to expect a live rendition or authenticating representation of recorded forms of the musical composition. What is being authenticated during a live pop performance? Pop performance can be a representation of a representation, to the extent to which a recording of a musical work – the artefact that is commodified through multi-track recording techniques – attempts to document (represent) an originary performance. Alternatively, multi-track recording processes may aim solely to produce a sonic utopia or best version of an original composition intended to attain an acceptable, marketable, commodifiable musical fidelity. From this perspective, pop-music performance is a re-enactment in which the recorded musical corpse is revived and re-presented through physical action in the 'hear and now'.

Co-presence of performer and spectator is an enduring generic convention in pop performance, proposing a shared experience, a sense of 'being there' in the moment. To be able to say, 'I was at the Newport Festival in '65 when Dylan went electric', for example, would confer a cultural credibility based on the speaker's embodied experience of the event in the presence of the artist, Bob Dylan. It would also reflect an aspect of the debate around the incorporation of electronic technologies, associated with rock and pop in the 1960s, into the folk music genre – in Manchester, 1966, a fan shouted 'Judas' when Dylan replaced his acoustic with an electric guitar – and of the incursion of electronic technologies into the live music performance paradigm.

As with theatrical performance, the element of liveness has been fundamental to pop concerts, but the latter form produces a sense of presence closer in register to live art than to theatre when it works against representation in favour of immediacy, intimacy, self-expression and certain kinds of performer-spectator interaction. For example, it is a convention at pop performances for the audience to request the band to play a beloved song during the encore, but it is difficult to imagine a similar interaction in theatrical performance, unless especially conceived to do so. On a tour staged during the late 1980s, Elvis Costello took this practice to an extreme, basing his performance on audience members spinning a carousel as a means by which to select songs from a list of hit records. This illustrates the importance of the recorded musical work in the framing of pop performance, which is in part intended to revivify recorded forms through replay by physically present musicians. Differentiation of pop performance and theatrical event is more problematic than it might seem during multimedia performances, as registers can be modulated by technological interventions, shifting modes of expression and representation to the extent to which replay and telematic media intersect with actualised physical performance elements that are considered live. The incursion of audiovisual technologies has produced mixed effects that either amplify and extend or attenuate notions of presence, representation and self-expression in pop performance. This technological incursion into live performance can lead to a condition of 'inter-mediality', which is 'associated historically with the exchangeability of expressive means and aesthetic conventions between different art and media forms' (Chapple and Kattenbelt 2006: 12). Inter-mediality leads to a blurring of boundaries between art forms and genres, resulting in a condition of media convergence that can articulate performer–spectator relations in new ways through interactions of live and mediated forms.

An early example of inter-mediality in pop performance, in which mediated images modulate a sense of presence, is provided by the Velvet Underground, whose nascent career in the psychedelic genre was influenced by Andy Warhol. In the mid-1960s, Warhol conceived of the Exploding Plastic Inevitable, an intermedial event that blurred generic boundaries of live performance arts to combine elements of disco, film show and happening with psychedelic pop concert. Warhol toured north America with the EPI, and one manifestation, on 1 November 1966, featured the Velvet Underground with Nico. The event comprised an intersection of playback technologies and live elements that framed and infused the band's performance. Jack Bernstein, writing for the *Tech*, MIT's in-house newspaper, describes the scene: 'The performance started with a couple of movies, projected on the same screen at the same time; somehow it was coherent . . . in addition to the films, a multi-faceted mirrored globe spewed splotches of light about in every direction' (Bernstein 1966). Bernstein identifies the performance as having begun prior to the physical presence of any performer being discernible, and this raises questions relating to performance ontology. What kinds of staged performance can take place without the spectator perceiving the visual embodiment of a performer? How can the manipulated interplay of technologies alone – producing light, sound and image – be considered to constitute performance? What kinds of framing are required for technologies to produce, or convey, a sense of presence? In the instance Bernstein describes, film projections shape the encounter, allowing the spectator a 'sensible amount of time' in which to become accustomed to a cinematically permeated mise en scène (Bernstein 1966). Bernstein is referring to a phenomenological apprehension that would contour the aesthetic and perceptual response to the Velvet's concert. Bernstein's cognisance of technological manipulation seems to indicate a sense of remote presence, or the anticipation of physical presence, realised via a visual montage in which projected images and light display intersect arhythmically in real time, live. Contemporary technologies would allow software programming to produce the effects Bernstein describes, but in 1966 it is likely that technicians would be performing the playback and light projection in real time. The absence of any*body* in the space does not seem to attenuate the sense of liveness – that the event is happening here and now – but in this instance, the sense of presence is perceived via media that indicate absent orchestrators.

Philip Auslander refers to the imbrication of live and mediated forms and the ontological implications for performance in his book, *Liveness: Performance in a Mediatized Culture*. Auslander observes that the live and the mediated are not so much opposed as intertwined: 'live performance cannot be said to have ontological or historical priority over mediatization, since liveness was made visible only by the possibility of technical reproduction' (Auslander 1999: 54). An example of this interdependence of live and mediated forms occurs in the ontology of the live event in pop performance, which depends on the replaying of recorded musical forms and making absent performers visible by presenting musicians bodily to the spectator in a shared concert space. The experience of listening to music playback media (mediated by radio transmission, vinyl disc, CD, and latterly via MP3 and audio streaming from Internet sources) offers, in terms of temporality at least, a linear auditory experience when the song/composition is played through from start to finish. The experience of embodied co-presence of performer and spectator contributes greatly to the pop concert's phenomenology, making the space of reception not only a hearing place, but also a seeing place and a being place. This multiple mode of address in music-driven performance offers a diffusion of experience that I refer to elsewhere as operating a phenomenology of 'auditory space' (Kelly 2005), and it is a phenomenon that shares an anticipation of embodied forms with theatrical performance conditions.

Warhol's EPI event progresses as the Velvet Underground 'set up for their performance', preparing their 'electric bass, electric guitar, electric piano and . . . drums' in readiness to play (Bernstein 1966). They are, clearly, not a folk band. The framing of this scene of presence, in which the spectator bears witness to the performer's preparatory procedures, could be described in theatrical, post-Brechtian terms as an act of defamiliarisation. But is it appropriate to identify this preparatory action as theatrical, when the performance, or at least this aspect of it, is functional in register? The performers prepare to play their instruments, but are they also engaged in an act of self-presentation? Their preparatory actions are learned or practised behaviour, rehearsed in the sound check, and as Alice Raynor articulates, 'representation is a kind of repetition that generates the phantom of a double' (Raynor 2002: 535). The presentation of pop music is a re-enactment, and the phantom of a rehearsal process is always present on-stage, however seemingly self-presentational the mode of the event. The donning of instruments and plugging in of leads to pre-positioned amplifiers demonstrates an intentionality to perform, but simultaneously displays a preparedness evocative of ritual that works against notions of improvisation and free play.

The spatiality and mode of address of intermedial pop performances can be organised into diametrical categories: those that intend to obscure their technological artifices, the better to create an illusory, immediate and immersive experience; and those that display mediating technologies as components that openly construct a performative frame. Jay Bolter and Richard Grusin articulate these poles in their McLuhanesque theory of remediation, which they define as 'the representation of one medium in another' (Bolter and Grusin 2000: 19). Extending their argument, in which aesthetic conventions are transferred across genres and media, they claim that all media simultaneously engage in the 'play of signs' and have a 'real, effective presence' (p. 54). They develop this into a semiotic/phenomenological binocular perspective, describing an oscillation between 'immediacy and hypermediacy' in which either processes of digital mediatisation are perceived as transparent and immediate (in which technologies are hidden), or their artifice is acknowledged as constructive of a performance system (p. 54). In inter-medial performances that produce wholly illusory experiences, the spectator can become immersed within a powerfully affective performance environment. The Velvet Underground's EPI performance, by intersecting affective, immersive and illusory technologies that operate within a self-reflexive performance mode, demonstrates a state of hypermediacy in which inter-medial processes are revealed and celebrated. As I have argued elsewhere, a feature of hyper-mediacy is that it creates a multi-sensory mode of address, which in music-driven performance produces a condition of *auditory space* (Kelly 2005). In the case of EPI, auditory space is produced through a complex interrelationship of sound, image and bodies: 'slides projecting patterns of optical design' create 'an interplay between the background movies, the dancers and the music' (Bernstein 1966).

Inter-medial pop performance can also provide an experience in which the physical presence of the performers and their music is framed by technologies of the spectacular. This visual dimension appears to enhance the aura of presence of the Velvet's singer, Nico, despite representing a past time and space. Bernstein notes that Nico's 'presence pervaded the hall as the projectors switched from a movie . . . to colour and black and white close-ups of her' (Bernstein 1966). This suggests that the interplay of iconic image projections amplifies and extends the singer's aura of presence, rather than attenuating it, which offers a paradox in that the cinematic referent is always absent, in contrast to the performer's body, which is right there, on stage in front of the spectator. This offers an early example of a pop performer's presence being amplified and shaped by projected images and mediating technologies.

The impression that inter-medialities can amplify the aura of presence in pop performance works against Walter Benjamin's claim that technological inter-vention will 'devalue the here and now of the artwork' (Benjamin 2003: 254). In his seminal paper 'The Work of Art in the Age of its Technological Reproducibility', Benjamin argues that the 'aura's present decay' is in part caused by the 'desire' of the 'masses to "get closer" to things spatially', particu-larly through photographic and cinematic media (p. 254). The perceptual shift afforded by moving image culture in its variety of contexts, spaces and loca-tions, whilst affecting our sense of existential, proximal and perceptual pres-ence to the world, does not necessarily lessen our impression of immediate engagement with it. In inter-medial pop events that use visual playback media to depict multiple perspectives, the sense of presence can be amplified in ways that enhance the celebrity or star status of the performer. Madonna's 1990 *Blonde Ambition* tour, for example, employed playback and telematic image projection to extend the visual scope of the performance, focusing the specta-tor's viewpoint. Far from attenuating the singer's presence, telematics seemed to enhance the aura of authenticity pervading the event by allowing close-up perspectives of the performer in real time.

When *Blonde Ambition* visited Wembley Stadium, I was positioned a signifi-cant distance from the stage, near to where the centre line of the football pitch would be. Madonna's actual, three-dimensional performing figure on stage was diminutive from my perspective, but video images filled vast screens mounted at either side of the stage, and a third screen was suspended above the centre line. The projection extended the visual perspective of Madonna's stage per-formance, mediating what was seen through a montage of medium shot and close-up perspectives. As the diminutive figure of Madonna moved, gesticu-lated, sang and positioned herself in a series of tableaux with her dance troupe, an equally complex and varied choreography of camera angle and cinematic syntax addressed the spectator. Madonna's presence was amplified as the screened images increased the scale, impact and virtual proximity to the figure on stage, but the greater detail and definition of the screened images made them, and not the unmediated elements, the visual focus of the event. This led to a doubling of presence in which the unmediated vied with the mediated for the spectator's attention, but the immersive nature of sound in the experience of reception added a cohesion to the event that attenuated this effect. Intercut with the telematic images were sequences from Madonna's pre-recorded promotional videos for the songs she was performing. These emphasised themes and ideas relating to the lyrical content of each song, but also evoked a sense of the artist's past oeuvre. The playback imagery initiated a process of recollection, the presentation of older material functioning as a *memoria technica* allowing the spectator to reflect on the star status of the performer, by depicting a body of international hit songs. It also elucidated a shared past with her audience, celebrated sonically and physically in the mediated present, breathing new life into the corpse of her recorded work.

Madonna's star status is attributable in no small degree to her exploiting the medium of video, used by the music industry (and MTV) as a promotional device by tying memorable images to strong musical motifs and, in Madonna's case, by creating an array of fictional personas associated with the tone, tenor and theme of the song. At Wembley, the combination of live performance, telecast and playback imagery offered a perceptual experience that cohered principally through melody, chorus refrains from hit songs – *Material Girl*, *Like A Virgin*, *Vogue* – and the somatic impact of amplified sound. Madonna theatricalised the representations on stage by reprising aspects of costume, dance sequences and gestures relating to the many personas and iconic images associated with her songs. She remediated elements of past screen performances, changing costume on-stage, and offered an ironic commentary and postmodern interplay to the system of inter-medial exchanges. Reflecting on the nature of star status, Stanley Cavell claims that the 'screen performer is not an actor at all', but '*is* the subject of study . . . the figure created in a given set of films' (Cavell 1971: 28). At Wembley, whilst I was in the presence of the physical entity known as Madonna, it is a mediated presence and one that is framed by the dramatic personas she has created. Madonna's actualised presence acquires its star status via recognition of the roles she has created in her pop videos, televised appearances and many photographic images, elements of all these forms remediated for live re-presentation. We also access the precise physical contours of the performer's body through the various lenses of inter-mediation (sonic and visual), in a process that enhances a sense of theatrically structured intimacy, paradoxically realised through an enormity of visual scale and auditory impact. Under such conditions of reception, at no point is it possible to segregate the roles Madonna performs from the being who performs them. Despite her inter-song role as MC and commentator, Madonna, the physical presence on stage and virtual presence on screen, is indistinguishable from her entity as star. The sense of presence associated with star status can be attenuated, subverted or diffused in inter-medial performances that use animations and avatars in place of physically present performers, as is the case with animated pop band Gorillaz.

WHOSE PRESENCE AMONGST SHADOWS? ANIMATION, INTER-MEDIALITY AND PERFORMANCE REGISTER

By 'performance register', I mean the relationships of presence between performer and spectator during the live event. As a prelude to encounters with specific examples of register in Gorillaz' *Demon Days*, I will contextualise aspects of the medium of animation.

Since the mid-1990s, the rapid expansion of digital technologies has produced a resurgence of interest in the animated form, owing to the relative ease with which animated images can now be produced digitally. No longer is animation the exclusive preserve of skilled draughtspersons creating imaginary worlds frame by meticulous frame: technology has eased the burden and lessened the difficulty and duration. Techniques essential to animation, such as in-betweening of key frames, lip-synching image to sound, and coloration of cells, are processes that can now be automated. The surge of interest in the graphic novel/comic form, and in video games at the end of the twentieth century, coupled with the availability and affordability of animation, video and music production technologies, have led to a creative context in which the aesthetics and technologies of media converge. Gorillaz provide an example of this convergence in their virtually animated concept band, and also in the virtual extension of the band as Internet presence.

Formed in 2001, the band comprises the fictional personas Murdoc (bass), 2D (vocals/keyboards), Noodle (guitar) and Russel (drums). The animated characters are avatars for musician Damon Albarn, formerly of pop group Blur, Jamie Hewlett, cartoonist and creator of the graphic comic *Tank Girl*, and latterly, disc-jockey and hip-hop record producer Danger Mouse (Brian Burton).

Unlike the majority of pop groups, whose image identity depends upon the spectator's recognition of a coherent signifying system, usually organised around the perceived identity of a fixed cohort of individual performers, Gorillaz has developed a collective working process in which guest artists record with the creative team in the studio, and perform alongside virtual representations in concert. This intermedial process leads to an intriguing tension between virtual and actual presences when Gorillaz perform live, as the spectator is forced to apprehend the liveness of the performance in the somatic impact of the sound produced by physically present musical performers, whilst at the same time encouraged to identify with virtual characters in the scopic essence of the event. To interrogate these intermedial processes, I refer to a performance attended on 3 November 2005. I use a composite recording in the form of a DVD, comprising footage edited from stagings that took place in Manchester Opera House from 1 to 5 November, as an aide-memoire and reference document.

Interactions of live performance and animation date back to the earliest era of the two-dimensional medium. In the early twentieth century *Gertie the*

Dinosaur (1914), whose animated image was projected onto a cyclorama in vaudeville shows, appeared to interact with her trainer, and creator, Windsor McCay. Gertie reacted to McCay's commands and the show concluded with an actual person seemingly being carried off stage on the back of a two-dimensional dinosaur. Interactions of live action and animated characters also occurred in the Fleischer Brothers' *Out Of The Inkwell* (1920) and *Big Chief Koko* (1925), in which the spectator is asked to imagine that the animated characters have free will and self-determination (Ashbee 2003: 7). What is apparent from these early examples of animated and live intermediation – which toured US theatres in the 1920s – is the playful awareness that the animated form is an artificial construct. The self-reflexive tension of perceiving animated artifice and live performance develops from the knowledge that three-dimensional physical performers and two-dimensional delineations cannot actually interact. The knowingness of this impossibility resides in the 'palpably produced nature of animation's artifice' (Jameson 1991: 77), and produces a sense of complicity that also drives Gorillaz' *Demon Days* performance.

In pop performances that communicate dramatic personas, such as *Blonde Ambition*, a similar complicity occurs in the demystification of the representational process – a showing how the object of pleasure is constructed, for example, when Madonna changes costume and transforms roles on-stage. The collaborative tenor of performer – spectator relations can be the principal mode of address in pop concerts. But it might be asked, aren't pop performers, at some level, presenting their individual expressive talents, and in the extent to which they demonstrate this, could we say that pop performers are operating in a self-expressive mode? This raises issues of authenticity in pop composition that are related to modernist ideas of originality and 'the unique individual' (Gracyk 1996: 220). Notions of authenticity and musical originality are difficult to explain exhaustively without examining cultural contexts and codes in detail, but such notions are relatively easy to identify as belonging to a well-rehearsed debate in pop and rock music journalistic discourse. The UK 1980s music scene was a context in which originality and authenticity were much valued, and bands such as Echo and the Bunnymen and the Cure, for example, were considered to be authentic expressions of identity, their music original. Conversely, contemporary bands such as Five Star, whose open emulation of the Jackson Five identified them as fake in the UK music press, and Go West, a band comprising white middle-class men attempting to adopt a Detroit soul sound, were considered inauthentic and unoriginal. All of these bands performed on BBC's television show *Top of the Pops*, making their musical expressions, however in/authentic, hostage to the framing of light entertainment and mass audiences in the UK. But the simulations of Five Star, particularly their intertextual reworking of an established US pop group, produce a pastiche, an emulation in blank irony, their endeavours presaging in spirit the drive towards intertextual referencing so prevalent in the sample-based postmodern pop forms that would emerge. The minor-key melancholies and angst-ridden, guitar-driven songs of Echo and the Bunnymen and the Cure firmly locate their operations in the 'existential model of authenticity' so redolent of modernist art and ideologies (Jameson 1991: 12). In the postmodern era, musical identity is as likely to be based on sound emanating from the selection, combination and reappropriation of pet-sounds sampled from existing sources as by the skilful playing of traditional instruments prompted by the urge to original expression of emotion. A current example of postmodern pop is offered by Señor Coconut, a Caucasian German who reprises electronic music from bands of the 1980s, including Kraftwerk and Yellow Magic Orchestra, using sampled samba and salsa beats and Latin instrumentation. Señor Coconut's musical identity is con- structed knowingly as artifice, and can be recognised by a Latin aesthetic, a pas- tiche eschewing the sound signature of original recordings written by other artists.

Gorillaz' music, although composed by the creative team behind the band, is informed by and openly references a gallimaufry of lyrical, rhythmical and melodic motifs from a range of genres. What makes Gorillaz so distinctive in performance, however, is that their music depends on performers such as Shaun Ryder and Neneh Cherry, associated with different-sounding bands/genres, who are also able to fuse inter-mediations of live and playback forms through physical interaction and sonic synchronisation. This inter-medial interplay in performance, and the shifting vocal and instrumental contributors to their records, situate Gorillaz' work in an emergent postmodern praxis of collabo- ration, identifiable through a convergence of forms, and a diffusion and frag- mentation of identities. Gorillaz' work emanates from a spirit of collaboration that decentres notions of authenticity and originality, positioning their work openly in a postmodern field of play and display.

Gorillaz have developed a collaborative performance register that induces a 'break down' in the 'distance between actor and audience', giving the specta- tor 'something more than a passive role in the . . . exchange' (States 1985: 170). Pop performers often engage in a post-Brechtian form of direct address, encouraging spectator interaction and complicity in the event. On a recent world tour, German electronic band Kraftwerk offered spectators a direct form of musical intervention: by disseminating synthesisers in the form of handheld electronic calculators, spect-actors were able to add an element of contingency by contributing random melodies to the song, *Pocket Calculator*. (Gorillaz employ a similar technique, using technology sponsored by Motorola at their Apollo Theater concert in Los Angeles, April 2006.) During another song, *Robots*, Kraftwerk performed off-stage, their physical presence replaced by three-dimensional avatars in the form of robot-like mannequins. Their embod- ied absence did not impact significantly on the performers' ability to sustain spectator engagement, or attenuate the liveness of the event. Kraftwerk's direct sonic engagement with, and physical disengagement from, the spectator problematises traditional modes of presence in pop-concert reception, which have often centred upon notions of embodied presence and individual authorship. Gorillaz contribute to the demise of the modernist meta-narrative of authorial presence in pop performance by making animated images, guest artists, shadow performers and avatars the locus of expression in a performance register that encourages the active participation of the spectator in a variety of new ways.

The extent to which an audience can be encouraged to interact with the staged presences at pop concerts is shaped by the spatial configuration of the event and the spectator's position/point of view in relation to the actual and virtual elements of performance. The organisation of the *Demon Days* concert follows a proscenium configuration, but one that is carefully modulated to produce a visual layering effect based on differentiation of two- and three-dimensional, actual/virtual presences and mediations. Owing to the collective process in which live performers come and go, song by song, the staging configuration follows an open and flexible organisation downstage (forming a kind of forestage), with a semi-fixed bank of translucent flats upstage. Suspended upstage centre is a projection surface upon which video playback occurs, or animated images are screened. The stable musical personnel of Gorillaz, performers who would usually be observed displaying their instrumental skills, are rendered as featureless two-dimensional shapes, their black shadows appearing on the variously coloured translucent flats, giving the upstage elements the look of an animated Mondrian painting. Upstage left is occupied by orchestral instrumentalists, whose presence is relatively anonymous, and upstage right by a flexible group of singers who function as choral accompaniment.

The technique of using silhouettes is similar to that of Indonesian shadow theatre, whose manually animated forms are always accompanied by music. In shadow theatre, the *wayang*, or silhouettes, are employed by *dalangs*, or narrators, with the purpose of disseminating 'religious and dynastic propaganda' (Banham 1992: 881). Gorillaz may or may not be aware of the political heritage of Indonesian shadow play, but the thematic content of the songs of which *Demon Days* is comprised is politically situated, falling short of open propaganda in its ironic relation to the left-of-centre positions conveyed. An example of this political positioning occurs on the song *Fire Coming Out of the Monkey's Head*, in which Dennis Hopper's disembodied voice delivers a spoken-word narrative to a medium-tempo, groove-driven musical accompaniment. The narrative is inter-medial; Hopper's spoken form is accompanied by musical melody and rhythm, projected animations, and sung vocals. As with Indonesian shadow theatre, the narrative is preceded by music, and after eight bars that establish the groove, Hopper's voice begins;

> Once upon a time at the foot of a great mountain, there was a town where the people known as happy folk lived . . . here they played out their peaceful lives, innocent of the litany of excess and violence that was growing in the world below. To live in harmony with the spirit of the mountain called Monkey was enough. (Gorillaz 2005: DVD)

The decision to follow the time-honoured opening of fairytale and folklore, in which basic exposition of scene and setting is delineated by an omniscient narrator, creates a fictional point of view associated with oral narrative custom. This works against pop-song conventions that also aim to appeal to as broad an audience as possible, but do so through lyrical content delineating broadly recognisable interpersonal relationships in their contemporary contexts, adopting non-linear means by which to convey an attitude, emotion or political position. Gorillaz' decision to follow an oral narrative convention could easily have lead them into similar territory to that pursued by Rick Wakeman in his 1970s progressive-rock opera *Journey to the Centre of the Earth*, also a concept album, but with a linear focus and monolithic structure. Hopper helps avoid this by adopting an ironic vocal mask to deliver a parable in which the magical mountain, Monkey, is a metaphor for the exploitation of nature: the mountain erupts when mined for its material goods – perceived as riches by interloping 'strange folk' – with catastrophic effect.

The resultant dystopia the open-ended narrative conveys is communicated through animated images, including that of a character's face expressing shock at being bathed in what appears to be toxic rain, and a sung commentary in the place where a chorus would usually be. Albarn's sung interventions to Hopper's narrative alter the perspective and distance of the spectator to it, as they shift from an objective to a subjective point of view. The first of Albarn's sung sections, in which a 'dance of the dead' is described, presents a perspective outside the fictional world delineated by Hopper and the animated scenes. This has the effect of connecting the specificity of the childlike, fictional world of Monkey Mountain to an objective actuality described by Albarn's shadowy presence. Albarn's shadow-hand gestures replicate the contours of the animated figures of the 'strange folk', which provides a gestural bridge back into the Monkey Mountain narrative. In performance, this bridging device was less significant, as Albarn's presence behind the flat, upstage centre was not so clearly focused as in the video montage on the DVD.

In the second of Albarn's sung sections, the connection to a political reality is strengthened through lyrical content that specifies context, location and culture uttered from a personal perspective: 'Oh, little town of USA the time has come to see, all the things you think you are. But where were you, when it all come down on me? Did you call me? No' (Gorillaz 2005: DVD). The virtual mediations that delineate the parable of Monkey Mountain are made relevant to the audience in the here and now of the performance space, offering a dialogue between the pre-recorded mediations, the sung/performed present and the sensory experience perceived by the spectator. By introducing a psychological component to the narrative, which gains politicised specificity through the cartoon-like personification of 'little town . . . USA', the spectator engages in a dialogue of the fictional and the actual, occupying the position of voyeur and potential co-respondent to Albarn's rhetorical questions. The political engagement of the spectator is not a particularly subtle form of didacticism, but the animated form carries with it the 'omnipresent force of human praxis', which signals the intentionality and constructedness of the message and eschews a condescending attitude (Jameson 1991: 77). Through the use of irony and animation, and the virtual/actual address of the ear and the eye, the spectator is made complicit in a form of social presence broader and more vital than can be offered by the embodied live performers alone, but whose sonically amplified physical presences are somatically engaging. The inter-mediations extend perspectives and broaden conceptual horizons in ways that, carried via a sonic field of engagement, can powerfully affect spectator emotions.

Gorillaz further subvert a fundamental component of the live pop concert, the physical co-presence of singer and spectator, in a song recorded by Ibrahim Ferrer, who sings on the track 'Latin Simone', and in a way that is powerfully affective. Ferrer died in August 2005, but the documentation of his physical presence is remediated in the form of a projected video sequence in which he is depicted recording for the *Demon Days* album. The video footage is the principal scopic focus, as the performers on stage left and right are not illuminated, and a blue light punches out the silhouettes of the musicians performing behind the flats. The video depicts Ferrer singing behind a piano as his voice is recorded, and the sound playback is synchronised with the music performed live. The effect of this is to breathe new life into Ferrer's performance, revivifying it, and if one were to close one's eyes, it would be impossible to distinguish between the live and the recorded elements of the sonic experience. In this way, the video functions as an avatar, providing a manifestation of the absent performer that is *felt* in the present, but that is, paradoxically, located ontologically in the past. The video playback oscillates between a direct form of address, a virtual presence felt through and synchronised with Ferrer's singing, and a documentation of diurnal activity, as Ferrer is seen walking through the studio and interacts with the musical production team. The rendition of this song attains its affective potential in the tension that lies between the music that is rendered live, the recorded melodies, made distinctive by the tonality of Ferrer's vocals, and the playback images. Although we are aware that Ferrer is not actually present in the visual field of perception, his voice is felt as part of the lived experience of the event that unfolds in the present as a somatic force working on the spectator's body with equal impact to the live music that fills the concert hall. A further tension exists in the revelatory documentary sequences, a behind-the-scenes showing of what went on in the studio. Ferrer is denied a voice in these sections of diurnal activity, lending the images a ghostliness, in which Ferrer's disembodied presence is enhanced. The ensuing nostalgia is attenuated as the diurnal images engage in a *pas de deux* with those depicting Ferrer singing, but it is the uplifting feelings produced by the harmonious melodies and airy tonality of Ferrer's voice that ensure his ability to intervene in the present, despite disembodiment.

CONCLUSION

Inter-mediality in pop performances can address the spectator in a variety of registers. Image projections can enhance the psychological impact of the performer's presence, whilst creating a state of perceptual tension in the scopic dissonance of two and three dimensionalities, as when Nico performs with her projected iconography. Inter-mediating technologies can produce a flexible, fluid and intimate perspective of live performance through interactions of large-scale telematic images, structured in the language of cinematography, that contrast with and contribute to the actual, physical presence of the performer as perceived by the naked eye. Madonna's projection of video from past works informs songs performed live, affecting a temporal discourse that reprises the past in the actualised present, working with the spectator's own memory. Through a process of remediation, screened personas intersect with live re-presentations, making the songs performed in the hear-and-now resonate with recollection of performances in the there-and-then. Whilst the Warhol-influenced Velvet Underground used film projection experimentally, Madonna continues to exploit telematic and video playback technologies as a memory device, or *memoria technica*. By reminding the spectator of her international hit-rate, Madonna's infusions of past images into her live performances enhance her entity as star whilst fragmenting her personal identity.

Pop performances develop a complicity of the spectator in the staging of the event that shares a register with postmodern inter-medial theatre, and to the extent to which the spectator is aware of the constructedness and artifice of pop performances, they can be identified as hyper-medial. In *Demon Days*, Gorillaz produce a hyper-medial state of play, as animated characters illustrate disembodied spoken narratives to musical accompaniment and interact with live performers and shadow performers. In *Latin Simone*, the reflexiveness of hyper-mediality is underscored, and to some extent undermined, by an immersive soundscape in which a recorded voice is synchronised with live sound and video projections, producing an experience that is both immediate and removed, offering a form of auditory memorial that is felt in the present whilst the performance occurs in the past. There is a strong tension in the creation of an illusory, monolithic soundscape that makes the disparate elements of the multi-screen video montage cohere. Ferrer's virtual embodiment impacts somatically on the spectator through sound and melody that, although identifiable with the singer, are part of a collaborative performance mode that challenges traditional notions of identity in pop performance.

By creating new interactions of recorded forms, visual and auditory representations, inter-medial pop performances operate in a postmodern field of play that engages the spectator intellectually, but also emotionally. Older media forms, such as pop video and audio recording, are remediated in hyper-medial systems that demonstrate, display and perform their processes of constructedness, whilst working on the spectators somatically and emotionally through sound. As traditional modes of performance, associated with stable identity, authenticity and originality, are challenged by new inter-medialities, the role of spectator is shifted from one of passivity to active participation in the performance of sound event. Gorillaz use a choral group in performance to further the sense of complicity and help bridge the perceptual gaps between the live and recorded media, the two- and three-dimensional. No longer does the spectator need or require an authenticating presence, or a physically present performer, in a mode that encourages complicity through direct sonic engagement and visual replay. The spectators of inter-medial pop are not only finding a voice, but encountering new apprehensions of sight and sound that have the potential to affect their own presence as embodied subjects. In performance, the shadows, ghostings, repetitions and inter-medial interventions that produce a complex and engaging scopic experience make *Demon Days* innovative, but the experience would be less effective without the ingredient that makes all pop performances engaging: the emotional potential of memorable songs and remembered sounds. Gorillaz extend this potential, and the immediacy and liveness felt in the field of performance, by offering further interactions using technologies of the Internet to explore virtual presences.

REFERENCES

Ashbee, B. (2003), 'Animation, Art and Digitality: From Termite Terrace to Motion Painting', in M. Thomas and F. Penz (eds), *Architectures of Illusion: From Motion Pictures to Navigable Interactive Environments* (London: Intellect Books).

Auslander, P. (1999), *Liveness: Performance in a Mediatized Culture* (London: Routledge).

Banham, M. (ed.) (1992), *The Cambridge Guide to Theatre* (Cambridge: Cambridge University Press).

Benjamin, W. (2003), 'The Work of Art in the Age of its Technological Reproducibility (Third Version)', in H. Eiland and M. W. Jennings (eds), trans. E. Jephcott, H. Eiland et al., *Walter Benjamin: Selected Writings. Vol. 3: 1935–1938* (London: Harvard University Press).

Bernstein, J. (1966), *The Tech*, Tuesday 1 November, http://www-tech.mit.edu/archives/VOL_086/TECH_V086_S0457_P006.pdf (accessed August 2006).

Bolter, J. D., and Grusin, R. (2000), *Remediation: Understanding New Media* (Cambridge, MA: MIT Press).

Cavell, S. (1971), *The World Viewed* (London: Harvard University Press).

Chapple, F., and Kattenbelt, C. (eds) (2006), *Intermediality in Theatre and Performance* (Amsterdam: Rodopi).

Gracyk, T. (1996), *Rhythm and Noise: An Aesthetics of Rock* (London: I. B. Tauris).

Horn, D. (2000), 'Some Thoughts on the Work in Popular Music', in M. Talbot (ed.), *The Musical Work Reality or Invention* (Liverpool: Liverpool University Press).

Jameson, F. (1991), *Postmodernism, or the Cultural Logic of Late Capitalism* (London: Verso).

Kelly, J. (2005), 'Auditory Space: Emergent Modes of Apprehension and Historical Representations in *Three Tales*', *International Journal of Performance Arts and Digital Media*, Vol. 1, No. 3, pp. 207–36.

Raynor, A. (2002), 'Rude Mechanicals and the *Spectres of Marx*', *Theatre Journal*, No. 54, pp. 535–54.

States, B. O. (1985), *Great Reckonings in Little Rooms: On the Phenomenology of Theater* (London and Berkeley, CA: University of California Press).

7. CASE STUDY: FILM SOUND, ACOUSTIC ECOLOGY AND PERFORMANCE IN ELECTROACOUSTIC MUSIC

Randolph Jordan

Typically, when we think of a live musical performance, our understanding of it is well grounded in the realm of the visual. When we go to a musical performance, for example, we *see* the musicians on a stage which acts as the locus of our attention. This attention to the visual presence of the performers offers a certain measure of validity to the uniqueness of the live event, and can direct our attention to aspects of the music's production that we may otherwise be unaware of. Yet this same visual engagement can call attention away from qualities of the sound being heard that reveal themselves only when they are attended to in their own right. Such visual engagement can also distract us from the way that music is behaving within the performance space itself.

The use of recorded sound as the basis for live performance blossomed in the second half of the twentieth century, and has raised many issues concerning the idea of what a musical performance should be. When performers began using recorded sound, many argued that a certain level of authenticity was removed along with the removal of conventional musical instruments. When we can no longer see what a performer is doing to create the sound we hear in a live setting, the notion of performance can be called into question. Nowhere is this more evident than the laptop performances that are so prevalent today in which, as Philip Sherburne has sardonically observed, 'a twitch of the wrist becomes a moment of high drama' (Sherburne 2002: 70). With the prevailing consensus that musical performances need to be visually stimulating, the sight of a lone, stationary figure stooped over a laptop computer is disappointing. Those working in the broad field of electroacoustic music – sound compositions

presented through loudspeakers – have long based their idea of musical performance on the sounds being played rather than the people playing them. Live
diffusion of acousmatic sound – sound presented in the absence of any visual
source – provides the basic model for concerts of electroacoustic music. The
sound itself is pre-recorded, but its particular treatment within a given space is
left up to the diffuser, who moves the recorded sound through the sound system
in real time using a mixing console or, more recently, specialised software. In
this way the performance becomes context-specific despite the lack of musicians
performing in real time.

A fair bit has been written on the art of live diffusion, but this writing tends
to be from a technical and/or psychoacoustic perspective. What technologies
can be used to move sound around space on the levels of both composition and
playback? How does our understanding of space relate to the treatment of
sound, and vice versa? How can spatiality be built into auditory composition?
These are all important questions. But for present purposes I would like us to
take a step back and consider the basic premise of live diffusion of electroacoustic material, which has so often been taken for granted: the desire to
remove evidence of the source of sound as well as how it is being manipulated
in a given performance.

This chapter will discuss the concept of the 'acousmatic' and the issues it
raises when considering the idea of live performance as hinging upon an audience's need for a visual point of reference as substantiation of a performer's
presence. The tradition of acousmatic music, pioneered by French composer
Pierre Schaeffer, will be discussed as an ideal that challenges the visually based
paradigm for music performance in Western culture, while, at the same time,
calling figurative art into question through its insistence on total abstraction.
The acousmatic ideal will then be posited against the ecological approach to
sound awareness found in the field of acoustic ecology. Like the term 'acousmatic', the concept of 'schizophonia', coined by Canadian composer R. Murray
Schafer (founder of the acoustic ecology movement), refers to the separation of
sound from source. For Schafer, however, this separation is extremely negative,
and it will thus serve as an instructive counterpoint to Pierre Schaeffer's acousmatic ideal. Along the way we will flesh out key debates in the theories and
practices of sound reproduction technology, most notably questions concerning the mediation of experience, the spatial contexts of sound reproduction,
and the role of multi-channel systems in the presentation of recorded sound.
Here it will become clear that many of these debates have crystallised in the
field of film sound theory, and that the particular issues faced when thinking
about sound in the cinema can yield productive ways of thinking about the
questions raised by the concepts of acousmatic sound, schizophonic experience,
and electroacoustic performance. The writing of Michel Chion will serve as the
basis for connecting the thinking of Pierre Schaeffer to the world of film sound,

and, by extension, R. Murray Schafer's concern for the world's sound ecologies. Ultimately I will suggest that the ideologies behind acousmatic music and the notion of schizophonia are not, in fact, irreconcilable. The work of Hildegard Westerkamp will be discussed as an exemplary practice that merges the seemingly opposing ideologies of Schaeffer's acousmatic ideal and Schafer's context-based approach to sound awareness. Her piece *Kits Beach Soundwalk* will serve as a case in point, both in its approach to soundscape composition and in the way that it has been diffused in the context of electroacoustic performance. So let us begin by considering the basic ideologies underlying the concept of the 'acousmatic' in more detail.

The Acousmatic

In *The Voice in Cinema*, electroacoustic music composer and film sound theorist Michel Chion describes the origin of the term 'acousmatic' in a story concerning Pythagoras from the 1751 *Encyclopedia* of Diderot and d'Alembert. Here the term 'Acousmatiques' is used to refer to those 'uninitiated disciples of Pythagoras who were obliged to spend five years in silence listening to their master speak behind the curtain, at the end of which they could look at him and were full members of the sect' (Chion 1999: 19). The reason for keeping the disciples in the dark may have been two-fold. In the context of his book on the voice, Chion uses this story to illustrate the idea that the voice without body is imbued with special powers of omniscience and ubiquity. Chion uses the term 'acousmêtre' to refer to cinematic characters presented as voices without bodies that, being kept hidden from view, are seemingly more powerful than the average human being. This sense of power through an emphasis on auditory presence would certainly befit a master wishing to assert his status as such. Yet Pythagoras' strategy might also have been an early expression of what has been distilled to the more familiar 'principles before personalities' tenet held by many religions: focus on the message, not the messenger. Not until the message is understood can the distraction of exposure to the messenger be allowed, a point that Chion makes in *Guide des objets sonores* (Chion 1983: 19), his companion piece to Pierre Schaeffer's *Traité des objets sonores*, the latter composer's landmark work of theory in which he formulated his ideas about acousmatic sound. For Pythagoras there was clearly some value to the idea of presenting sound in the absence of a visual source, and a sense of this value remained intact through the twentieth century. Chion reminds us that in French the word 'acousmate' has come to designate 'invisible sounds', and it was writer Jérôme Peignot who 'called this term to the attention of Pierre Schaeffer' (Chion 1999: 19). It is once Schaeffer began using the term that its relevance to musical performance became especially charged.

Pierre Schaeffer was interested in how musical composition might gear itself towards just such an understanding of sound in its own right. He pioneered the tradition of composition and performance referred to as acousmatic music, the basis of which is to present compositions recorded on a fixed medium and played back through loudspeakers. Yet it is important to understand that Schaeffer wanted to move beyond the physical detachment of sound from source offered by the loudspeaker, and into something more abstract. The designation 'acousmatic sound' can apply to any sound presented in the absence of a visual source. The designation 'acousmatic music' was, for Schaeffer, geared towards presenting sound compositions in which the audience is called upon to detach themselves from the need to think about the sources of the sounds they hear and focus on the sounds as self-contained objects. Schaeffer posited three main modes of listening: causal (listening with an ear towards the cause of a sound); semantic (listening for the meaning contained within the sound); and reduced (listening to the qualities of the sound in its own right) (Chion 1994: 25–34.) Schaeffer was most interested in reduced listening, and the ideal for acousmatic music is often thought of as the presentation of sound which fostered this kind of listening alone.

In acousmatic music, then, the idea of referentiality is not thought of in terms of a visual counterpart, for such a counterpart is done away with through the use of loudspeakers as the mode of sound transmission. The sound is necessarily detached from its original source, whatever that may be. The use of electroacoustical transmission is a crucial aspect of Schaeffer's concept of acousmatic music. For reduced listening to take place, sound must not only be detached from source, it must also be fixed on a recording medium so that the sounds can attain 'the status of veritable objects' (Chion 1994: 30). No live sound is ever truly repeatable, so to analyse a given sound's particular qualities properly it must be made repeatable through technologies of recording and transmission. In this way the sound is made 'concrete', and this is one of the principal tenets of the movement that came to be known as *musique concrète*.

To qualify as a composition upholding the ideals of acousmatic music the sound must be organised in such a way that it does not evoke a sense of its own causes; it must achieve a level of abstraction that allows the audience to attend to its status as pure sound rather than sound which emanates from something recognisable in the world. This is the essential difference between acousmatic *music* and acousmatic *sound*; the former is about an intentional removal of causal and semantic elements within a composition, while the latter simply designates a sound which has been separated from its source. We all experience electroacoustically transmitted sound on a regular basis, but most of this consists of music to which we attach a basic understanding of source: we hear the latest pop stars singing through the sound system in the local mall and we attach this voice to our knowledge of their being. This is acousmatic sound. When we hear a well-designed piece of acousmatic music, we don't attach a sense of the sources to the sounds. We just hear them as they are.

The cinema, being an inherently audiovisual medium, sheds some interesting light on the concept of the 'acousmatic' and its relationship to the sense of sight. An examination of acousmatic presence in film will prove useful in expanding our understanding of the ideals and limitations of Schaeffer's thought. In his adaptation of the term 'acousmatic' for use in film sound theory, Michel Chion has led the way in bridging the gap between Schaeffer's world of acousmatic music and the role of sound in film. Needless to say, in a purely auditory medium, the idea of the 'acousmatic' means something quite different from how Chion has adopted it for use in the cinema. In *Audio-Vision: Sound on Screen*, Chion discusses acousmatic sound for the cinema in terms of 'passive' and 'active' modes. The passive mode would include ambient sound, such as bird song and traffic noise, which don't invite the listener to question their sources. When we hear birds chirping as part of the soundscape of an environment presented on screen, we don't ask where these sounds are coming from. Our reaction to them is passive. In the active mode, as you might imagine, questioning the source of an acousmatic sound occurs in the audience and/or characters in the film (Chion 1994: 33). We hear an unidentified sound that makes us ask: what was that? Where did it come from? Such use of acousmatic sound often drives narrative forward by engaging a character in the film to ask these same questions, and then to seek the answers.

In either the active or the passive mode, acousmatic sound in the cinema is a perfect example of the medium's necessarily audiovisual nature. As Chion makes clear: take the image away and there can be no such thing as an off-screen sound. Without the image we can never know whether or not the traffic sounds we hear emanate from the space that would be represented on screen, and any question as to the source of the sound would no longer be based on the presence or absence of accompanying visuals. The cinema thus reduces the complexity involved in the distinction between different conceptions of the acousmatic. Films focus on acousmatic sound without the intention of treating it as an abstract object to be extracted from the context that comes with knowledge of its source, the ideal in Schaeffer's conception of acousmatic music. In the end the cinema's simplification of the concept of the acousmatic is a function of well-established conventions of audiovisual synchronisation: if a given sound and image are synchronised on screen, then the source of the sound can be found in the image. Remove this synchronisation and we have an instant recipe for acousmatic sound, regardless of whether or not the sound itself is abstract or referential in nature.

The main difference between Pierre Schaeffer's original sense of acousmatic music and Chion's adoption of the term 'acousmatic' for the cinema is that, for Schaeffer, the main purpose of presenting sound acousmatically is to deflect attention from source while keeping the sound itself the object of intense scrutiny. This situation is impossible under the two categories of acousmatic sound that Chion identifies in film. Passive off-screen sound remains neutral, designed to be ignored by the listener. Active off-screen sound does exactly the opposite: creating a desire in the listener, and perhaps in a character in the film, to seek out the cause of the sound. In either case, sound is not the object of scrutiny in and of itself. So it might seem that Schaeffer's ideal is impossible in the audiovisual realm of the cinema. Later I will suggest otherwise. For the moment, let us take this premise as a given and position it against the perform-ance of acousmatic music.

LIVE DIFFUSION OF ACOUSMATIC MUSIC

With recorded music presented to an audience in the absence of live perform-ance, Schaeffer's ideal acousmatic situation is easily enough achieved. The problem then becomes how to integrate live performance into this acousmatic situation. We've probably all listened to music in the dark, and thus have some experience of something approaching Schaeffer's ideal acousmatic situation. Yet when we go to see music performed live, even by musicians manipulating recorded materials in real time, the model is almost always the same: the artists stand on a stage, and we all stare in their direction. Even if we close our eyes, there is no escaping the orientation of the listening environment to the stage as source of the sound we've come to hear. Enter the live diffusion model of elec-troacoustic performance: a person sits at a mixing desk amidst the audience, and as the piece is being played back this 'diffuser' decides how the recorded composition should be translated into the multi-channel speaker array specific to that particular performance space.

As Barry Truax has noted, in the traditional live performance model, the per-forming musicians are up on stage and the sound engineer, responsible for how the sound is presented in the concert space, is kept separate at the mixing desk on the house floor. Thus diffusion and performance are generally thought of as being separate (Truax 1998: 141). This separation actually suits the acousmatic ideal: when the performers are removed from the stage by presenting music recorded on a fixed medium, attention to the source of this sound can be averted. The position of the diffuser within the middle of the audience is also a necessity for the performance: the diffuser must have the perspective of an audi-ence member so as to be able to manipulate the sound properly. This is why performers, when adhering to the conventional stage/audience divide, cannot properly gauge the way their performance is being heard by the audience. The live diffusion model in electroacoustic presentation conflates the performer and the sound engineer to solve this problem and help achieve the acousmatic ideal.

In most concerts of acousmatic music, the composer is not the one diffusing the composition. Concerts are often presented with a single diffuser responsible for interpreting each piece in the programme according to the particularities of the performance space. Composers Adrian Moore, Dave Moore and James Mooney have addressed the potential conflict between an artist's intentions and those of the diffuser. So as not to be confused with an artist interfering with the original composition, the status of the diffuser has remained that of an engineer whose task it is to make the artist's work sound as good as it can without getting in the way of the composition (Moore et al. 2004: 317). Yet this causes the diffuser's art to disappear, which, while suiting the acousmatic ideal, doesn't do justice to the performative virtuosity of live diffusion. The ultimate solution may lie in having the composers perform the diffusion themselves, as does happen from time to time. Moore et al. have also talked about a 'more transparent' model for merging composer and diffuser by bringing the recording studio into the performance space. One of their arguments against this is that it would not be 'visually striking' (Moore et al. 2004: 318), again suggesting the need for a lack of obtrusive visual evidence of the performance within the acousmatic model. In this way the diffuser can remain unseen, thereby maintaining the spirit of the acousmatic ideal. So the problem remains: the idea of diffusing a recorded piece of music is not considered a performance art on the same level of respectability as musicians playing conventional instruments. This is largely due to a lack of understanding of what it is that diffusers do, as well as the association made between the diffuser at an electroacoustic music concert and the sound engineer at a conventional concert. It is partially the acousmatic ideal that keeps the art of the diffuser in the dark. So what is it that they actually do, anyway? And what issues arise when considering the art of diffusion in relation to the acousmatic ideal?

Surrounding the Sound-stage

What differentiates the diffuser within the field of electroacoustic music from the sound engineer who controls the sound in a concert venue is the real-time spatial interpretation of the music being presented. Generally speaking, a sound engineer at a concert involving performers on a stage is not spreading the sound across a multi-channel array on the basis of interpreting the performed composition in real time. Ideally, the sound engineer gets all the settings right during the sound check and then acts as a monitor to make sure things match this ideal as the show progresses. The diffuser's job, on the other hand, is to act as a kind of composer who, on the basis of the content of the original composition, creates a spatialisation of the piece specific to the conditions of that particular performance. Traditionally, this has meant translating a stereo recording into a multi-channel configuration. This poses many problems for the ideals of conventional musical performance.

We've addressed the desire for the diffuser to remain unseen so as to present the compositions according to the acousmatic ideal. To flesh out how presenting sound in a multi-channel array further challenges the notion of the traditional performance, we need to understand the concept of the sound-stage as it relates to the world of hi-fi stereo culture and the purist ideals held by the audiophile community about what makes a good recording of a performance, and what makes a good playback of that recording.

There are many people in the world who still prefer the sound of analogue media to that of newer digital formats. It seems that along with the 'analogue is best' mentality comes a particular philosophy about what kinds of music are best as well. It turns out that the best kinds of music are those which adhere to an understanding of music being something produced by musicians on unamplified instruments with no intentions of having their sounds captured and represented in any recording format whatsoever. In essence, the version of the audiophile ideal that I'm exploring here is that the best recordings are the ones that should never have been made in the first place. This seems like a contradiction, and of course it is. In my opinion, however, the kind of purism I'm describing is founded upon a very particular contradiction that Jonathan Sterne has called the 'vanishing mediator' in his book *The Audible Past*. Ultimately, Sterne observes that the goal of fidelity became part and parcel of this vanishing mediator, 'where the medium produces a perfect symmetry between copy and original and, thereby, erases itself' (Sterne 2002: 285). The basic idea is that any technologies of recording/transmission should vanish from perception when listening to the final product. This is more commonly referred to as 'transparency'.

At the heart of the idea of transparency is the concept of the 'sound-stage'. In audiophile parlance, there are two main things that this term refers to. One is the ability to understand the spatial position of every musician and their instruments in a recording. This is dependent upon designing the recording according to the ideal of music as performed live by musicians localisable within a single space, and maintaining the integrity of this ideal by placing any given instrument sound in a specific spot – and keeping it there. The other main feature of a good sound-stage is a system's ability to draw attention away from its sources, especially with regard to the position of a pair of speakers. Being able to tell where the speaker is positioned in the room is bad. Being able to tell where an imaginary musician is positioned in the room is good.

This mentality has spilled over into the realm of film sound production and exhibition, particularly where surround sound is concerned. One of the main principles behind surround-sound speaker placement is that of the sound-stage. No speakers, particularly not any of the side or rear speakers, should call attention to themselves. The sound field should remain stable and not disrupt the spectator's feeling of immersion within the soundscape of the film. Indeed, in the vast majority of films we find a tendency towards using sound to create the feeling of a stable environment even where the picture might suggest otherwise. This is most evident in the use of continuous soundscapes during scenes in which the picture editing is intended to be as 'invisible' as possible. This is one reason why the standard shot–countershot scenario for conversation between two characters is not as disorienting as it should be. If a cut in the soundscape was heard every time a cut in the image was seen, the experience would be far more jarring, if only for the reason that we have not been trained to internalise the convention of abrupt sound edits in the way that we have come to terms with continuously changing shots on the image track.

The problem of jarring sound is explored by Michel Chion in *Audio-Vision* when he discusses the idea of 'in-the-wings' effects in surround-sound mixing. He notes that much more use was made of side and rear channels in the early days of the formats, but sound designers found that too much emphasis on these channels drew attention to them and away from the frame of the image. This situation was not conducive to the ideals of a cinema that seeks to keep the processes of its production hidden. I experienced just such a situation recently when I threw on my DVD of *Monty Python and the Holy Grail*. I had forgotten about the film's false start in which the credit sequence from a completely unrelated film is the first thing we see and hear. All of a sudden it stops, and from the right rear channel in the Dolby Digital 5.1 mix we hear the sound of the projectionist's voice grumbling about having put on the wrong film by mistake. The isolated position of this voice startled me at first, and I was jolted into an awareness of the system of reproduction, which was very appropriate for the reflexive nature of this comic routine. Of course, the 1975 film was originally mixed in mono, and so arguments can be made about whether or not this use of surround sound is faithful to the original concept of the film. I generally prefer to stick with whatever format the film was originally designed for, but in the case of this particular gag I prefer the updated multi-channel mix, as it suits their purposes splendidly. Chion suggests that this feeling of distraction by 'in-the-wings' effects may simply have gone away as people became used to the new sound formats, and that perhaps with some changes to picture-editing practices it could have spawned a new realm of productive audiovisual collaboration. 'So perhaps it was a mistake to have given it up so quickly' (Chion 1994: 84).

I suspect, however, that the ideals of the vanishing mediator are so deeply ingrained that no amount of pushing sound through the rear speakers would have undone the deeply held ideals of the audiophile community, whose Holy Grail it is to lose all awareness of the equipment responsible for the sounds it hears. My position, and it is by no means a new one, is that this equipment is as much an instrument of sound production as any of the 'real' instruments held in such high regard. This is the basic principle behind the idea of the 'scratch' in contemporary DJ culture, and long before that in the practice of scratching the surface of film found in much avant garde/experimental cinema. I believe that to ignore the instrument of sound reproduction is to lose a major part of what makes the experience of a great sounding system so profound. And of course, this is the very principle behind using the mixing console as an instrument of performance in the act of live diffusion of electroacoustic material.

So where live diffusion succeeds in erasing the performer from view and acknowledges studio equipment as instruments of performance, the movement of sound through space can actually distract from the ideal of acousmatic music. With no referentiality to speak of, these abstract sounds cannot disappear into an imagined context like environmental sound presented in the side and rear channels of a multi-channel cinema array. Because the sound can find no context but that of its own being, any movement through the performance space effectively becomes an 'in-the-wings' effect. Attention is thus diverted away from the sound itself and to the equipment used to reproduce the sound, as well as towards the space in which this sound is being reproduced: two faux-pas when wanting to keep attention focused on the sound in its own right.

This problem highlights the importance that we attach to our ability to contextualise our sensory experience, and the study of the contextualisation of sound within the environment is the domain of acoustic ecology. The goal of the acoustic ecologist is to foster awareness of sound within the context of environments in which we are necessarily making use of our other senses at the same time. To understand sound in context, to be able to attach it to a source, goes against the principle of acousmatic music as explained thus far. Yet there is much in common between the acoustic ecologist's quest for sonic awareness and Pierre Schaeffer's desire to pay sound the attention it deserves. It will now be useful to consider the issues raised by Schaeffer's acousmatic ideal in the light of its apparent antithesis: R. Murray Schafer's concept of 'schizophonia'.

SCHIZOPHONIA

As an ideal, the reduced listening situation of acousmatic music stands in stark contrast to the contextual grounding of sound within the environment sought by those working in and around the field of acoustic ecology. R. Murray Schafer was one of the pioneers of the field of acoustic ecology, a broad area of study that takes as its basic premise the study of the environment through attention to sound. Crucial to this study is an understanding of the way that humans are affected by the sound of the spaces they inhabit, to what extent these 'soundscapes' (a term that Schafer coined) are shaped by our behaviour, and to what extent changes in our behaviour can thus shape the sounds of our environments towards more positive ends.

Schafer invented the term 'schizophonia' in the late 1960s and elaborated upon it in his most famous book, *The Tuning of the World*. He uses the term to refer to 'the split between an original sound and its electroacoustical transmission or reproduction' (Schafer 1977: 90). For Schafer, the term has extremely negative connotations and is used to describe contemporary soundscapes that have become rife with represented sound to the extent that the electroacoustic is drowning out that which is merely acoustic. The logical conclusion of this overabundance of represented sound is 'the complete portability of acoustic space' through technologies of recording and transmission: 'Any sonic environment can now become any other sonic environment' (p. 91). The fundamental fear underlying the experience of schizophonia is that we will lose our grounding in the context of the here and now, with 'machine-made substitutes' for 'natural sounds . . . providing the operative signals directing modern life' (p. 91).

From the outset it must be said that the experience of acousmatic music within the controlled circumstances of a performance event is not of the same order as the quotidian real-world dissociation of sound from source that Schafer uses the term 'schizophonia' to describe. So, in one sense comparing Schaeffer's acousmatic ideal to Schafer's concept of schizophonia is like comparing apples to oranges. However, though Schafer uses the word 'schizophonia' to describe negatively the dissociation that occurs at the hands of electroacoustic technologies within our daily environments, the ideology underlying his bias is also present within his work as a composer. In his own works of environmental theatre (see Schafer's *Patria: The Complete Cycle*), Schafer rarely makes use of electroacoustical transmission. He generally composes for purely acoustic instrumentation with the performance space in mind, allowing this space (often in the wilderness) to contribute as much to the composition as vice versa. It is a context-based approach that supports his use of the term 'schizophonia' as a negative, and illustrates his view that even within a space of performance, the decontextualised experience of electroacoustic transmission is not a good thing. For this reason, I suggest that positing these differing ideas against each other yields a productive way of thinking about both Schaeffer and Schafer that cannot arise when they are treated in isolation.

Schafer's bias is clearly directed towards the idea of a pre-industrial soundscape, one in which he supposes schizophonia could not exist. This bias is linked to his distaste for the idea of transcending the present tense, of losing touch with one's grounding in the context of the present moment. Yet the soundscapes that he would have us return to are a product of a distant past that we can only glimpse in today's world. He relies heavily on written ear-witness testimony from times past, a necessarily mediated perspective on experience to which he has no access. He has also pioneered the use of recording technology for the purposes of documenting, analysing and ultimately preserving a selection of today's changing soundscapes. With his appeal to technologies of representation in order to access the past, and preserve the present for the future, Schafer's line of thinking exhibits an incongruity with his stated distrust of such technology and its effects on our experience of both space and time. However, this incongruity is only apparent if the idea of schizophonia retains the negative connotations that he intended. I suggest that Schafer's apparent hypocrisy need not be read as such. Rather, we should understand Schafer's position of being caught between the past and the present as exemplary of the schizophonic experience that he decries, and recognise that it is precisely this experience that has allowed him to explore environmental sound in the way that he has. If we approach Schafer this way, he need not be subject to the updating that many have suggested is necessary to make his work relevant to today's world. The relevance has always been there. It need only be recognised.

What is crucial to note about Schafer's concept of schizophonia is that it is based on the idea that a represented soundscape can effectively replace an existing soundscape. I call this the 'space-replacement' model of schizophonic experience, the idea being that the listener loses grounding within the context of the listening environment and enters the time and place of the recording rather than the space in which the recording is being transmitted. While something approaching this space-replacement model of schizophonic experience might exist in very controlled circumstances, such as acoustically treated recording studios, in cinemas or when using headphones, the idea is essentially impossible in the context of our general experience of represented sound within existing soundscapes. No reproduced soundscape can ever fully replace the pre-existing soundscape of the place in which it is being transmitted. What does happen, however, is a layering effect whereby the soundscape of a given place is mixed with a represented soundscape, thus creating an interaction between the two that calls attention to itself as such. Schafer's version of schizophonia posits an average listener that cannot separate the real from the represented, and thus representation should be banished lest this listener become confused, disoriented, and disconnected from the context of the environment. I propose a different model for the average listener, one whose experience of schizophonia exemplifies an *increased* awareness of environment.

Our understanding of the way a space should sound leads to an awareness of how it sounds differently in the face of represented sound. If we can, in fact, maintain an awareness of what sounds emerge from technologies of representation within a given environment, and do not walk into a mall outlet fashion store and believe we have been transported to the recording studio of whatever pop star is blaring away through the store's sound system, then what we face is an experience of schizophonia that is based on a grounding within the context of our environments, marked by an awareness of what aspects of this environment are the result of technologies of representation. This doubling effect is how I think the idea of schizophonia should best be understood.

It is in Schafer's breakdown of soundscapes into the categories of 'hi-fi' and 'lo-fi' that I suggest the essence of my point about schizophonia can be found. His use of these terms connects his thinking with the discourse of fidelity found in the audiophile approach to sound reproduction technology mentioned above.

For Schafer, the hi-fi soundscape is one in which sounds exist on a 'human scale'. The main example of this is given in chapter 14 of *The Tuning of the World*, where he says: 'There are few sounds in nature that interfere with our ability to communicate vocally and almost none that in any way pose a threat to the hearing apparatus' (Schafer 1977: 207). Though Schafer's claim here can easily be argued against, what is important to understand is his equation of high fidelity with what Jonathan Sterne refers to as 'the spatiality of the unamplified voice' (Sterne 2002: 342).

If we think about schizophonia in terms of Sterne's vanishing mediator, we find two possible scenarios. The first is that Schafer believes in the possibility of technologies of electroacoustic transmission becoming transparent, thus allowing for the space-replacement model of schizophonic experience; a given space is replaced by a recorded invader when the mediating technology vanishes, leaving only the space of the original recording in its wake. The second possibility is that schizophonia actually suggests the impossibility of the vanishing mediator; space cannot be replaced, and schizophonic experience becomes an awareness of the mediating technology's presence within that space. This second possibility involves understanding schizophonia as a marker of a particular kind of attention to soundscape, which comprehends the role of mediation. This awareness of mediation amounts to a sense of contextual grounding within one's environment, while also being aware of the abstraction of that environment through the presence of electroacoustically transmitted sound.

Space Replacement and THX

As suggested earlier, one of the few places where one might experience Schafer's space-replacement model of schizophonia is within the sonically dead spaces of specially designed cinemas. It is within such cinemas that many concerts of acousmatic music take place, so it is useful to consider what issues arise when acknowledging the potential for such spaces to bring schizophonic experience to life.

The THX certification programme for cinema spaces and equipment has been at the forefront of efforts to try and reduce the differences between the controlled standards of the sound studio and the less controlled conditions of exhibition. The idea is to get all cinemas standardized to THX specifications with as little differentiation as possible. In theory, if a THX certified film is played back on THX certified equipment within a correspondingly designed space, there will be no difference between master and duplicate, original and copy (Johnson 1999: 104). This has extended into the realm of home cinema in recent years, with THX certifying home electronics and companies like DTS claiming that their process for encoding DVD soundtracks essentially clones the master tracks, offering the original without any process of reproduction getting in the way.

One of the main problems with the THX ideal is that it requires not only equivalent equipment on both ends, but also equivalent spaces. What this means is that the only real way to guarantee that exhibition spaces will behave the same way as studio spaces is for the sounds of these spaces to be banished altogether. Cinema spaces become increasingly dead, with no architectural particularities that grant them a signature of their own. This is the space-replacement model of schizophonia at its most tangible: the sound of a space is literally replaced by a dead zone designed to be filled with a represented space from elsewhere. In this case it is not so much the represented space that is replacing a real-world space, but rather the cinema itself that has replaced any sense of a space grounded in the context of material reality. Space replacement has become the guiding principle for the construction of cinema spaces, and this is the main reason why the home cinema environment can only rarely live up to this principle: most people cannot afford to build a studio-level cinema space within their homes, and thus the listening experience, even on THX certified equipment, is always subject to the sound of the spaces in which people live.

Michel Chion has expressed dismay at the degree to which projects like THX have been extended. He laments the quest for sonic purification and banishment of coloration, and exhibits nostalgia for the sounds of the large acoustical spaces of older cinemas (Chion 1994: 101). Chion suggests that standardisation models for film sound eschew notions of sonic fidelity in favour of homogenisation (pp. 100–1). What is crucial here is that Chion's use of the term 'fidelity' refers to privileging the sound of the space of exhibition over that contained on the film's soundtrack: being faithful to the space in which sound is reproduced, not to an idea of the original sound from whence the reproduction has come. This is a reversal of the way that fidelity has been used in the discourses responsible for the ideal of the vanishing mediator to which THX subscribes.

Chion's desire for the sound of the acoustical exhibition spaces of old is, in the end, a desire for what I call concrete schizophonia, that in which a soundscape is doubled in the presence of reproduction technology, rather than the total soundscape replacement that Schafer fears and for which THX standards reach. Chion enjoys the interaction between electroacoustically produced sound and the space in which it is transmitted, a grounding in the here and now which allows schizophonia to exist without being fuelled by the desire to 'transcend the present tense' that Schafer suggests is characteristic of the schizophonic experience (Schafer 1977: 91). Ultimately Chion's stance on this issue suggests a model for the kind of spatial awareness that I think the concept of schizophonia is most suited to: an awareness of the relationship between all the auditory elements of our environment that captures the spirit of acoustic ecology very well indeed.

SOUNDSCAPE COMPOSITION AND THE QUEST FOR AN ELECTROACOUSTIC ECOLOGY

Chion's desire for the acoustic spaces of old cinemas offers a sense that one can experience contextual grounding when confronted with electroacoustically transmitted sound. Chion is positioned in the middle ground between Pierre Schaeffer's acousmatic ideal and the absolute banishment of electroacoustic technologies espoused by R. Murray Schafer. This is a middle ground explored by composers who have emerged from the discipline of acoustic ecology and are interested in the use of field recordings – once used only for documentation and analysis – as the basis for soundscape composition. Katharine Norman refers to such composition as 'real-world music', an approach that relies on a balance between the realism of the recorded environments that make up the compositional building blocks, and their mediation through technologies of electroacoustic recording and transmission. In her words, 'real-world music leaves a door ajar on the reality in which we are situated' while seeking a 'journey which takes us away from our preconceptions', ultimately offering us a new appreciation of reality as a result (Norman 1996: 19).

This 'real-world music' is suited to the idea of schizophonia as the experience of mediation rather than as the fear of space replacement, which, in turn, points schizophonia back to Schaeffer's acousmatic ideal. Katharine Norman's description of soundscape composition as real-world music suggests that total realism is impossible, even within a documentary approach to composition. If this is true, then surely the opposite is true as well: total abstraction from context is also an impossibility. I have argued that the idea of schizophonia as space replacement is essentially impossible. The reality is that the acousmatic ideal is no more achievable than schizophonic space replacement. Rather, the reduced listening experience that acousmatic music induces is one of negotiation between listening modes. While seeking to appreciate the qualities of sound in its own right, the acousmatic ideal should not seek to divorce this sound completely from its context in the world. Rather, attention to the qualities of sound in its own right helps the listener discover the sound's context anew, what Katharine Norman refers to as 'reflective listening' (Norman 1996: 5); an alternative to the reductionism that many feel is inherent in Schaeffer's ideal listening situation.

As Rolfe Inge Godøy has recently pointed out, while reduced listening was Schaeffer's goal for acousmatic music, his *objets sonores* are impossible to abstract from fundamental images of movement that we necessarily build within our minds while listening. Godøy describes this relationship between reduced listening and visuality as being linked to '*embodied cognition*, meaning that virtually all domains of human perception and thinking, even seemingly abstract domains, are related to images of movement' (2006: 150). If we are constantly referring auditory experience back to images of movement within our minds, then it might seem that the acousmatic ideal is a physical impossibility. And we are thus back to the conventional concert scenario with its performer/audience divide, where even with our eyes closed we cannot separate sound from an understanding of its source in some form of physical movement responsible for generating the sound events that we hear. So perhaps the condition of acousmatic sound as it exists in the cinema, whereby there is always an image accompanying a sound (regardless of whether or not this image is understood to represent the sound's source), is the only possible way that acousmatic sound can really be experienced. Chion claims throughout his writing on sound in film that the cinema is necessarily founded upon an artificial relationship between sound and image, where the sounds we hear are connected to the images we see as part of the process of filmic construction. If we adopt this approach, then the relationship between sound and image in film is inescapably abstract. So perhaps this abstract relationship emulates the process of embodied cognition, the images on the screen providing visual movement along with the sounds put forth by the loudspeakers. This could be thought of as a relationship less about cause and effect than about giving abstract domains anchorage through the concept of gesture.

Embodied cognition might seem like a problem for Schaeffer's acousmatic ideal, and suggests that the cinema may have got the concept of acousmatic sound as right as could be hoped, abandoning a total removal of sound from the context of its production and offering a model for listening while remaining visually engaged. However, Godøy also points out that in Schaeffer's original development of the idea of reduced listening he recognised the fact that listeners would not be able to eradicate attention to context or signification completely, and that the act of shifting attention in and out of the mode of reduced listening was a necessary part of the experience (Godøy 2006: 151). In essence, Godøy is arguing that Schaeffer's concept of reduced listening recognizes the real-world nature of human perception, and that this kind of listening is more about an awareness of the different ways of listening than about adhering to one particular way for an extended period of time. This is essentially the same argument that I am making about R. Murray Schafer's concept of schizophonia: it works best as a description of the awareness of the role of electroacoustically transmitted sound within our sonic environments, and an ability to shift attention between them rather than letting the electroacoustic soundscape dominate our attention at the expense of those elements that remain unamplified.

A soundscape composer who works actively with principles of shifting attention in soundscape awareness is Hildegard Westerkamp, one of the founding members of the World Soundscape Project with R. Murray Schafer in the early 1970s. In her 1974 article 'Soundwalking', she lays out the foundations for beginning the process of soundscape awareness:

> Start by listening to the sounds of your body while moving. They are closest to you and establish the first dialogue between you and the environment. If you can hear the quietest of these sounds you are moving through an environment that is scaled to human proportions. In other words, with your voice or your footsteps you are 'talking' to your environment, which in turn responds by giving your sounds a specific acoustic quality. (Westerkamp 1974: 19)

Here she aligns herself with the ideals of human scale that Schafer holds so dear. She also shares Schafer's profound interest in the contextual understanding of auditory environment. The title of a later article, 'Speaking from Inside the Soundscape', indicates her position that if one is to express properly the way that sound works within a particular ecology, one must speak from inside the soundscape to others who are also within that soundscape. She cites Gregory Bateson, who writes: 'The problem of how to transmit our ecological reasoning to those whom we wish to influence in what seems to us to be an ecologically "good" direction is itself an ecological problem. We are not outside the ecology for which we plan – we are always and inevitably a part of it' (quoted in Westerkamp 2001: 146). While her alliances with Schafer are thus clear, we'll see that she does not equate human scale with a non-amplified existence. Further, her ideas about the give-and-take relationship of soundscape experience carry over very well to her compositional practices in the electroacoustic sphere.

Westerkamp suggests that, as children, 'listening and soundmaking (input and output, impression and expression) were ongoing activities, like breathing, happening simultaneously, always in relation to each other, in a feedback process' (Westerkamp 2001: 145). This simultaneity of listening and soundmaking is something Westerkamp would have us hold on to as adults. Westerkamp has an approach to ecology that reorders the ecological systems under observation in order to express their potential permutations in other contexts. Again, this is a model based on her notion of the soundwalk, which includes the practice of deconstructing the soundscape within our minds as we separate sounds that are often heard as one, and then sorting them into categories based on their pleasantness to our ears. The goal is to understand the soundscape as a composition so that we might compose better soundscapes in the future. This amounts to a psychological reordering of the heard environment that she emulates in her soundscape compositions. We've heard Derrida suggest that to read is to rewrite. For Westerkamp, to listen is to compose.

Westerkamp's work is part of an ever-increasing tradition of soundscape composition that recognises one basic fact: that the experience of pure abstraction is impossible even if sound is presented in such a way that it deflects attention away from source and onto the properties of the sound itself. As human beings our minds are always in search of ascribing representational meaning to the world around us, so the best that we can achieve is a balance between our grounding in the materialism governed by our survival instincts and an ability to transcend that materiality through separation from source and abstraction from context. Thus whether such abstraction is seen as positive, as in Pierre Schaeffer's case, or negative, as in R. Murray Schafer's case, it must be understood as a negotiation between the abstract and the concrete, an engagement with the materiality of context that always informs any transcendence of this context. Westerkamp's piece *Kits Beach Soundwalk* addresses these issues directly, while also bringing together the wide range of issues that have been dealt with here. As such, a brief examination of the work will make a fitting conclusion to this discussion.

Kits Beach Soundwalk is a documentary, of sorts. We hear Westerkamp's voice as narrator describing the scene on Kits Beach (the colloquial term for Kitsilano Beach) in Vancouver, Canada. She calls attention to different aspects of the soundscape, and makes a particular distinction between the din of the traffic noise in the background, and the sound of the waves on the beach in the foreground. She suggests that, on the basis of where we focus our attention, we can replace background with foreground. As her voice explains this trick of the mind, Westerkamp manipulates the traffic noise on the recording to grow louder and quieter, and eventually to disappear as she moves us in for a closer listen to the details of the beach. She highlights the tiny clicks and pops of the barnacles, and begins to relate associations she makes between these sounds and others she has experienced in her life. She comes to rest on her memory of a piece by pioneering electroacoustic composer Iannis Xenakis: *Concret PH II*. As she describes the piece it is brought in for us to hear, gradually replacing the soundscape of Kits Beach with that of Xenakis's work, and by extension, that of Westerkamp's memory. We have slipped from a document of an existing soundscape to a work of acousmatic music, by way of the technological manipulation of a recorded soundscape which emulates the powers of human perception to compose our auditory environments through the acts of listening and remembering.

David Kolber has analysed Westerkamp's piece in some detail, illustrating how, through the shifting of perspective, she offers us a way to experience our sonic environments anew. He situates her work within acoustic ecology's mandate to offer ways of dealing with our increasingly noisy industrialised soundscapes, and suggests that through the act of listening as composition we can reclaim environments from which we have become alienated, that those aspects of our environment that tend to dominate our awareness are 'ultimately alterable by human desire and intent' (Kolber 2002: 43). Perhaps most importantly, he recognises how Westerkamp's engagement with electroacoustic technologies is a fundamental part of this reclamation process through their ability to change our habits of listening.

Westerkamp has used the technological component of soundscape composition as a way of dealing with the need to speak about soundscapes from inside of them, as well as a way to position her audience within the environments she wants to share. She has also demonstrated the impossibility of a technologically reproduced soundscape to give us a sense of what that soundscape is really like. By exposing the manipulation inherent in recording and playback, she calls attention to the mediated nature of the experience. And yet, as she does so, she makes a very clear point about how we all mediate our experience every second of every day of our lives, and how this mediation is related to our own personal histories. She narrates her own experience, connecting the sound of barnacles to the Xenakis piece, but she also leaves room for our own associations to develop. This is what happens in any piece of acousmatic music: we are always engaged in exploring associations within our minds and thus we can never experience sound on completely reduced terms.

Kits Beach Soundwalk offers what Andra McCartney has called the potential for an 'electroacoustic ecology', a balance between the use of reproduction technologies and an understanding of how these technologies fit within the rest of the world (McCartney 2002: 22). McCartney, who has written extensively about Westerkamp's work, is a soundscape composer in her own right, and creates admittedly schizophonic pieces for galleries and the Internet in the hopes that, even though they present sounds that have been severely recontextualised, they may still offer some resonance for people within their own soundscapes and aid them in learning about their environments. This puts a positive spin on what, for Schafer, is an intensely negative aspect of modern society: the overrepresentation of sonic space, creating artificial spaces in which one context interferes with another.

Finally, the art of live diffusion in electroacoustic performance is an open acknowledgement of the act of mediation, calling our attention to space in a site-specific environment. When matched with composition that seeks to do the same, the result is a rich blend of the ideals of Pierre Schaeffer's goal of reduced listening and the need for ecological awareness espoused by R. Murray Schafer. I have heard *Kits Beach Soundwalk* diffused on several occasions in concerts put on by the electroacoustic studies programme at Concordia University in Montreal, Canada. Each presentation translated Westerkamp's stereo recording into a multi-channel array of at least eight loudspeakers, and sometimes more. The strategy used by diffuser Ian Chuprun for the placement of Westerkamp's work in the space of Concordia's Oscar Peterson Concert Hall speaks to the issues raised by the tensions between Schaeffer's acousmatic ideal and Schafer's distaste for the electroacoustical separation of sound from source.

In brief, Chuprun followed the conventions that have come to dominate surround-sound mixing in mainstream cinema: the sound of a voice speaking is anchored to the central plane, while ambient environmental sound is free to roam across all channels. When Westerkamp is heard narrating her experience of the soundwalk, her voice is kept to speakers at the front of the hall in an aesthetic acknowledgement of her 'presence', while ensuring a level of intelligibility that would be disrupted were her voice to be thrown around the space. This strategy keeps Westerkamp's voice grounded within the realm of human scale. During the moments when Westerkamp would stop speaking and let the environmental sounds shine through, Chuprun would open these sounds up to the full speaker array, much as ambient sound is allowed to surround the listener in the cinema. These moments would act as teasers that eventually lead to the moment when the Xenakis piece arrives. Westerkamp stops speaking for a stretch, and we listen to this piece of acousmatic music which points away from referentiality through its abstract treatment of sound, yet has been grounded for us through Westerkamp's association of this abstraction with the sound of the barnacles we heard just prior.

This simultaneous grounding and abstraction is complemented perfectly by the multi-channel treatment of Xenakis's piece here. No longer listening to naturalistic environmental sound, we are presented with acousmatic music which, because of its abstract nature, does not readily simulate a natural environment. So the fact that this music surrounds us means that we experience it as an 'in-the-wings' effect, calling attention to the apparatus responsible for its dissemination. Yet, at the same time, it has been linked to the environmental sound which earlier in the piece was allowed to surround us less conspicuously. As we are moved from the barnacles of Kits Beach to *Concret PH II*, we are moved from representation to abstraction on the level of Westerkamp's composition. Yet, as we make this shift, we are also moved from a naturalistic approach to multi-channel diffusion (that seeks to replace the space of the hall with the space of Kits Beach), to the diffusion of acousmatic music which draws us back into the space of the hall by rendering this diffusion 'visible'. Within the cinema, the passive mode of experiencing acousmatic sound in the surround channels is the domain of naturalistic ambient sound effects, and this is where the Kits Beach soundscape positions us. The shift to *Concret PH II* breaks us out of the passive mode by way of its lack of grounding in naturalistic context: we become aware of the speakers as the source of the sound, thus grounding the sound within the site-specific context of its exhibition. This shift maps out the transition from schizophonia as space replacement to schizophonia as awareness of the mediated environment within an electroacoustic ecology. Through her compositional strategies and their complementary diffusion, Westerkamp and her diffuser can speak to us from within this electroacoustic ecology, of which we are also a part.

The Xenakis portion of Westerkamp's piece thus becomes the nexus point where abstraction and representation merge. This is precisely the point that Westerkamp makes when she explains that the barnacles reminded her of

Concret PH II: we are always at once grounded in the world and lost in our thoughts. This co-existence of the real and the imagined is at the heart of sound-scape composition, in which the act of listening is a dialogue between us and our environments. The ultimate goal for Pierre Schaeffer, R. Murray Schafer, Michel Chion and Hildegard Westerkamp would seem to be that we become aware of our co-existing planes of attention and learn to focus on how and when we shift between them. It is in this awareness that we find our way out of the dilemmas posed by the acousmatic ideal, the space-replacement model of schizophonic experience, and the distance between original and copy created through the electroacoustical transmission of sound.

References

Chion, M. (1983), *Guide des objets sonores: Pierre Schaeffer et la recherche musicale* (Paris: Buchet/Chastel).
—— (1994), *Audio-Vision: Sound on Screen*, trans. C. Gorbman (New York: Columbia University Press).
—— (1999), *The Voice in Cinema*, trans. C. Gorbman (New York: Columbia University Press).
Godøy, R. I. (2006), 'Gestural-Sonorons Objects: Embodied Extensions of Schaeffer's Conceptual Apparatus', *Organised Sound*, Vol. II, No. 2, August, p p. 149–57.
Johnson, L. B. (1999), 'Harmonic Progressions', *Stereophile Guide to Home Theatre*, Vol. 5, No. 2, February, pp. 100–6.
Kolber, D. (2002), 'Hildegard Westerkamp's *Kits Beach Soundwalk*: Shifting Perspectives in Real World Music', *Organised Sound*, Vol. 7, No. 1, April, pp. 41–3.
McCartney, A. (2002), 'Sharing Experiences Towards the Possibility of an Electroacoustic Ecology', *Soundscape*, Vol. 3, No. 1, July, p. 22.
Moore, A., Moore, D., and Mooney, J. (2004), 'M2 Diffusion: The Live Diffusion of Sound in Space', *Proceedings of the International Conference on Music and Computers* (Miami, USA), pp. 317–20.
Norman, K. (1996), 'Real-World Music as Composed Listening', *Contemporary Music Review*, Vol. 15, No. 1, pp. 1–27.
Schafer, R. M. (1977), *The Tuning of the World* (Toronto: McLeland and Stewart).
—— (2002), *Patria: The Complete Cycle* (Toronto: Coach House Books).
Sherburne, P. (2002), 'Sound Art/Sound Bodies', *Parachute*, No. 107 (Summer), p. 70.
Sterne, J. (2002), *The Audible Past: Cultural Origins of Sound Reproduction* (Durham, NC: Duke University Press).
Truax, B. (1998), 'Composition and Diffusion: Space in Sound in Space', *Organised Sound*, Vol. 3, No. 2, pp. 141–6.
Westerkamp, Hildegard (1974), 'Soundwalking', *Sound Heritage*, Vol. 3, No. 4, pp. 18–27.
—— (2001), 'Speaking from Inside the Soundscape', in D. Rothenberg and M. Ulvaeus (eds), *The Book of Music and Nature* (Middletown: Wesleyan University Press), pp. 143–52.

SECTION FOUR:

PRODUCTION AND CONSUMPTION

8. SOUND AND MUSIC IN WEBSITE DESIGN

Lee Tsang

The Internet has, from its very outset, prioritised the visual over the aural. Sound has been avoided for a variety of reasons, but as the practical problems of bandwidth and space are diminishing, the aesthetic experience of web interfacing is rapidly undergoing a transformation. Sound itself is now marketed on the web, with website design businesses stressing the value of adding a range of sound-based products including voiceovers, sound effects and music loops, as a means of standing out in a competitive market.

This chapter includes an overview and analysis of the emerging uses of sound and music in websites. It explores the advantages and disadvantages of using auditory icons and musical earcons, and tackles how to minimise irritation and to identify user types. Issues relating to music in advertising play a significant role in the discussion, and draw upon a wide range of sources from environmental psychology to film theory. Bearing in mind existing studies exploring cross-cultural issues in website analysis, the study includes a brief analysis of specific promotional websites, focusing mainly on the McDonalds Corporation 'I'm lovin' it' campaign and how its use of music reflects the cultural and political climate. Building on research into irritation and user types, these sites provide a springboard for further investigations into effective loop construction and approaches to interactivity.

Web Promotions of Multimedia Entertainment in Western Art Music Industries

The multimedia entertainment industry benefits most from the Internet's capacity to make use of sound. Although film's embracing of the technology is perhaps obvious, Western art music's attempts to harness the marketing opportunities are perhaps a little less expected. There is now a growing competitive spirit developing amongst UK orchestras and the opera companies Opera North, Covent Garden, Welsh National Opera, English National Opera and English Touring Opera. These organisations are now making short films of performance clips, production montages, and 'documentary-style' introductions to works, providing music downloads and video streaming; and in the case of Opera North, producing an archive of Flash animations that is itself worthy of in-depth multimedia analysis.

Of all the trailer-type movies that these organisations have generated, Flash animations are most clearly helping opera as an art form to compete with the cinema on its own terms. In the Opera North archive the trailer movies feature soundtracks extracted from the operas and vary visually from simple, often quirky forms of animation to montages of stills. The most artistically challenging and rewarding animations are those that take full advantage of the short movie form, distilling a whole opera into a single concept. For instance, for Poulenc's *La Voix Humaine*, which tells the story of a woman's despair when her ex-partner calls for one last time, we witness the image of the protagonist reduced momentarily to a mere electrical signal. The iconic silhouette of a woman on the telephone is increasingly abstracted as the emotion of the woman's voice takes over. As the voice travels down the telephone cord, the cord is transformed into a representation of vocal resonance – a vocal cord, as it were, a pseudo-sound wave. The voice ceases as the wave smooths out; the orchestra continues, then suddenly a dramatic chord coincides with an image of the telephone cord, disconnected. The visual transformation that takes place in this movie enhances our understanding of the piece as a whole: it draws attention to the voice as being everything in the opera, as well as conveying the woman's hysteria, loneliness and – ultimately – madness. This is just one example of the Internet motivating the development of multimedia art by offering an outlet for the kind of advertising that is not normally commercially viable for artistic organisations to produce for TV or cinema.

Of all the other UK Western art music organisations, the Philharmonia Orchestra arguably stands out most by fully embracing a gamut of multimedia possibilities. Capitalising on its longstanding relationship with the cinema, the orchestra's sub-website 'The Sound Exchange' features clips of animated films for which live soundtracks are performed, as well as its own animation clip mini-series 'TristanTheMovie' for young listeners. This story of Tristan and Isolde told in a contemporary way features the notably optional use of Wagner's music and additional (humorous) sound effects. Some would contend that its treatment of Wagner's opera is symptomatic of Western art music 'dumbing down' (after all, the music does not seem essential to this movie), whilst others would argue it is an example of good educational practice, helping to engage the young. Whatever a user's take on this, the rest of the site certainly shows a broadness of educational reach. It includes forums for exchanging sound files; a Sound Library database of notes and phrases played by individual instruments and full orchestra; MP3 concert downloads; tutorials on how instruments work (currently most comprehensive in the strings section); mobile phone downloads; and 'Play the Orchestra' games for very young users.

These uses of sound reflect a range of artistic possibilities, but are not necessarily typical of non-multimedia business or information resource sites; we are dealing here specifically with sound-based products. Sound opens up a world of design possibilities even for sites that are not specifically dedicated to sound as an art form, and one of the principal ways in which it can play a role in general web interfacing is the use of auditory icons and (musical) earcons.

Auditory Icons and Musical Earcons

Auditory icons are similar to Chion's (1994: 75–87, 224) 'territory sounds' in filmic contexts; that is, sounds that characterise real environments, such as a door slam or a paper scrunch; earcons, by contrast, typically use musically pitched/rhythmic tones and function as arbitrary leitmotifs. Both types of sound are part and parcel of web-based and non-web-based interfacing and in most cases are of the so-called 'redundant' sort, meaning that they are inessential to the use of the system. They increase a site's user-friendliness and efficiency by supplementing or supporting information provided by visual means (including visual icons). Comparison tests have shown that most users favour auditory icons over earcons (Buxton et al. 1994; Bussemakers and de Haan 2000) because icons are better at facilitating interfacing efficiency; earcons are preferred by some (e.g. Hankinson and Edwards 2000) for their potential aesthetic 'added value'.

Through mimicry of real-world sound, auditory icons enable the senses to function more holistically in virtual environments. Effective mimicry requires 'parameterisation' (Gaver 1993), which means taking into account the implied weight, speed and size of the signified object so that the perceptual similarity of its dimensions and motion is conveyed. This helps to avoid confusion caused by audiovisual 'mismatching' so, for example, 'largeness' here would sound large rather than small (Takala and Hahn 1992; Hahn et al. 1995a, 1995b). In addition to studying these 'underlying dynamics of physical processes', effective mimicry of basic sound quality requires careful analysis of sampled sound spectra (Balzano 1986: 312; see also Handel 1995: 426; Hajda et al. 1997: 264–5; and Tsang 2001: 9–11).[1]

Although auditory icons may be favoured in efficiency tests, both auditory icons and musical earcons are perceived as enhancing performance in multimedia entertainment, particularly gaming activity (Edworthy 1998; Bussemakers and de Haan 2000) – an important strand in certain website designs for helping users to engage with a product or brand. In such cases, the 'perceived complexity of music and its inherent associations and expectations', as promoted by Hankinson and Edwards (2000), is likely to be appreciated more than in strict information-gathering contexts. In contrast to the short sounds encountered in most typical information or general sites, the longer durations that tend to characterise gaming sounds allow for greater complexity and in turn potentially greater arousal (alertiveness and stimulation). This is certainly the case in the child-oriented sites of such major film brands as Harry Potter or Disney, where the high level of arousal is particularly useful for hooking young users; the sounds often reflect in easily recognisable ways a sense of movement and trajectory, are diegetic (as though generated within the depicted 'storyworld'), iconic often in the sense of auditory caricatures, or use 'mickeymousing' effects.[2] The characteristics of the auditory icons used here have usually been 'rendered' to have an expressive function that exaggerates or implies a quality beyond the literal objects to which they refer.[3] They become more than merely functional; like earcons, they too have 'added value'.

In filmic contexts Chion uses the term 'added value' specifically to refer to cases when the expressive and informative meaning of the sound(s) emanates 'naturally from the image itself' (Chion 1994: 221). This implies that a 'mismatch' with the visual stimulus has less added value than a match. In computer-interfacing contexts, such 'mismatches' have been proven to reduce efficiency (Lemmens et al. 2000; Bussemakers and de Haan 2000), but the studies that have found this tell only part of the story. One's criteria for defining a 'mismatch' are essential for making aesthetic judgements about web design because the extent or type of 'mismatch' plays a major role in whether or not an instance of multimedia (IMM) is perceived negatively.[4] It is conceivable that 'mismatching' itself can be used to desirable effect. Within an artistic context, to move beyond the literal, to confound or to subvert expectation – in Cook's terms (1998), 'to contest' – can introduce emotional complexity, a more interesting kind of hook. For instance, major mode sounds for an image that attempts to illicit a negative emotional response from a listener slow down performance efficiency presumably because such sounds are counterintuitive. Depending on the perceiver and the overall context of the site and what it is meant to achieve, the sounds might be deemed either inappropriate (an artistically negative response) or ironic (an artistically positive response). Although in most cases efficiency is one of the most desirable aims for a website, as one moves into the entertainment sphere an 'efficiency' test may be beside the point; for certain sites to satisfy their aims, user stimulation and engagement may take a higher priority.

Understanding icons and earcons in terms of these IMMs is certainly useful, though not all IMM types as identified by Cook are appropriate in web design. IMMs that do not fit within the conformant (matching in the sense of consistent) and contestant (actively 'mismatching' in the sense of contradictory) forms are described by Cook as 'complementary' – a category which itself can be subdivided into 'essential' and 'temporal' types (my terms). In contrast to redundant sound for visual-privileged systems, 'essential' sound–visual complementation, such as a voiceover giving instructions about how to complete a task online, is rare and ill-advised because it reduces usability by not catering for those using a non-audio-functioning system or non-audio-friendly environments and, of course, the hard of hearing; 'temporal' complementation (where the timing of visuals leave gaps for sounds) can usefully cater to both the visually impaired and the hard of hearing, and can make for a pleasant browsing experience, though the increased time factor may prove frustrating for the efficiency-conscious user.

Sound Irritation

Whether using icons, earcons or extended musical pieces, IMMs can sometimes prove irritating to users. Web designers are keen to eliminate shared irritation factors wherever possible and there are certain (thus far) unwritten rules that the web designer might follow. We can search for supporting evidence for these from a range of studies that explore sound alertiveness, stimulation and annoyance, including Berlyne (1971), Sorkin (1988), Buxton et al. (1994), Edworthy and Stanton (1995), Yokom (2000–3), Ronkainen (2001) and Ahlstrohm (2003). The findings of these studies suggest that the characteristics listed under types 1 and 2 below are to be avoided. I have divided sound irritation factors here into type 1: 'Basic'; type 2: 'Complexity-inducing'; and type 3: 'User type-sensitive'.[5] On the whole, irritation increases with the prominence of types 1 and 2 and the absence of type 3.

Type 1: Basic
- abruptness of sound envelopes;
- overall loudness;
- length of interaction sounds – irritation increases with length;
- frequency height.

Type 2: Complexity-inducing
- dissonance;
- overtones;

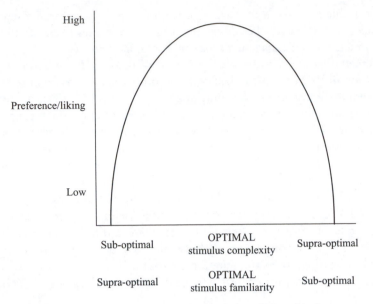

Figure 3   Hypothesised inverse U-curve indicating the relationship between complexity/familiarity and preference, after Berlyne (1971); Buxton et al. (1994) and Tan et al. (2006: 410)

- irregular beats;
- irregular changes;
- (slow) repetition rate;
- fast changes;
- speech.

Type 3: User type-sensitive
- existence of muting facility (especially for background music), *which helps users to modify*:
- arousal, *which is dependent on*:
- familiarity-complexity, *which affect judgements about*:
- fitness for purpose (including effectiveness of auditory icon parameterisation and, where appropriate, awareness and understanding of intertextual reference).

The perceived (un)acceptability of many type 2 factors is both a matter of degree and tied into type 3 issues of familiarity and complexity. Familiarity and complexity are negatively correlated (see figure 3); the extremes are disliked, suggesting that a moderate approach is best (Buxton et al. 1994), but it is important to take into account that in real life the perceivers' sense of what is moderate can change according to environment or the activity in which they are engaged. Moreover, aspects of type 3 – muting, arousal and complexity – raise the problem of effect overabundance: a web-page design with proliferating sounds initiated by (non-click-initiated) cursor movement may increase irritation levels, especially if the sounds have high levels of type 2 characteristics.

Web designers should take into account the views of Heyduk (1975: 90) and Buxton et al. (1994), who suggest that for website audio, initial irritation caused by highly complex sounds will usually be replaced by acceptance, whereas unvaried simple (e.g. unparameterised) sounds can often lead to irritation. However, in music, such assertions about the acceptance of complexity through familiarity are challenged to an extent by Hargreaves (1984, 1986) who found that 'dislike of certain [musical] styles . . . seems to override any repetition effects' (Hargreaves 1986: 121). In the case of the least familiar and most complex musical styles (e.g. atonal pieces) repeated exposure may even reduce liking further (Daynes forthcoming).[6]

User Types

As with any form of marketing, key to most mainstream website designs is the balance between satisfying the needs of what is known of target user types whilst remaining open, wherever possible, to general appeal. This has meant that within website design the divergence between sound for 'information' and sound for 'entertainment' has become increasingly blurred, with many businesses now being encouraged to occupy the middle ground. 'Entertainment' – often through the use of sound, especially music – offers a means of hooking the target user.

Designers can best incorporate entertainment by first identifying the kinds of sounds, styles and activities that the public find currently most appealing. The Internet itself caters for niche markets and now functions as a low-risk test-bed for possible future commercial investment in the more expensive media forms. This means that it not only expands popular culture's already extreme heterogeneity, but more importantly is itself a resource for predicting styles of optimal popularity.

Excepting highly unfamiliar and highly complex styles for reasons discussed earlier, web designers who are catering for mass markets would do well to consider, in relation to Berlyne's inverse-U curve model, whether or not their site's signature track is about to reach a phase of supra-optimal familiarity (see figure 3 above). Better still, they could choose a track that is likely to have popular longevity: this might mean avoiding the most popular songs or pieces of the day in favour of constructing a track that capitalises on the basic stylistic characteristics of such pieces. Apart from having the advantage of avoiding the problems and expense of copyright, such a track is unlikely to pass rapidly into supra-optimal familiarity because its various elements, though basically optimal, are essentially a variation of a prototype. Such a song or piece should also be considered for goodness of fit in relation to the site's overall message or purpose: we are optimally aroused when the track is what we expect (the prototype), though in the long term and in the context of the site we may in fact prefer the variation of the prototype, as it introduces a necessary element of complexity to maintain interest.

The relative importance of establishing optimal familiarity-complexity and the significance of the prototype depends entirely on users' need for cognition (NFC) – their involvement in the site or product. When considering users' NFC, one needs specifically to ascertain whether or not users are 'motivated' to process the site's 'cognitive load' (North and Hargreaves 1997a: 272). If users are unmotivated, their involvement in the site or product is low; in order to increase motivation one might increase the cognitive load through sound, for example by increasing the volume (p. 272), as this takes more processing than soft music (p. 277). If users are already motivated, their involvement in the site or product is high; one can make it easier for the user to process necessary information by reducing the cognitive load; for this, North and Hargreaves advocate slow, simple music rather than fast, complex music (pp. 94, 272). According to the Elaboration Likelihood Model (ELM; North and Hargreaves 1997b: 270–4), the types of persuasion employed here are described in environmental psychology as 'peripheral' (for low-NFC users) and 'central' (for high-NFC users) respectively. From a design perspective, simplicity of visual information lends itself well to the peripheral persuasion of the low-NFC user via high-arousal sound; by contrast, visually busier sites (which might include significant proportions of text) are perhaps more suited to high-NFC users, whose central persuasion to process the information would require the cognitive space of unintrusive sound. At all costs, the designer should avoid complex rational tasks for low-NFC users, and high-arousal sound when presenting complex tasks for high-NFC users. Designers should also bear in mind that the more arousing the music in high-NFC situations, the less the time likely to be spent in the environment (pp. 274–5).

In terms of goodness of fit, users' NFC may relate directly to understanding the relevance of the audio object: 'the effects of musical fit should be more beneficial for high- than for low-involvement consumers [users], since appropriate music focuses attention on the message: low involvement consumers [users], by definition, are less motivated to process the product in terms of accompanying music' (North and Hargreaves 1997b: 273). NFC, along with familiarity through prior knowledge or recognition, could be decisive also in determining how different types of media relationships are received – that is, whether the 'fit' is achieved through 'conformance', 'complementation' (contrariety) or 'contest' (contradiction).

In order to target specific markets, website designers benefit from weighing up the relative significance of different categories of user types. Apart from determining whether or not a site is most likely to be used by high- or low-NFC users, this involves considering the impact of age, gender and other social groupings.

Age, gender and social groupings
In a study of sound preferences in environmental spaces, Kang and Yang (2003) found that cultural background and long-term environmental experience play an important role in people's judgement of sound preferences. These researchers divide these judgements into two categories: 'micro-preferences', which denote sound preferences shared by people of the same age, gender and other personal differences; and 'macro-preferences', which denote sound preferences shared by people who have lived and worked in the same environments. Yang and Kang (2004) found that age increase correlated with preferences for sounds relating to nature, culture or human activities, such as church bells, water sounds and the voices of children; younger people favoured music and mechanical sounds, including music played on the streets, noise from vehicle parking and music from stores. Such micro-preferences most probably feed into preferences in interfacing, though more research into this area is necessary.

Some discrepancies between real and multimedia environment studies exist in findings on gender. Whereas Kang and Yang's real-environment study (2003) found that males and females exhibit only slight differences, Wang and Chang (2006), in research on differences in gender responses to online music, found the opposite. The important difference between these studies is that Wang and Chang specifically investigated goodness of fit – an issue of more concern in multimedia environments than in non-multimedia environments. Their findings confirm the stereotype that men, often requiring constant arousal in order to persist with an activity, are not usually concerned with whether or not the arousal source 'fits' with its context; and that women are usually intolerant of anything that doesn't 'fit'. More specifically, the research found that males respond well to music whether it is congruent or incongruent and women respond badly to incongruent music, believing it is better to have no music at all or better still to use congruent music. On this basis Wang and Chang advocate using congruent music for web advertising.

Wang and Chang's study should not be taken as prescriptive; the situation is perhaps more complex than their findings suggest. Their study could be taken further by exploring the possibility that in certain IMMs, complementation and contest may be perceived as a good 'fit'. The problem lies in the fact that their notion of 'congruence' is unclear in this respect, whereas for Cook the term is used specifically to help define the notion of conformance. On the other hand, Wang and Chang's study may suggest that more scope for experimentation with reduced risk is possible for sites designed for the male market. This possibility finds support in North and Hargreave's (1997b: 273) point about NFC. In the light of Wang and Chang's study, it suggests that men might be more likely to be low-NFC users than women because they are less concerned about 'goodness of fit' and more with general arousal.

All this does not mean that one should not consider carefully the sound used for male-oriented sites or that sites designed for women need to be exceptionally restrictive. According to a study of film genre preference by Fischoff et al., 'women are less restrictive in their gender cross-over behaviour than are men whose preferences tend to be male gender exclusive'. Fischoff et al. also note that the distinction is greatest amongst the youngest age group (25 years and below). Their study highlights 'action-adventure' and 'romance' as creating the widest differences in preferences (Fischoff 1994, as reported in Fischoff et al. 1998), so it is possible that sounds associated with these genres could affect appeal. Examples of action-adventure sounds include gunfire, up-tempo music, or sounds that have a wide dynamic range and include sharp contrasts; 'romance' sounds include softer sounds, subtler contrasts, and typically, in musical terms, legato orchestral strings. Whilst one should be wary of drawing conclusions from non-website-specific studies, the parallels with the Internet's multimedia possibilities are clear; by drawing together the findings of Wang and Chang and Fischoff et al., we can predict that 'male-gender-exclusive' sounds work (especially) well for (young) men whether or not they are congruent and that sounds relating to either gender work (especially) well for (young) women provided they are congruent. Moreover, by drawing together the various findings from these studies, we can begin to construct user profiles, indicating some likely sound preferences (see table 1).

These basic profiles do not incorporate any macro-preferences, which are also highly significant. Although Kang and Yang's study focused on environmental spaces in a single city, the basic idea of macro-preference is far reaching. Environmental and cultural similarities can often unite nationalities, as well as individuals from entirely different nations. Given the Internet's global reach, such macro-preferences should be taken into account in any design decisions.

WEBSITE SOUND LOOP ANALYSES

Who's 'lovin' it'? A Cross-Cultural Comparison of Audio Usage in McDonalds Websites

In order to find a suitable example of sound macro-preferencing in web design, the top twenty-five brands in 2005 according to Interbrand Corporation (2005: 94) were surveyed. Although a number of brand sites make use of sound, most do not allow for cross-cultural comparison because they are marketed principally through a generic site with a low degree of cultural sensitiv-

Table 1 *Website user sound preferences*

Type	User profile	Some likely sound preferences
A	High NFC; female; under 25	Music, mechanical, urban; non-gender-specific; 'good fit'; lower volume/complexity
B	High NFC; female; over 25	Nature, culture, human; non-gender-specific, though decreasingly male-gender-specific; 'good fit'; lower volume/complexity
C	High NFC; male; under 25	Music, mechanical, urban; male-gender-specific; lower volume/complexity, continuous arousal
D	High NFC; male; over 25	Nature, culture, human; male-gender-specific, though increasingly non-gender-specific; lower volume/complexity, continuous arousal
E	Low NFC; female; under 25	Music, mechanical, urban; non-gender-specific; 'good fit'; higher volume/complexity arousal
F	Low NFC; female; over 25	nature, culture, human; non-gender-specific, though decreasingly male-gender-specific; 'good fit'; higher volume/complexity
G	Low NFC; male; under 25	Music, mechanical, urban; male-gender-specific; higher volume/complexity, continuous arousal
H	Low NFC; male; over 25	Nature, culture, human; male-gender-specific, though increasingly non-gender-specific; higher volume/complexity, continuous arousal

ity; this is perhaps to be expected in the case of the commercial sites of Disney and Nokia, where a specific culture is being marketed, rather than appealed to. Of those companies with sites dedicated to different countries only two – McDonalds and Nescafé – were found to make use of sound. This section of the chapter will focus on the largest of these data sources: McDonalds. It builds on the cross-cultural analysis of websites by Würtz (2005) in which the analysis of McDonalds sites from a visual perspective took place in November/December 2003; many of the sites have since been modified significantly, but the broad thrust of her findings – which contends that high-context (collectivist) and low-context (individualist) cultures differ in imagery, layout, colour, communication of values and the 'assimilation of human presence' – still holds true.[7]

In July 2006 McDonalds had web pages dedicated to 60 different countries; of these, 12 did not have a dedicated website and 8 were grouped under a single website entitled 'Middle East'.[8] Of the 41 websites, 20 did not use sound at all (including Israel, which had a 'muting' icon) and a further 5 limited the use of sound to providing explicitly various forms of 'entertainment'. These forms of entertainment consisted of: (1) an interactive animation game with associated sounds (Germany and the USA), (2) an introductory montage with voiceover outlining the different areas of the site (Germany), (3) links to MTV (Belgium), (4) McDonalds radio commercials (India), (5) a dedicated radio station – Radio McDonalds (Brazil) – and (6) clips of nationally recognised pop artists, games and downloads, etc. (Brazil). These forms of entertainment seek to satisfy as wide a range of clients as possible, and arguably the Brazilian site was the most successful at this; it was the only one to use celebrity to give the product credibility via the establishment of authority (Huron 1989). According to Huron 'musical style may be used as a very effective nonverbal identifier' (p. 568), but the advantage of being identified with one group of 'race, sex, age, and social class or status' means that there is the possibility of alienating another. By presenting a selection, the Brazilian site avoided this to a large extent: credibility spanned a wide range of popular musical tastes.

The web's capacity to present a range of styles simultaneously has the advantage of being far less restrictive than a TV commercial, which would normally have to isolate a particular song or style; it also makes for a subtler and more sophisticated link between the music and the brand. Rather than directly endorsing a particular product, the music is presented on the web as 'for your entertainment' and in so doing it can improve attitudes towards the brand, whilst minimising the dangers of any stylistic choices. It is more easily able to adapt to – and, by providing options, reduces the risks of – the waxing and waning of familiarity. It also has the advantage of having numerous songs subliminally advertising the brand every time they are heard in their usual contexts.

Setting these special cases aside, 18 sites made use of sound on their home pages. Based on similarity, these sites may be clustered into the following non-hierarchical groupings:

- China and Taiwan (shortened version of China);
- Hong Kong, Malaysia and Turkey (same/closely connected);
- Middle East – mother site for all Arab countries;

- new Europe – Czech Republic, Poland, Slovakia, Slovenia, Bulgaria (all closely connected) and Netherlands (some similarities);
- Argentina;
- Colombia;
- Guatemala;
- France;
- Italy;
- United Kingdom.

Most of these sites still retain the basic elements of the global 'I'm lovin' it' campaign which has characterised McDonalds advertising since September 2003.[9] If we compare the above with Würtz's findings of November/December 2003 we find a number of interesting consistencies. According to Würtz, in 2003 the Korean site, more than other sites, showed a favouring of sound usage by implementing the entire 'I'm lovin' it' jingle (in Korean). As support for this finding Würtz quotes research which shows that 86.5 per cent of Asians (China, Hong Kong, Indonesia) strongly liked the use of sound compared with 64.9 per cent of an Australian control group (Evers and Day 1997).[10] Würtz's parallel may appear gratuitous, as the isolation of a single site is not especially statistically significant, but it is certainly true that in the current data set, most McDonalds Asian sites form two related clusters that make extensive use of the jingle. In particular, China stands out for bringing together the most radically contrasting sound types of any of the loops (natural sounds, such as car horns; ancient classical instruments, such as gong and zither; modern rap vocals with backbeat) and for producing the second most extended loop of all the countries in the entire data set (only the UK's was longer).

A highly influential cultural-context study by Hall and Hall (1990) groups nations in ways that correspond with the sound-usage proximity clusters of the McDonalds sites, though it is not possible to draw many direct comparisons because there are also many differences in terms of the countries that make up their data set. A few isolated similarities appear to be significant. For instance, in both data sets, the UK, France and Italy are fairly individual in their approach whereas the Scandinavian countries (no sound) and the emerging 'new Europe' (highly consistent use of sound) form very distinct groups. It is interesting that the Latin American countries, despite geographical proximity, do not have the same degree of consistency in approach to sound and design as the Scandinavians or the new Europeans. Germany, a low-context culture, and as such expected to be very text-based, makes considerable use of sound, but it does so by dividing the site into two distinct parts – one for information, the other for entertainment; this kind of explicit division is perhaps to be expected of a low-context culture, though it is perhaps also indicative of a need to cater to a large number of non-German residents, of which the largest nationality group by far is Turkish (a high-context culture). These few examples and the Asian groupings suggest that the 2006 clusters reveal sound (and also often image) macro-preferences that articulate certain national identities and alliances. Many of the 18 sites listed above articulate these national identities specifically through their treatment of (often looped) home-page soundtracks; the strongest of these national accents can be found in the soundtracks of sites by France, the United Kingdom, China and the Middle East.

Whilst the selected four sites seek to project a certain kind of image associated with nationality, McDonalds France defines its image primarily by drawing upon an audio stereotype or cliché. The use of women's voices singing is rare in this data set. McDonalds France is one of only two examples (Guatemala is the other), and it is significant that in the only other top-twenty-five multi-site brand that makes use of sound (Nescafé), France is the only country to use a woman's voice. The iconic power of vocal timbre cannot be underestimated here. The slightly breathy vocal quality of a highly sexual, chic female has been a cliché for communicating French appeal throughout the world since Jane Birkin's 1969 hit 'Je t'aime', if not before. This idea is adopted for the McDonalds France site but takes on a more urban, cosmopolitan feel: English words are sung against a moderately funky backing track by a streetwise, slightly naïve-sounding young French woman. By contrast, for the Nescafé France site, a jazz loop characterised by a wordless, slightly breathy, perceptibly French scat conveys a relaxed, sophisticated mood. In both cases the voice presents the woman as sexual object, an allure that is specifically related to the idea of the beautiful French actress.

McDonalds France's streetwise youth image is especially interesting, as the kind of sexual allure it represents is a variation of the tradition, akin to Ludivine Sagnier's contemporaneous portrayal of a cocky, promiscuous but ultimately naïve girl in Ozon's film *Swimming Pool* (2003).[11] Were it not for the fact that the ambiguity of sound means that sexual connotations are only suggested, one might criticise the brand for prostituting the female icon. It would not be the first time that McDonalds has come under fire for misuse of sexual connotation; in 2005, its global 'I'd hit it' campaign was withdrawn on those very grounds. Even more significant than any of these sexual references, though, is the fact that the McDonalds France site is one of the few not to incorporate the 'I'm lovin' it' jingle, preferring instead to use the woman's voice to loop the words 'When you see it's for real'. It seems important for McDonalds France to be seen to preserve an identity that is set apart from the US prototype.

Perhaps more interesting still are the socio-political resonances of the music used in the UK, China and Middle East sites. In each case, the home-page music loop is used as a means of (or desire for) uniting communities, with each site approaching the problem in a different way. In the case of the UK, this takes the form of stylistic heterogeneity, recognising difference and merging one musical style into another, principally through juxtaposition; the emphasis here seems to be generational, a medley of influences from rock and 1970s funk to 1990s girl bands, etc. In the case of China, superimposition is the main means by which old and new elements are fused, though there are passages where the sounds of these radically different styles dominate; the stylistic contrast is extreme, the emphasis being on respecting the traditions of the old China and embracing the hip, perceived 'cutting edge' of urban youth culture that characterises the new China. In the case of the Middle East, a desire to unite nations is suggested by grouping many sites under one 'mother' site and linking them uniformly to identical versions of the same site. The music for this 'mother' site emphasises children as the future (the home page features pictures of children, no adults); the voice of one child is joined by the voices of many, helping to convey the sense of both the individual and the larger Arab community.

The McDonalds community agenda, called McCommunity in some sites, is not entirely the benevolent institution it wishes to appear. In order to dominate the global market, McDonalds needs to speak a nation's language, and this means being aware of socio-political sensitivities. In all three – McDonalds UK, China and Middle East – the traces of these sensitivities are present. The UK site has a certain maturity in its drawing together of musical styles, an accepted 'evolutionary approach' to difference, and the understanding of complementary tastes. By contrast, the China site's diverse sound combination seems – to these Western ears – crude and indicative of a huge cultural gulf. The challenge of fusing the old and the new may be accepted with determination, but if regarded by the young in China as an accurate reflection of what is understood as global modernity, it may do nothing more than to drive a further wedge into an existing generational gap. In the case of the Arab countries, the desire to present a united front for diverse communities represents an urge towards an Arab nationalism, but in preserving (in name at least) a separate site for each state it resists the kind of unity that Saddam Hussein opposed in 1982: 'We must see the world as it is. . . . The Arab reality is that the Arabs are now twenty-two states, and we have to behave accordingly. Therefore, unity must not be imposed, but must be achieved through common fraternal opinion. Unity must give strength to its individual partners, not cancel their national identity' (quoted in Baram 1991: 121). In keeping with this implied fraternity, the 'I'm lovin' it' jingle, which features so prominently in many of the other sites, is again not used here – an omission which reduces only the perceived force of the brand as a symbol of Western domination.

On Repetition – or, How to Make Good Musical Wallpaper

By comparing the soundtracks of McDonalds UK and McDonalds China, one can pick up some tips on how best to approach the looping process. The UK track begins with a very slow introduction that gradually builds in texture and in dynamic and harmonic tension. This potentially gives high-NFC users the opportunity to find their initial bearings and to absorb any essential text. After allowing sufficient time for users to settle, the music becomes considerably louder and up-tempo, invigorating arousal levels for users who have not yet ventured beyond the home page. The point at which the track loops back is not to the introduction, but seamlessly to a moment in its up-tempo section; thus, the process of looping is not disruptive and is likely to keep users' arousal levels fairly consistent. By contrast, the looping of the McDonalds China track is poorly handled, with an abrupt cut-off point followed by a silent gap and an obvious signalling of a return to the very beginning of the track by gong and Chinese zither.

In contrast to these examples, one sure way of minimising irritation for background tracks is to fade out to silence without looping back; however, this may not satisfy the need of ensuring a low-NFC user is motivated enough to engage with the site. Fading out before looping can be a good idea in the sense that the silence reduces the arousal level – it is especially useful if a loop is short (as suggested by Yokom 2000–3); however, it can – as in the case of McDonalds China – make the reinitiation of the loop more noticeable than if the loop were seamless. This high level of arousal flux might prove irritating for some users, and by drawing attention to the looping point, it draws attention to one's familiarity with the music, potentially pushing the perception of the track into a state of supra-optimal familiarity.

Given that looping is inevitably going to produce a cumulative effect of familiarity, resulting in a very high risk of irritation, the substance of the loop must somehow include elements that counteract familiarity if it is to be optimally effective. The trick is to introduce an element of surprise, that is, a moment of musical complexity, ideally just before the loop begins or at the point of looping.

To minimise the likelihood of uncomfortably high arousal flux and irritation:

1. Choose a musical style in which short term repetition is expected.
2. Ensure the loop is long enough or contains enough contrasting elements or variations of sub-repetitions to provide interest.
3. Vary an additional statement before looping.
4. Introduce an irregularity (via rhythm and/or ornamentation) to distract from the loop point.
5. Hide the loop point by:
    a. energising the end of the loop so it leads towards a harmonic resolution;
    b. making the return point the (temporary) harmonic resolution;
    c. maximising timbral fusion.
6. Avoid having the soundtrack stop abruptly when browsing beyond the home page.

The McDonalds UK and China 'I'm lovin' it' tracks, like many good examples of high-arousal loops, are rooted in a tradition of repetitive club music which is specifically designed to keep listeners in situ. However, other musical styles can prove equally effective. Nescafé France's jazz loop works well, not only because the basic mood fits the relaxed, feel-good image the brand is trying to convey (narratively complemented by the images of a cup of coffee nestled between two hands, and a portrait photograph of an attractive, sophisticated woman with a beaming smile) but because inherent in the musical style is the whole idea of repetition and a balance of regular and irregular elements. The female singer's scat (the timbre of which communicates her unseen smiles) occupies a phrase consisting of three bars of four-time followed by a bar of two-time; an instrumental consisting of three bars of four-time then takes us back to the beginning of the loop. Despite its moderate rhythmic irregularity, the overall track is balanced by the contrast between vocal and straight instrumental passages. The presence of the instrumental allows the user's ears to rest from the scat; the texture is reduced and gives the impression that it is reaching a phrase end, only to become rhythmically more active (piano chords and right-hand elaboration) as it leads naturally back to the beginning of the loop for a temporary harmonic resolution. The natural ebb and flow of this loop potentially provides a gentle undulation in arousal levels, a balance between gentle reinvigoration and space to think – arguably a more desirable effect than keeping arousal levels constant.

There are examples using Western art music too. The Mercurius Company website cleverly avoids the familiarity-complexity problem by using an extract in which repetition and variation through ornamentation are expected. The music for the site is taken from the baroque piece *La Zaide*, the second movement from Royer's first Suite in D minor, performed by Ricardo Barros. The piece is written in a rondeau form, with the ritournelle being played between each couplet. Here, as with the Nescafé France jazz loop, arousal levels may fluctuate moderately because of the irregular phrase structure. The loop recording consists essentially of three nine-bar phrases taken from the opening ritournelle (bars 1–18, with the second phrase being a variation of the first phrase) and the first nine bars of the 'Finalle'. In this performance, the underlying pulse of the ritournelle is a little unruly, but rather than causing irritation, its irregularities are absorbed into the general impression of a florid, improvisatory style.[12]

If the loop designer wishes to balance continuity with mild arousal flux, she or he may take into account the following traits which characterise the Nescafé France and Mercurius Company examples:

1. Inject energy (rhythmic and ornamental) before the return.
2. This energy, combined with harmonic resolution at the point of return and overall timbral similarity, may facilitate continuity.

3. Irregular phrase patterns and sub-repetitions set up a slightly unpredictable sense of return which, rather than undermining, may also facilitate continuity; and yet:

4. Such continuity does not cause interest in the repetition to flag: the arrival point raises arousal by the (moderate) surprise it induces.

Interactive Loops

In contrast to these examples, looping may also involve user interaction. Sometimes (entertaining) confusion may arise when identical auditory icons are used for cursor-initiated actions and incorporated into the track itself; in such cases, a danger of cognitive overload as well as irritation may be caused by the resultant auditory dissonance and perceived irregular changes or beats. Another possibility is to hand over full control, especially if one intends to adapt to users of different NFC and empower them to modify their own arousal levels. This is most effective when the links or visual icons for switching to different loops have high visibility on the home page. It is an option that occurs in sites as diverse as McDonalds Guatemala and London Sinfonietta.

The handing over of control is sometimes taken even further in sites dedicated to Western art music and film. In music the idea of user interactivity has its roots as far back as Mozart's musical dice games, which enabled players to piece together pre-composed music to create a minuet; and later Cage's indeterminacy experiments, which highlighted the idea of listeners taking an active role in what they choose to hear. As Eno predicted, the idea of perceiver control has since developed into 'systems by which people can customize listening experiences themselves', changing the parameters of 'highly evolved raw material' (Kelly 1995: 4).

Such systems are now appearing on mainstream websites of Western art-music companies. Estell et al.'s *Velocity* (2006) on the Andriessen–London Sinfonietta site is just one example. It is a composition that explores the relationship between timbre, speed and harmonic change, using block chords in a minimalist fashion, with options for changing the timbre of the pulse. Such a piece affects arousal levels in many ways. First, the system's limited parameters mean that the perceiver focuses on the change in timbre that speed can cause. Second, the timbre choice can modify emotional impact; in this case certain auditory icons of real sounds potentially even introduce an element of humour. Third, the very act of making a judgement heightens the emotional impact of the change. Once constructed, the *Velocity* track can potentially be used in a continuous loop while the user engages in another activity.

Other pioneering forms of interactivity include exploring music in relation to colour, shape and user-controlled kinesis. In Braunarts and London Sinfonietta (2007), users are encouraged to experience musical loops within

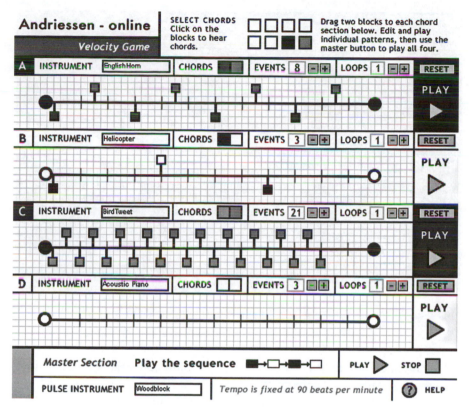

Figure 4   Estell et al.'s *Velocity* (2006) from London Sinfonietta's sub-website 'Andriessen-online' (courtesy of London Sinfonietta, www.londonsinfonietta.org.uk)

an abstract 3D space; the loops change in response to cursor key navigation. The user's control of kinetic rhythm and temporal structure plays an essential role in such intermedia experiences, and presents possibilities for synaesthesic (Föllmer and Gerlach 2004) and narrative perception. This example suggests that the Internet is offering something new to what was once the preoccupation of high-art Expressionists: the possibility of users operating within – and constructing – a sort of *Gesamtkunstwerk*. If the principles of such highly conceptual artistic experiences can be absorbed into more general marketing strategies, there is hope that they may cater to more than just the converted.

A case of immersion: Ozon's Swimming Pool
Such explorations of image manipulation and its effect on sound perception return us to film and the various ways in which the promotion of multimedia forms of entertainment may use site interactivity to help convey product concepts. Ozon's *Swimming Pool* is a rare example of a film produced by a

Figure 5   Stills from '3d music' by Braunarts and London Sinfonietta (2007)
(courtesy of Braunarts)

mid-context culture that has different web-promotional strategies for its low-context (German) and high-context (Japanese) audiences. As one might expect, the official German *Swimming Pool* site conveys information principally via text.[13] The official Japanese site, which will be the focus here, has far less text on its home page (in keeping with a high-context culture) but expresses the concept of the film via an interactive Flash animation.

The music for the animation is taken from Philippe Rombi's highly evocative score for the final scene and credits of the film. It is a culmination of various musical threads that are woven throughout the film and is inextricably linked with the idea of a female murder-mystery writer (Sarah) writing about writing.

When fully loaded, the animation is set against a swimming-pool-like backdrop. The movement of the cursor across the water's surface of this backdrop is speed-sensitive, causing ripples that vary from gentle, ever-decreasing circles to the effect of a skidding stone. The positioning of the cursor on text (which is in English) creates the impression of its fluid dispersion and reveals hidden text in Japanese within certain regions of the pool. As with any interactive animation which has no text instruction, the process of discovery is part of the experience, though it is particularly well suited to this film site's theme. The unearthing of hidden text is in keeping with the idea of mystery (the decoding of the Japanese language adding a further level for English-speaking users) as well as that of Sarah finding her words. Moreover, users' opportunities to respond to the music visually and kinetically enable them to take part in the process of constructing their own 'narrative'.

During loading, the music is heard and the animation slowly emerges, like the process of writing itself. The animation consists of two adjacent, blood-like, blue liquid drops dripping in Japanese anime style. On first loading, the dripping speeds up, though each drip is always drawn out to create a degree of unpredictability and suspense. As the animation builds momentum, so does the music (gently): new timbres are brought in to create a gradual textural crescendo. Whilst it is possible to perceive the animation entirely separately from this music, the 'forced marriage' of the media gives rise to synch points, creating an interesting audiovisual interplay of rhythms and tempi. The first drop initiates a change in the music, beginning its journey to the sound of an isolated piano tone followed by a three-note motif; eventually the drop synchronises with a tentative, imitative guitar entry. The music develops organically into a four-note string motif which descends in sequence and meanders harmonically; each drop provides temporary relief at times when the music searches for its harmonic resolution; when the harmony resolves, the visuals convey the tension as yet another drop begins its descent.

Whilst the subject matter of the film itself is the animation's primary concept, the music provides the basic structure and approach to the interactive visual elements. The music's counterpoint and imitation are ideal for setting up audiovisual counterpoint, the animated drops and cursor movements gently introducing further contrapuntal 'voices'. Various pages on the site feature montages of film shots, and in keeping with the music, fade in and out as the images change. On 'Story' and 'Review' the speed of change may be modified by the user, but the smooth 'fade' transitions always ensure that these never conflict with the music's fluidity. On 'Review', a rhythm is set up between the text and image transitions; these complementary elements, like the two adjacent drops, create the sense of duality which is itself conveyed in the music (at one point, alternating young solo female voices differentiated by breathiness of timbre) and the film (two young women – the imaginary character of the writer's story and the real person who inspired her).

The music's direct association with the process of writing – the initiation of an idea, its development, the writer Sarah working at her keyboard – helps to draw interesting parallels between the music as reflecting Sarah's muse and the site user's musical experience. For this reason, it is useful to consider Sarah in terms of the user profiles discussed earlier. The gently arousing, evocative music, with its seductive harmonies and lush legato strings, matches Sarah's general profile (low-context type B); although an English woman in France (mid-context), her high level of isolation, 'individualism' and focus on text (Hofstede 1991) suggest that she has low-context culture tendencies. However, it is interesting that in order to become engaged with her writing, Sarah must paradoxically reduce these tendencies; this mature high-NFC female struggles to engage (not knowing with what to engage), which suggests initially at least that she begins with the characteristics of a low-NFC profile (type F); the swimming pool at Sarah's publisher's holiday home inspires her to create 'Julie', a type E character, which in turn enables Sarah as author to develop into her more usual type B. In keeping with this transition, the music gradually builds arousal levels, on the one hand reflecting the writer's increased immersion in her narrative/activity, and on the other drawing the film perceiver into Sarah's world. As was the case in the Nescafé and Mercurius Company loops, arousal levels are modified throughout this track; they vary like gentle undulating waves as Sarah's inspiration for writing comes and goes.

The implications of this example for understanding user types are: (1) user involvement may vary over time, suggesting a switch from one user profile to another; (2) an individual's cultural preferences may differ from those that typify her or his country of origin.

One can informally test out one's responses to the music's arousal flux by having the site playing while working in another window. One's own work environment is thus transformed into a parallel of the filmic experience: having switched subject position, the detached perceiver is now in a narrative of her or his own making; what was once non-diegetic music for the fictional writer is now diegetic for the non-fictional site user. This self-reflexive interaction is fitting from the perspective of the film's reflexive content (Sarah writing about writing), and it is a testament to the power of the music that it can seduce users into performing such acts, though for the author of this chapter there is clearly a danger that it could lead to absurdity: 'I am now a writer writing about writing about a writer writing about writing . . .'!

CONCLUSION

Germaine Greer (2006) famously proclaimed that: 'The true art form of our time isn't music or dance or painting or poetry; it's marketing.' Nowhere is this truer than on the Internet, where the concept of the interactive work is fusing the worlds of Western arts and marketing in web environments. Audiovisual interactivity hooks target users by encouraging them to invest time and effort in a product's basic concepts. In some cases users literally constitute the artwork, and the sense of ownership this instils may strengthen users' bonds with a site, brand or product.

By causing users to act rather than merely observe, the website designer exerts a subtle power. Sound and music not only facilitate this exertion of power, they are sometimes its source. As Huron (1989) points out for TV advertising, the elements music introduces include 'entertainment', 'lyrical' persuasion, comprehensible 'structure/continuity', 'credibility' (via certain known artists) and, perhaps most important of all, a capacity for improving 'memorability', helping to embed brand or product associations in the unconscious. Sound plays a major role in defining a site's image and, especially through music, the identities of its users.

Perhaps the most important issue that has been raised in this chapter is that although the incorporation of sound into websites can reap great rewards, it can ruin a perfectly adequate site if mishandled. Website designers need to consider not just what certain sounds or musics say about a site, but also what they do not. Designers need to be especially sensitive not to alienate target users, which involves taking into account the ELM divisions, low and high NFC, as well as micro- and macro-preferences and the ways in which they relate to low- and high-context cultures. In addition, designers should be sensitive to common irritation factors, careful balancing of the relationship between familiarity and complexity, and the mediation of arousal in relation to the amount of information to be presented. The tools at one's disposal range from the use of auditory icons and musical earcons to musical loops, interactive movies and much more. In order to achieve the most aesthetically satisfying web experiences each IMM should be considered in terms of 'goodness of fit', in the right context taking this concept beyond mere congruence as conformance to include more complex, multi-layered possibilities such as complementation and contest.

Much that is relevant to our understanding of how all of these issues relate to web-user types and the contextual subtleties of irritation has yet to be discovered. It is hoped that the overview of related literature and brief analyses set out in this chapter offer a springboard for much-needed experimental research. In the meantime, the website examples explored in this study highlight some key aesthetic issues. For instance, the cross-cultural analysis of McDonalds sites showed us the importance of national branding, of political and cultural sensitivity. Global companies are especially savvy to meeting market expectations, which suggests that their sites may convey to observers from other countries important information about the host nation; the accents of national identity in certain musical choices and prototype modifications provide traces of cultural (and socio-political) aspirations.

Building on the study of home-page loops, the investigation into how to achieve good musical wallpaper set out some useful preliminary guidelines. Of these, perhaps the most important of all was the idea of mild arousal flux as a signifiicant element in the construction of effectively repetitious material. Study of the Nescafé France and Mercurius Company loops also showed that under the right circumstances, the complexity of certain type 2 'irritation' factors (irregular beats/changes) may in fact help to avoid irritation by supra-optimal familiarity.

Finally, *Velocity* on the London Sinfonietta site and the official Japanese *Swimming Pool* site drew attention to aspects of (timbral) rhythm and tempo which, in the case of *Swimming Pool*, interacted with visual kinesis. More importantly, these sites provided a taste of the exploratory experiences that sound and music usage might provide in the future, even raising issues of subjectivity. Eno describes these experiences as falling 'in a nice new place – between art and science and playing' (Kelly 1995: 4); a place I now call 'the web'.

NOTES

1. The spectrum of a sound's acoustical components may be plotted using the Fourier transform. It shows specifically the strength of a sound's fundamental and other harmonic components in decibels (dB) and vibrations per second (Hz or kHz).
2. 'Mickeymousing consists in following the visual action in synchrony with musical trajectories (rising, falling, zigzagging) and instrumental punctuations of action (blows, falls, doors closing)' (Chion 1994: 121–2).
3. Chion (1994: 224): 'Rendering frequently translates an agglomerate of sensations. For example, sound accompanying a fall is often a great crash, conveying weight, violence, and pain.'
4. For more on IMMs see Cook (1998: 98–106).
5. These divisions have the advantage of facilitating parallels with timbre dimensions (notably the McAdams et al. model as developed by Tsang 2002) that may prove useful in future research.
6. With this in mind, it would be interesting to explore specifically whether London Sinfonietta's looping of such music has any beneficial effects.
7. See Hofstede (1991) and Hermeking (2005) for a statistical study of collectivism and individualism and how this relates to the low-/high-context divisions of Hall and Hall (1990).
8. Users for the Lebanon site are directed to this mother site, though the country is not listed on the home page.
9. The original music of the 'Ich liebe es' launch was by Tom Batoy and Franco Tortora (Mona Davis Music), later with English vocals by Justin Timberlake.
10. Incorrectly attributed to Evers (2001) by Würtz (2005).
11. This too is expressed through vocal timbre. See the section on 'A case of immersion' below.
12. Apart from the written trills and mordents (the commas to the right of the notes), there are additional diminutions, such as on the third beat of bar 14, and the third beat of the fifth bar in the 'Finalle' (cascade); some mordents are played twice, lingering on the blue note (something like a *pince double*) – these happen on the first beats of bars 6 and 7 of the 'Finalle'.
13. Unfortunately, this site is no longer accessible.

REFERENCES

Ahlstrohm, V. (2003), 'An Initial Survey of National Airspace System Auditory Alarm Issues in Terminal Traffic Control', *Technical Note* (Springfield, VA: National Technical Information Service).

Balzano, G. J. (1986), 'What Are Musical Pitch and Timbre?', *Music Perception*, Vol. 3, No. 3, pp. 297–314.

Baram, A. (1991), *Culture, History and Ideology in the Formation of Ba'thist Iraq, 1968–89* (London: Macmillan).

Berlyne, D. E. (1971), *Aesthetics and Psychobiology* (New York: Appleton-Century-Crofts).

Bussemakers, M. P., and de Haan, A. (2000), 'When it Sounds Like a Duck and Looks Like a Dog . . . Auditory Icons vs. Earcons in Multimedia Environments', *Online Proceedings of the International Conference on Auditory Display*, 2–5 April, Georgia, www.icad.org/websiteV2.0/Conferences/ICAD2000/PDFs/Bussemakers.pdf (accessed August 2006).

Buxton, W., Gaver, W., and Bly, S. (1994), 'Auditory Interfaces: The Use of Non-speech Audio at the Interface', unfinished book manuscript, www.billbuxton.com/Audio. TOC.html (accessed January 2007).

Chion, M. (1994), *Audio-Vision: Sound on Screen*, trans. C. Gorbman (New York: Columbia University Press).

Cook, N. (1998), *Analysing Musical Multimedia* (Oxford: Clarendon Press).

Daynes, H. (forthcoming), 'Listeners' Perceptual and Emotional Responses to Tonal and Atonal Music: The Effects of Familiarity', PhD dissertation, Hull University.

Edworthy, J. (1998), 'Does Sound Help Us to Work Better with Machines?', *Interacting With Computers*, Vol. 10, No. 4, pp. 401–9.

Edworthy, J., and Stanton, N. (1995), 'A User-Centred Approach to the Design and Evaluation of Warning Signals', *Ergonomics*, No. 38, pp. 2262–80.

Evers, V. (2001), 'Cultural Aspects of User Interface Understanding: An Empirical Evaluation of an E-learning Website by International User Groups', PhD dissertation, Open University, Milton Keynes.

Evers, V., and Day, D. (1997), 'The Role of Culture in Interface Acceptance', in S. Howard, J. Hammond and G. Lindegaard (eds), *Human Computer Interaction INTERACT'97* (London: Chapman and Hall).

Fischoff, S. (1994), 'Race and Sex Differences in Patterns of Film Attendance and Avoidance', paper presented at the APA Convention, Los Angeles, 15 August.

Fischoff, S., Antonio, J., and Lewis, D. (1998), 'Favourite Films and Film Genres as a Function of Race, Age, and Gender', *Journal of Media Psychology*, Vol. 3, No. 1, www.calstatela.edu/faculty/sfischo/media3.html (accessed August 2006).

Föllmer, G., and Gerlach, J. (2004), 'Audiovisions: Music as an Intermedia Art Form'. *Media Art Net*, www.medienkunstnetz.de/themes/image-sound_relations/audiovisions/print (accessed August 2006).

Gaver, W. W. (1993), 'Synthesizing Auditory Icons', in *Proceedings of the SIGCHI Conference on Human Factors in Computing Systems* (Amsterdam: ACM Press).

Greer, G. (2006), 'The Genius of Madonna', *Independent*, 30 July, comment. independent.co.uk/commentators/article1204434.ece (accessed January 2007).

Hahn, J., Fouad, H., Gritz, L., and Wong Lee, J. (1995a), 'An Integrated Approach to Motion and Sound', *Journal of Visualization and Computer Animation*, Vol. 6, No. 2, pp. 109–23.

—— (1995b), 'Integrating Sounds and Motions in Virtual Environments', *Sound for Animation and Virtual Reality*, Siggraph'95 Course #10 Notes, August, citeseer.ist. psu.edu/hahn95integrating.html (accessed January 2007).

Hajda, J. M., Kendall, R. A., and Carterette, E. C. (1997), 'Methodological Issues in Timbre Research', in I. Deliège and J. Sloboda (eds), *Perception and Cognition of Music* (Hove: Psychology Press).

Hall, E. T., and Hall, M. R. (1990), *Understanding Cultural Differences* (Yarmouth, ME: Intercultural Press).

Handel, S. (1995), 'Timbre Perception and Auditory Object Recognition', in B. C. J. Moore (ed.), *Hearing* (New York: Academic Press).

Hankinson, J. C. K., and Edwards, A. D. N. (2000), 'Musical Phrase Structured Audio Communication', *Online Proceedings of the International Conference on Auditory*

Display, 2–5 April, Georgia, www.icad.org/websiteV2.0/Conferences/ICAD2000/PSs/Hankinson.ps (accessed August 2006).

Hargreaves, D. J. (1984), 'The Effects of Repetition on Liking for Music', *Journal of Research in Music Education*, No. 32, pp. 35–47.

—— (1986), *The Development of the Psychology of Music* (Cambridge: Cambridge University Press).

Hermeking, M. (2005), 'Culture and Internet Consumption: Contributions from Cross-cultural Marketing and Advertising Research', *Journal of Computer-Mediated Communication*, Vol. 11, No. 1, article 10, jcmc.indiana.edu/vol11/issue1/hermeking.html (accessed January 2007).

Heyduk, R. G. (1975), 'Rated Preference for Musical Compositions as it Relates to Complexity and Exposure Frequency', *Perception and Psychophysics*, Vol. 17, No. 1, pp. 89–91.

Hofstede, G. (1991), *Cultures and Organizations: Software of the Mind* (New York: McGraw-Hill).

Huron, D. (1989), 'Music in Advertising: An Analytic Paradigm', *Musical Quarterly*, Vol. 73, No. 4, pp. 557–74.

Interbrand Corporation (2005), 'The 100 Top Brands', *Business Week*, 1 August, p. 94, www.businessweek.com/pdfs/2005/0531_globalbrand.pdf (accessed January 2007).

Kang, J., and Yang, W. (2003), 'Sound Preferences in Urban Open Public Spaces', *Journal of the Acoustical Society of America*, Vol. 114, No. 4, p. 2352.

Kelly, K. (1995), 'Gossip is Philosophy', interview with Brian Eno, *Wired*, pp. 1–13, www.wired.com/wired/archive/3.05/eno.html (accessed January 2007).

Kramer, M. (1993), 'Arab Nationalism: Mistaken identity', *Daedalus* (Summer), pp. 171–206.

Lemmens, P. M. C., Bussemakers, M. P., and de Hahn, A. (2000), 'The Effect of Earcons on Reaction Times and Error-rates in a Dual-task vs. a Single-task Experiment', *Proceedings ICAD 2000*, pp. 177–83.

North, A. C., and Hargreaves, D. J. (1997a), 'Experimental Aesthetics and Everyday Listening', in D. J. Hargreaves and A. C. North, *The Social Psychology of Music* (Oxford: Oxford University Press).

—— (1997b), 'Music and Consumer Behaviour', in D. J. Hargreaves and A. C. North, *The Social Psychology of Music* (Oxford: Oxford University Press).

Ronkainen, S. (2001), 'Earcons in Motion: Defining Language for an Intelligent Mobile Device', *Proceedings of the International Conference on Auditory Display*, Espoo, Finland, 29 July–1 August, pp. 126–31.

Sorkin R. (1988), 'Why are People Turning Off Our Alarms?', *Journal of the Acoustical Society of America*, Vol. 84, No. 3, pp. 1107–8.

Takala, T., and Hahn, J. (1992), 'Sound Rendering', *ACM Computer Graphics*, Vol. 26, No. 2 (Proc. SIGGRAPH, '92), pp. 211–20.

Tan, S-L., Spackman, M. P., and Peaslea, C. L. (2006), 'The Effects of Repeated Exposure on Liking and Judgments of Musical Unity of Intact and Patchwork Compositions', *Music Perception*, June, Vol. 23, No. 5, pp. 407–21.

Tsang, L. (2001), 'Musical Timbre in Context: The Music of the Second Viennese School, 1909–1925', PhD dissertation, Southampton University.

—— (2002), 'Towards a Theory of Timbre for Music Analysis', *Musicae Scientiae*, Vol. 6, No. 1, pp. 23–52.

Wang, L. C., and Chang, L-H. (2006), 'The Effect of Music Congruence and Gender on Online Users' Flow Experiences', in J. L. Johnson and J. Hulland (eds), *Proceedings of the 2006 AMA Winter Educators' Conference: Marketing Theory and Applications* (Chicago: American Marketing Association), 17, pp. 193–4, www.marketingjournals.org/clara/wintered/PDFs/AMA_2006.pdf (accessed January 2007).

Würtz, E. (2005), 'A Cross-cultural Analysis of Websites from High-context Cultures and Low-context Cultures', *Journal of Computer-Mediated Communication*, Vol. 11, No. 1, article 13, http://jcmc.indiana.edu/vol11/issue1/wuertz.html (accessed July 2006).

Yang, W., and Kang, J. (2004), 'Sound Preferences in Urban Squares: A Case Study in Sheffield', in B. Martens and A. G. Keul (eds), *Evaluation in Progress: Strategies for Environmental Research and Implementation* (IAPS 18 Conference Proceedings on CD-ROM), 7–9 July.

Yokom, B. E. (2000–3), 'The Aesthetics of Sound in Web Presentations', *Blue Gel Media*, Golden Colorado, www.bluegelmedia.com/tutorials/av/aesthetics_of_sound.htm (accessed January 2007).

WEBSITES

Andriessen-online, www.londonsinfonietta.org.uk/andriessen-online/home.html.

Disney Online, disney.go.com/home/today/index.html.

English National Opera, www.eno.org.

English Touring Opera, www.englishtouringopera.org.uk.

Francois Ozon Official Website, www.francois-ozon.com/english/index.

Harry Potter – The Official Site, harrypotter.warnerbros.com.

London Sinfonietta – Making Musical History, www.londonsinfonietta.org.uk.

London Symphony Orchestra, www.lso.co.uk/home.

McDonald's, www.mcdonalds.com.

Mercurius Company – Baroque Dance and Music, www.mercuriuscompany.co.uk.

Nescafé, www.nescafe.com/nescafe/nescafe+worldwide.htm.

Opera North, www.operanorth.co.uk.

Philharmonia Orchestra, www.philharmonia.co.uk.

Philharmonia Orchestra – The Sound Exchange, www.philharmonia.co.uk/thesoundexchange.

Royal Opera House – A World Stage, info.royaloperahouse.org/Opera.

Un film de Francois Ozon: Swimming Pool, www.gaga.ne.jp/swimmingpool.

Welsh National Opera, Cardiff: Wales Millennium Centre, www.wno.org.uk.

9. MUSIC MEDIA IN YOUNG PEOPLE'S EVERYDAY LIVES

Dan Laughey

It should come as a surprise that there is still a lack of research on how (young) people use music media in everyday situations. Contributions have been made in recent years with the advent of new technologies, but still not enough is known.[1] The surprise is made greater by the recognition that music in various multimedia forms has pervaded everyday life in economically developed countries for a considerable period of time. Music in cinemas, shops, cafés and restaurants has been established since the 1930s.[2] The pre-war era also witnessed the rise of music in the home, via the gramophone and later the radio. Gramophones were to have a major cultural impact in that they spread American influences across the Atlantic to Europe and other parts of the world following the mass importation of recorded music in the early 1930s. By the mid-1930s gramophones were relatively cheap to buy and portable too – they could be taken on holiday or moved around the home – which increased their use among young people and the working classes.

An even greater cultural impact was made by the radio. Commercial radio broadcasting began in 1920 in the United States and Europe. Throughout the 1930s the British Broadcasting Corporation (BBC) – the only company with a licence to broadcast across radio waves whilst located in Britain – provided daily airings (excluding Sundays) of dance band music that proved extremely popular: 'Each band was allocated its own day and fans tuned in religiously' (Nott 2002: 62). The BBC's monopoly was threatened, however, by the International Broadcasting Company (IBC), which helped to develop radio stations in continental Europe – such as Radio Luxembourg – with transmitters capable of being received by wireless sets in Britain. These stations initially exploited a major BBC weakness: the absence of popular music programmes on Sundays and during weekday mornings. About 90 per cent of programmes on commercial stations were dedicated to popular and dance music (Nott 2002: 74–5). Frith (1987) argues convincingly that the radio was the most important medium to drive forward the British record industry in its early years.

In the twenty-first century, of course, music is available on a wider array of multimedia formats than ever before. The cumbersome portable gramophones of seventy years ago have been replaced with mobile devices such as the slender iPod, some models of which can store over ten thousand tracks. As well as the traditional media of cinema, recorded music (vinyl, cassette, CD) players, radios and magazines, music is now mediated through specialist music television channels, DVDs, karaoke equipment, the Internet (including MP3 file-sharing sites, fan sites, music news and band sites, and interactive discussion forums like MySpace), phones (ring tones as well as digital music files) and other mobile devices (Walkmans, iPods, DAB digital radios and so on). New media technologies promise to cater for ubiquitous listening (Kassabian 2002), with young people at the forefront of these technological developments, as both consumers and producers. Shawn Fanning was only nineteen years old when he created the online music distribution site Napster. The majority of individuals prosecuted by the International Federation of the Phonographic Industry (IFPI) for heavy illegal downloading are under forty years of age.[3] This chapter aims to understand better how young people use music in all its multimedia forms. Rather than focus on fanatical, obsessive or exceptionally creative music media users, though, I am interested in how music is mediated to young people in mundane, everyday contexts. I will draw on empirical research by way of focus-group interview discussions in order to achieve this aim.[4] Before doing so, I will address three central themes that emerge from previous studies of music media use. These themes attempt to evince the different uses of music media: private and public; intensive and casual; and alternative and populist.

PRIVATE AND PUBLIC

Although contemporary media use is associated mainly with private settings, historically this has not been the case: 'The radio was originally utilised to convey music more to public places than to the home . . . mass media have neither any sort of natural roots nor any obvious natural roles in the private sphere' (Reimer 1995: 58, 59). Moreover, it would be a mistake to perceive today's youth music media use as private and domestic. Elsewhere I have detailed the consumer-oriented role that music media play in public places as well as the way in which media influences penetrate the public lives of young people (Laughey 2006). The impact made by music media on the public sphere has been largely neglected by classic youth cultural studies of privatised media use in teenage bedroom cultures (e.g. McRobbie and Garber 1975). In response to this neglect, two recent studies of pre-teen and teenage bedroom cultures (Baker 2004; Lincoln 2005) have stressed the intertwining relationship between the private and public. In particular, young people's bedrooms are seen as productive spaces where publicly available resources, such as pop music, are shaped into personal projects of self-identity and creativity. Baker (2004) applies the concept of 'playing' (Schechner 1993) to her young female respondents. Their forms of playing vary from role-playing, as a singer or DJ, to reproducing music texts in innovative ways, to mixing two tracks together or replacing original lyrics with one's own. Nine-year-old Kate, for example, 'played at creating her own radio programmes' (Baker 2004: 82) as a means of exploring possibilities of self-representation and anticipating future roles, both career- and hobby-related.

The overlapping character of public and private play in bedroom spaces is also evidenced by Lincoln's discussion of 'zones'. In contrast to 'codes', which are constructed by dominant ideologies in order to privatise and pacify teenage cultures – codes of romance, beauty and so on (McRobbie and Garber 1975) – zones are multi-layered 'pathways' governed by 'social, reflexive, active agents' (Lincoln 2005: 401) that flow between public and private realms of influence. For example, media technologies can function as zones in the bedroom space by introducing public dimensions (e.g. a television programme) amid more privatised zones, such as a dressing table. Music, in particular, provides a reflexive 'pathway out of the private sphere of the bedroom and into the public sphere of the city' (Lincoln 2005: 409) for teenagers as they prepare to go out at night. In a separate study, music media use in domestic spaces as a means of 'getting in the mood' to go out to social events 'was referred to by nearly all respondents' (DeNora 1999: 39). Music is also used by some of DeNora's women respondents to determine the atmosphere of private spaces such as bedrooms (DeNora 1999: 40), which effectively reduces unwanted distractions from outside these spaces but, in turn, can potentially impact on the atmosphere of these outside spaces too. In this instance, the assumption that bedrooms are private spaces is clearly questioned. The 'private' use of mediated music in bedrooms can potentially intrude upon public spaces outside bedrooms, as well as outside homes. Notions of 'the private' and 'the public' are clearly relative to how particular actors are situated, and do not conform to an inherent demarcation.

Perhaps the most interesting fusion between public and private uses of music media has been explored in respect to mobile technologies such as the personal stereo and iPod. Bull (2000: 23) refers to 'users accounts of "losing" themselves in public and of becoming distracted or disorientated'. Personal stereos, paradoxically, are intended for use in public environments but actually reconstitute the private–public divide by altering the sensory experience of public environments (in that they partially affect one's sense of sound). Personal stereos function as a Goffmanian 'involvement shield' in public interactions and essentially enable 'new modes of experiencing the city' (Thibaud 2003: 330) – or the countryside for that matter. Bull has expanded his thesis on how sound technologies reconstruct the experience of contemporary urban life by considering the contexts of car stereo-radio and iPod use (Bull 2003, 2005). In both cases, the mundane routines of workaday life are, temporarily at least, circumvented by these technologies and the music soundtrack they predominantly afford. At least on the level of sense and perception, individuals feel empowered by mobile music media technologies in such a way that 'the distinction between private mood or orientation and their surroundings is often abolished' (Bull 2005: 351). As such, music can enable a feeling of occupancy and control in 'public' spaces – like train carriages – as well as 'private' ones, such as bedrooms. Technological advances in music media clearly problematise any claim to a separate public and private sphere in everyday experiences of contemporary life. The multiple forms of music media available in public and private contexts also afford differing degrees of user involvement.

Intensive and Casual

As stated earlier, music media use as a whole has been underresearched. This is an even more accurate statement in the case of levels of involvement in music media use. The commonsense assumption would be that music media used in private, personal contexts are likely to undergo more intensive consumption (i.e. concentrated listening and some elements of participation) than the casually consumed media technologies used in public contexts. It is clear from the previous discussion, however, that the majority of new media technologies can operate in both private and public places – and, furthermore, their use blurs the boundaries between these two spheres. So far, knowledge about variable degrees of involvement in music media use has been gleaned mostly from studies of private contexts of use. Baker notes that her research participants used music in their bedrooms both as a background accompaniment to other activities, such as homework, and as a foreground resource 'to sing, master dance moves, record compilations of favourite songs and learn lyrics' (2004: 81). Similarly, Lincoln's (2005) zoning model is multi-layered in the sense that several media technologies often compete for attention in teenage bedroom cultures. Typically, a television set might be operating in the background whilst another zone – governed by, say, the CD player – takes precedence, although the fading out of one zone in order to bring another to the fore is a frequent feat of youth consumer agency. Listening to music on the radio is commonly a technique of background zoning, 'associated with "doing other things"' (Lincoln 2005: 408) such as homework.[5]

Studies of casual music consumption are in desperately short supply, though.[6] A little more is known about intensive use of music media. DeNora's discussion of 'personal music maps', whilst not specifically about music media use, is compelling all the same in its attempt to explore how individuals act 'like disk jockeys to themselves' by listening to music that reflects their everyday, fluctuating moods (1999: 35). Intensive, concentrated listening is associated with emotional events in people's lives and demonstrates 'music's ability to invoke past feelings and ways of being' (p. 48). Music of different styles and on different formats is able to 'get into' people's thoughts and feelings to such an extent that it aids identity formation (see also Tarrant et al. 2002: 139). Intriguingly, DeNora's female respondents did not necessarily associate their favourite music with intense emotional responses. Sometimes listening to certain songs that were situated on the margins of their personal music maps none the less enabled the recalling of vivid memories about a particular time in their lives. On other occasions, music that was central to a person's music map – for example, a record collection belonging to a lately dead husband – would be resisted, perhaps for fear of the emotions it would conjure on being heard again. It is clear from these examples that there is no simple correlation between intensive music use and preferred music tastes, particularly given that music is able to generate intimate meanings and that 'the past comes alive to its soundtrack' (DeNora 1999: 49). Intensive and casual use of any particular piece of music, style or artist are also clearly situated temporally, and longitudinal studies are required to understand how changes occur in levels of user involvement over time.

Intensive use of music media in more public, social networks has been examined recently in relation to bootleg (Marshall 2004) and vinyl (Hayes 2006) record collectors. According to the former, 'The individuals who collect bootlegs are in general the most committed fans that an artist has' and 'it is *fans* rather than casual consumers who are the market for bootleg records' (Marshall 2004: 166–7). Marshall's interviews with bootleg record collectors depict a network of highly committed individuals who are fanatic about owning entire collections of every recording that was ever produced, legally or illegally, under the name of a particular artist. For example, Dylan collectors demonstrate extremely intensive media use by typically owning the same albums on various formats (vinyl, cassette, CDs and so on). Unlike intensive music fans, casual consumers are unlikely either to purchase a bootleg record – only obtainable on the 'black market' these days – or to describe themselves as following a particular artist. In Hayes's study, a small network of youth consumers exhibit 'engagement in the listening process' (Hayes 2006: 52) through intensive use of vinyl records as a means of accessing rare music of past times. They demonstrate this intensive use by 'their active involvement in negotiating the pops, skips, and crackles endemic to most second-hand records' (p. 58).

This contrasts with the lack of physical participation required in operating a CD player with a remote control device. Hayes argues that these young vinyl collectors used their LP records to regain a level of agency in resisting the 'ideal consumer' type favoured by a profit-driven global music industry. He continues: 'Sadly, many of their peers have yet to develop this degree of autonomy, quickly embracing each new singing sensation simply because MTV has his or her video in heavy rotation' (p. 67). Hayes clearly adopts the elitist stance of his research participants here, which leads on smoothly to the debate about how users distinguish alternative from populist music media.

ALTERNATIVE AND POPULIST

If most studies of user involvement centre on intensive media use, it is also fair to say that these studies are more likely to discuss alternative than populist music tastes. Research on Internet music users certainly follows this trend. Before commenting on this research, though, it is helpful to begin discussion on this issue by analysing Thornton's (1995) much-cited distinction between mass, micro and niche media in the context of clubbing cultures. Mass media such as television are associated mainly with populist music artists and genres that 'sell out' to the mainstream. Mass-mediated music is therefore dismissed by those with alternative music tastes as shallow, commercialised trash. In contrast, micro media such as flyers, fanzines and low-budget websites are narrowly targeted at specific groups of music consumers – in Thornton's case, clubbers – often in localised contexts (e.g. the London club scene). Distinct from mass and micro media, though, are niche media in the form of consumer magazines such as *The Face*. Niche media are considered by Thornton to be integral to the creation of subcultural capital. *The Face* not only reports on clubbing and raves – it helps to construct the alternativeness of these youth cultural pursuits. Whilst these distinctions between the taste cultures of different media are thought-provoking and to some extent accurate, Thornton bases her evidence on textual analyses of these media and offers little empirical research into how these media are used by clubbers. It is very easy to become suspicious of claims about certain youth lifestyle magazines playing a lead in the formation of underground club cultures when it is these exact same claims that these magazines make in their marketing campaigns to increase sales. Furthermore, obsessive attempts to search out alternative, underground, subcultural editorials leaves Thornton with very little to say about mainstream, populist music media *per se*, other than to pander to the biases of her research subjects and reject such media as the 'Sharon and Tracy' kind.

Despite the shortcomings of Thornton's thesis, it remains one of the few attempts to account for the varying levels of taste that different music media are perceived to command. With the rise of online music distribution in recent years, however, distinctions between mass, micro and niche media are less clear-cut. The Internet is now a commonplace medium for niche music styles and genres, despite the fact that it is accessible on a 'mass' scale. In its early years, though, downloading of MP3 (compressed digital music) files via the Internet was considered to be a subversive practice, not least by the major record corporations, which soon filed law suits against 'large-scale uploaders'. Peer-to-peer (P2P) file-sharing software enabled users to search out unprecedented libraries of music on sites such as (most notoriously) Napster, in order to download tracks free of charge and without restriction, given that copyright laws had been flouted. Internet music piracy had become a widespread, alternative use of new media technology by the start of the twenty-first century. Unlike previous music piracy activities that operated in criminal circles within developing countries (Laing 1986), Internet piracy spread first in North America and Europe, therefore hitting the major record companies in their core markets (Leyshan et al. 2005: 187). In turn, MP3 file-sharing has 'a transformative effect on the circulation of cultural products' (Bradley 2006: 3) and 'weaken[s] the traditional divide between the producer and the consumer, the licit and the illicit, since options of opportunistic reproduction and exchange are vastly multiplied' (Rojek 2005: 364). Use of P2P software, although still far from lawful, has become normalised and is perceived, on the whole, to be less 'alternative' than before, although more advanced applications are developing rapidly to replenish consumer desire for empowerment effectively. As such, online music use in all its intricate ways 'introduces the level of innovative flexibility and choice to the *consumption* of popular music that previously were obtained only in its *production*' (Rojek 2005: 366).

Populist music media use is less well understood than alternative use. Perhaps inevitably, researchers tend to focus their interest on the exceptions rather than the rules. The previously discussed study of vinyl collectors is an illustration of this tendency. Hayes located his respondents in three music stores in a Canadian city. Eventually he selected for interview twenty-three young people who were 'serious about music in their lives' (Hayes 2006: 57), and, if this was not selective enough, his article is devoted to 'eight of my research participants' enthusiastic responses towards the consumption of music on vinyl' (p. 58). The consequences of this tailored sample have more to do with those young people who are *not* selected for analysis than those who are. What about non-vinyl collectors? What about those young people who visited these music stores but were not 'serious' about their music consumption? What about young people who do not shop at music stores but obtain their music through other means? What about young people who live in rural areas? Of course, a researcher who 'searches out' alternative music use through such a selective methodological approach is going to find it. Unfortunately, the vast majority of studies that approach music consumption in terms of fandom, subcultures and scenes fall victim to this blinkered perspective. Perhaps paradoxically, far less is known about 'ordinary', populist use of mainstream music media, and there is a lack of sustained theorisation of what is meant by 'the mainstream', other than in negative relation to 'the underground' (Thornton 1995: 87–115). It may be the case that there is a relationship, but no clear correlation, between populist tastes and casual involvement in mediated music. I will try to address this issue as well as draw other comparisons between alternative and populist, private and public, intensive and casual music media uses in the research findings that follow.[7]

MUSIC MEDIA USES (1): INTERNET, IPOD AND MP3 PLAYERS

The Internet provided a range of music uses for the young people that I interviewed. More so than any other medium, the Internet provided a resource for fans of particular performers or genres to update and hone their knowledge and tastes. Large databases of songs can be accessed free of charge using P2P software such as WinMx, SoulSeek and Torrentz. With P2P software 'you can almost play what you want' (Ricky, Richmond College AB2) and 'it's the best way of getting music you don't know' (Gemma, Southwell College 1). One respondent used the allmusic site to develop tastes for new bands by reading their profiles, as they are sorted into particular music traditions. Jack used all-music to preview music in line with existing tastes: 'It's a bit like going to see a band at a gig but also going to see the support acts, who start to gain the same sort of following' (Pollington College 1). The Internet is a consumer-led music medium in that users of P2P sites can access an unprecedented collection of music for free or a nominal charge – a facility that could only have been accessed in the pre-Internet age at a huge expense in terms of time and money. Simon considers this facility to be a means of building a sense of one's 'music heritage' – young consumers are using online sites, with their vast array of freely available tracks, to search out bands from yesteryear (Pollington College 1). Simon's favourite bands are the Rolling Stones and Black Sabbath, while Jack likes the Clash and Stiff Little Fingers. These bands are hardly 'contemporary' and they became famous long before Simon or Jack were born. None the less, these young people think that they sound better and more authentic than today's bands, many of whom openly declare musical influences that may spur their fans to look for the original 'Green Day sound', the authentic 'Kaiser Chiefs', the real 'Killers' and so on.

As well as facilitating consumer demand for new – and old – music, the Internet threatens any continuing semblance of the 'cultural gatekeeper' figure. Traditional gatekeepers such as influential figures in the music industry (like A&R people) or those who broadcast music programmes are being dislodged from their thrones, if not overthrown, by online users themselves. Internet radio sites such as Turn Up the Ska! enable consumers to make available their favourite playlists for online peers to download and listen to; it's like being a radio DJ without the vocal input between tracks. Message boards like MySpace empower fans to exchange news, information and recommendations – word of mouth is an important part of online communication. The power of MySpace as a consumer-driven breeding ground for popular culture is appreciated by the music industry. All the major artists and bands have a MySpace home page to profile their latest music up to a limit of four tracks. Hugely successful mainstream acts such as the Arctic Monkeys owe much of their early popularity to the power of message boards. In the case of the Arctic Monkeys, fans used MySpace and other message boards to distribute songs that derived from free demo CDs handed out at small gig venues where the band first performed. The band has since signed for a well-known independent record label and released the fastest-selling debut album ever in Britain but, instead of following the traditional route of being 'spotted' by record industry A&R people, the Arctic Monkeys were brought to the attention of industry figures through online consumer interest. The Arctic Monkeys represent perhaps the ultimate example of music media empowerment via the Internet, given that individuals in everyday contexts can become 'petty producers' (Abercrombie and Longhurst 1998). Chris and his 'mates have got our own band – we've got music on the Internet' (Pickles High School 1). Petty production indeed!

Music downloading on the Internet was not, though, a craze that exploded overnight. Online music distribution only found its killer application when downloaded music could be transferred from computer hard drives to mobile devices such as the iPod and other MP3 players. These devices enabled large quantities of digital music files to be consumed in public as well as private contexts. One's CD player along with one's entire CD collection could be compressed and stored on a pocket-sized machine to be carried with one on everyday journeys.[8] In his empirical work on iPod users, Bull describes the iPod use of a 35-year-old bank executive, Jean, as she commutes to New York on a typical weekday morning:

> She would scroll through her song titles looking for a particular song to listen to that would suit her mood at that particular moment and, whilst listening to that song, would scroll through her list for her next choice – her musical choices would merge seamlessly into one another during her journey time . . . The ability to continually adjust music, whilst on the move, to moods with such sophistication and precision is relatively new if, indeed, the desire to do it is not. (Bull 2005: 344)

In my own research it was similarly the case that iPod use corresponded to particular moods and situations. For example, Paul stored a playlist which he called 'SLEEP', containing five songs that helped him fall asleep (Wilson High School 1). By contrast, iPods were used by some young people at parties where they were connected to stereo systems and switched to the 'shuffle' mode so that songs would be played randomly from a collection of thousands of tracks. Moreover, iPod users are able to give ratings to songs so that, in the public context of a house party or even in some public bars with the requisite facilities, they can play only their favourite tracks. Perhaps the most significant cultural impact of the iPod results from its capacity to store vast music collections. Daniel (Wilson High School 1) spoke about a strange experience that occurred after he had stored his entire CD collection – stretching back over ten years – on his newly purchased iPod. When it was set to shuffle mode, he experienced odd feelings of happiness, regret, anger and embarrassment as he recalled songs that were attached to memories of particular events and episodes in his teenage years. On some occasions he was forced to skip over certain tracks which threw up unwanted recollections. Soon after, he scrolled through his iPod and deleted several CD albums that he had come to resent. iPod and MP3 players with similarly large memory capacities are often associated with intensive, personal use, although these technologies retain a public use dimension – with regard to both the P2P Internet downloading process[9] and the playing of these devices through stereo systems – that counteracts the assumption that they are simply the latest developments on the personal stereo prototype.

Music Media Uses (2): Music Television and Radio

In contrast to music mediated through the Internet and MP3 players, young people are more likely to use music television and radio, as well as music magazines, as casual media of consumption. However, this contrast is relative and should not be exaggerated. Certain niche digital channels were still used intensively by some respondents as a means of accessing specific music styles and performers. MTV Base, for example, was considered by Sam to offer an attractive alternative to the run-of-the-mill nightlife entertainment provided in her local area:

> DL: [. . .] why is MTV Base so popular?
> Sam: Cause it's got music that nobody else plays in Manchester.
> (Natton College 2)

One group drew comparisons between pop-orientated television and radio outputs, and more alternative outputs across these same music media:

> DL: . . . if you're not into [pop and R n B] – if you want to hear alternative sounds, how do you get to know about them?

Ricky: Er/ perhaps the Internet.

DL: The Internet mainly.

Sean: And there's like, you know that rock – there's a Radio 1 rock show which is on at midnight on Radio 1.

DL: Yeh.

Rebecca: And, erm, Kerrang! And MTV2.

(Richmond College 1)

Kerrang!, MTV2 and MTV Base were considered more alternative than generic television channels such as MTV and VH1. Even mainstream music programmes, however, were sometimes considered to offer a potential route into new, alternative sounds: 'it's like you watch *Top of the Pops* don't you, all your little TV acts, and then you see a certain song which is like – you know, and maybe you start to get into a certain genre' (Chris, Scarcroft College 3).

When these exceptions are accounted for, though, it became clear from my interviews with young people that these forms of music media mostly catered for populist tastes and enabled music to function as a background noise where other activities would occupy the foreground. At Pickles High School, for instance, a group of girls disliked the music CDs played by the boys in their common room and preferred to listen to music on the radio as a more democratic soundtrack to their everyday conversations:

DL: . . . What sort of music gets played here mainly then?

Mel: Garage.

Sophie: Garage.

Clare: Garage, yeh.

DL: Who decides that – is it=

Clare: The lads.

DL: So you'd put on – what would you put on instead of garage?

Mel: The radio.

Sophie: Yeh, it's easier to listen to when you want a chat.

(Pickles High School 1)

Radio is often the preferred soundtrack for young people in public places. Music television channels are also often a background presence in communal areas of schools and colleges as well as in public bars, shops and restaurants, especially those that target young consumers. The recurrent role of mainstream music television and radio programmes as a means of previewing songs that might then be pursued and used more intensively through other media is typified by Stacey's comments about consuming mass-mediated music with friends: 'We hear it on the radio or listen on the television, someone says that they have it so we just borrow it, tape it and listen to it' (Natton College 3). These music media also function in private contexts as forms of domestic entertainment that require little mental or physical exertion: 'watching [music television] I can just sit there and relax and I don't have to move apart from going like that to change the channel' (Jen, Scarcroft College 3). Jen's preference for passive, casual consumption served as 'rest time' from the busy working schedule that she undertook every weekend between her studies.

Whilst casual music consumers like Stacey and Jen did not perceive music television or radio to be populist or cheap in entertainment value, other respondents who valued their music tastes more highly were critical of such consumers: 'There are people that are, like, sheltered a bit and don't really know about other music . . . say, when you hear it on the radio or on the TV or something maybe they think, "Oh that's good" cause they haven't heard it before, but like most people, they know what kind of music they're into' (Jolene, Natton College 3). Jolene draws a distinction between users of music radio and television, with their fickle tastes and ignorance of the latest sounds, and young people like herself who enjoy a broad knowledge of music trad- itions and are secure in their tastes for particular styles. Her friend Sam is like- minded: 'I hate radio . . . They play the same things every time' (Natton College 2). It was evident from discussions that Jolene and Sam accessed what they perceived as alternative music styles from other friends, or sometimes from niche media such as specialist music magazines, rather than from the mass media. None the less, the alternative sounds – hip-hop, rap and soul – that they consumed tended to derive from either 'classic' artists of the past (such as 2Pac) or up-and-coming artists who were shortly to enter the charts and 'crossover' into mainstream media exposure. In this sense, the perceived populism of casual media use via television and radio in relation to alternative media use is more a matter of timing than musical content. 'Alternative' music is very often of the past or of the future rather than the present. Mass media such as most music radio stations, on the other hand, are dedicated only to the *presently* popular.

Summarising Music Media Uses

Bearing in mind the differences in the uses of these multiple music media by young people in my research, it is possible to propose a model that accounts for these differences in relation to variations in typical user context (private/public), involvement (intensive/casual) and taste (alternative/populist). This model is illustrated in Table 2.

It should be emphasised that this model is based on *typical* uses of these media and so there will always be atypical exceptions. For example, it seems reasonable to suggest that in some situations – for example, whilst shopping in a supermarket – CD players will be consumed in public contexts with casual

Table 2 *Typical characteristics of music media use*

Media	Context	Involvement	Taste
Vinyl LP record players	Private	Intensive	Alternative
CD/cassette players	Private	Intensive	Alternative Populist
Internet/MP3 players	Private Public	Intensive	Alternative Populist
Niche music TV/radio/DVDs	Private Public	Intensive Casual	Alternative
Magazines/newspapers	Private Public	Intensive Casual	Alternative Populist
Mainstream radio	Private Public	Casual	Populist
Mainstream music TV/films	Public	Casual	Populist

involvement. It will also be reasonable to suggest, however, that most of the time CD players will be used in private contexts with intensive involvement: singing along while driving a car, listening emotionally in intimate settings such as bedrooms, honing CD collections in one's personal rack or storage case, and so on.

This model does not imply a McLuhanesque interpretation in which the various media determine their musical messages. Media technologies do not shape the meanings that users bestow on the music to which they listen. On the contrary, as Rojek suggests, it is the flexible means in which music is consumed through these new technologies – means that traditionally were only available at the point of production – that create a scale of variable usage such as that detailed in Table 2. Effectively, 'young people appropriate and rework communication media, constructing new narratives of personal and social experience' (Williams 2006: 195). This quote from Williams is applied to his study of online music users who identify with the 'straightedge' subculture, but it could equally apply to many of my own interview respondents who did not affiliate themselves with a subcultural category. As I have argued, even casual, populist music media use requires a sophisticated analysis of agency and should not be dismissed as inferior. Lincoln's 'zones' seem like a fruitful line to explore further in understanding how this agency is practised in private contexts such as bedrooms. DeNora's notion of personal music maps also takes an important step towards understanding how today's casually consumed music can become part of tomorrow's life narrative: a song heard on the radio can construct a sense of what it was like to live at a given moment in time, and when heard again it can bring all those memories flooding back. Further research of some magnitude is needed, though, to paint a thorough picture of how an ever expanding range of music multimedia are used – particularly in public places – by young (and older) people with different means for different ends.

Notes

1. A similar point is made in a recent article on Internet music use: 'Although some examples of empirical research on music audiences exist, remarkably little has been published to date about popular music and media use, and even less has been published about popular music and the Internet' (Jones and Lenhart 2004: 185). Since the publication of this article there have emerged several other works on Internet music use, but there remain very few published articles or books to date that consider how different music media technologies compare and contrast with each other at the phase of consumption.
2. The Muzak Company formed in 1934 for this purpose.
3. According to the IFPI 'Thousands of people – mostly internet-savvy men in their 20s and 30s – have learnt to their cost the legal and financial risks involved in file-sharing copyrighted music in large quantities' (BBC News website, 'Legal fight hits "music pirates"', 15 November 2005, http://news.bbc.co.uk/1/hi/entertainment/music/4438324.stm, accessed July 2006).
4. The empirical research on young people's music media use, to be discussed later in this chapter, was gleaned from a wider project in which I conducted 52 interviews with either groups or individuals, a questionnaire-based survey with 232 respondents, and simple observation at 54 diverse research locations where public music functioned to some degree, in the Greater Manchester conurbation of north-west England. Research participants of both sexes ranged from 15 to 30 years of age. Most of these young people were accessed in further education colleges and sixth form centres that cater for full-time students aged 16–19 years (see Laughey 2006).
5. My own research on music radio use in domestic contexts – elaborated later – supports this idea that music on the radio (and on television) is mostly a casual consumer experience (see Laughey 2006: 122–6).
6. DeNora and Belcher's (2000) study of music in retail stores is one of the few qualitative attempts to explore the subliminal influences of casually consumed music in public places. Some advances in the study of casual music consumption have been made by researchers in the social psychology of music (e.g. Sloboda and O'Neill 2001), but much more research is necessary in this area.
7. To enable comparisons of both similarities and differences between music media technologies, I have separated them into two groups. Not all the various music media used by my research participants are discussed here, but they are all accounted for in the overall analysis, illustrated in table 2, and further research findings are discussed in Laughey (2006).
8. As Bull remarks, 'iPod users often refer to the magical nature of carrying their entire music collection with them wherever they go, thus giving them an unprecedented amount of choice of music to listen to' (Bull 2005: 344).
9. A survey of students at a British university found that 63 per cent of respondents downloaded MP3s on campus (only 18 per cent off campus in presumably more private settings), and that MP3 usage was a major phenomenon in the university population (Coates 2002). University students with easy access to high-speed internet connections therefore become 'movers and shakers' among their peers, who do not proceed to higher education.

References

Abercrombie, N., and Longhurst, B. J. (1998), *Audiences: A Sociological Theory of Performance and Imagination* (London: Sage).

Baker, S. L. (2004), 'Pop In(to) the Bedroom: Popular Music in Pre-teen Girls' Bedroom Culture', *European Journal of Cultural Studies*, Vol. 7, No. 1, pp. 75–93.

Bradley, D. A. (2006), 'Scenes of Transmission: Youth Culture, MP3 File-sharing, and Transferable Strategies of Cultural Practice', *M/C Journal*, Vol. 9, No. 1, http://journal.media-culture.org.au/0603/05-bradley.php (accessed June 2006).

Bull, M. (2000), *Sounding Out the City: Personal Stereos and the Management of Everyday Life* (Oxford: Berg).

—— (2003), 'Soundscapes of the Car: A Critical Study of Automobile Habitation', in M. Bull and L. Back (eds), *The Auditory Culture Reader* (Oxford: Berg).

—— (2005), 'No Dead Air! The iPod and the Culture of Mobile Listening', *Leisure Studies*, Vol 24, No. 4, pp. 343–55.

Coates, G. (2002), 'MP3: Devil or Liberation?', paper presented at Reshaping the Social: British Sociological Association Annual Conference, University of Leicester, March.

DeNora, T. (1999), 'Music as a Technology of the Self', *Poetics*, No. 24, pp. 31–56.

DeNora, T., and Belcher, S. (2000), '"When You're Trying Something On You Picture Yourself in a Place Where they are Playing This Kind of Music": Musically Sponsored Agency in the British Clothing Retail Sector', *Sociological Review*, Vol. 48, No. 1, pp. 80–101.

Frith, S. (1987), 'The Making of the British Record Industry 1920–64', in J. Curran, A. Smith and P. Wingate (eds), *Impacts and Influences: Essays on Media Power in the Twentieth Century* (London: Methuen).

Hayes, D. (2006), '"Take Those Old Records Off the Shelf": Youth and Music Consumption in the Postmodern Age', *Popular Music and Society*, Vol. 29, No. 1, pp. 51–68.

Jones, S., and Lenhart, A. (2004), 'Music Downloading and Listening: Findings from the Pew Internet and American Life Project', *Popular Music and Society*, Vol. 27, No. 2, pp. 185–99.

Kassabian, A. (2002), 'Ubiquitous Listening', in D. Hesmondhalgh and K. Negus (eds), *Popular Music Studies* (London: Arnold).

Laing, D. (1986), 'The Music Industry and the "Cultural Imperialism" Thesis', *Media, Culture and Society*, Vol. 8, No. 3, pp. 331–41.

Laughey, D. (2006), *Music and Youth Culture* (Edinburgh: Edinburgh University Press).

Leyshan, A., Webb, P., French, S., Thrift, N., and Crewe, L. (2005), 'On the Reproduction of the Musical Economy after the Internet', *Media, Culture and Society*, Vol. 27, No. 2, pp. 177–209.

Lincoln, S. (2005), 'Feeling the Noise: Teenagers, Bedrooms and Music', *Leisure Studies*, Vol. 24, No. 4, pp. 399–414.

McRobbie, A., and Garber, J. (1975), 'Girls and Subcultures: An Exploration', in S. Hall and T. Jefferson (eds), *Resistance through Rituals: Youth Subcultures in Post-war Britain* (London: Routledge).

Marshall, L. (2004), 'The Effects of Piracy upon the Music Industry: A Case Study of Bootlegging', *Media, Culture and Society*, Vol. 26, No. 2, pp. 163–81.

Nott, J. J. (2002), *Music for the People: Popular Music and Dance in Interwar Britain* (Oxford: Oxford University Press).

Reimer, B. (1995), 'The Media in Public and Private Spheres', in J. Fornas and G. Bolin (eds), *Youth Culture in Late Modernity* (London: Sage).

Rojek, C. (2005), 'P2P Leisure Exchange: Net Banditry and the Policing of Intellectual Property', *Leisure Studies*, Vol. 24, No. 4, pp. 357–69.

Schechner, R. (1993), *The Future of the Ritual: Writings on Culture and Performance* (London: Routledge).

Sloboda, J. A., and O'Neill, S. A. (2001), 'Emotions in Everyday Listening to Music', in P. N. Juslin and J. A. Sloboda (eds), *Music and Emotion: Theory and Research* (Oxford: Oxford University Press).

Tarrant, M., North, A. C., and Hargreaves, D. J. (2002), 'Youth Identity and Music', in R. A. R. MacDonald, D. J. Hargreaves and D. Miell (eds), *Musical Identities* (Oxford: Oxford University Press).

Thibaud, J-P. (2003), 'The Sonic Composition of the City', in M. Bull and L. Back (eds), *The Auditory Culture Reader* (Oxford: Berg).

Thornton, S. (1995), *Club Cultures: Music, Media and Subcultural Capital* (Cambridge: Polity).

Williams, J. P. (2006), 'Authentic Identities: Straightedge Subculture, Music, and the Internet', *Journal of Contemporary Ethnography*, Vol. 5, No. 2, pp. 173–200.

Woodworth, G. M. (2004), 'Hackers, Users and Suits: Napster and Representations of Identity', *Popular Music and Society*, Vol. 27, No. 2, pp. 161–84.

10. CASE STUDY: THE DEVELOPMENT OF THE APPLE IPOD

Kieran Kelly

Since its launch in 2001 the Apple iPod, in a variety of guises, including a video player, has sold around 60 million devices. It accounts for 75 per cent of the market for personal music devices in the US, more than half in France and the UK; only in Germany is it outsold, and only then by all the similar devices put together. Although it has not yet become the generic descriptor for a personal music device ('MP3 player' still has currency) it has given rise to the term 'pod-casting' for the distribution of audio content across the Internet. Accounting for some three-quarters of all legal music downloads, the related iTunes website has been a commercial success for Apple Corporation, a company formerly associated with personal computers and widely perceived as a stylish alterna-tive to the more common arrangement of Intel chip and Windows Computing. As early as 2005 Apple Computers announced that downloads from iTunes, the digital distribution network for music, had hit 300 million, a figure that put commercial digital music networks on the map. The story of the Apple iPod, a digital music player, its integration with the iTunes servers and its impact on the legitimation of a previously clandestine aspect of digital convergence, is deserv-ing of attention by all those interested in multimedia.

This chapter examines the development of the iPod, and in the subsequent discussion it will be demonstrated that Apple had actually to consider the inter-ests of a variety of other actors, including developers and the owners of content rights. By doing this, Apple Corporation was able to enter the market with an offering, in particular the iTunes store, above and beyond that of the multitude of other MP3 players offered by hardware companies.

There are one or two assumptions about the study of new technology which are not debated in any great detail in this chapter and which should therefore be outlined in advance. The first is that the motivation for Apple's development of the iPod is the pursuit of profits. The second is that the Apple Corporation, despite a number of peculiarities in its history and practice, is a corporate enterprise operating in accordance with the fundamental requirements of a capitalist economy, in particular the competition for, and the accumulation of, value. The third is that the business practices of a media technology corporation are not those of a media content creator. It is also accepted that cultural objects are cultural commodities and that their use and development are impacted upon by sales potential as well as the provision of cultural use. Some use is made of earlier theories, particularly in the work of the British writer Raymond Williams on the relationship between economics and cultural work. American academic Douglas Kellner summarised this approach rather well:

> Political Economy highlights that capitalist societies are organized according to a dominant mode of production that structures institutions and practices according to the logic of commodification and capital accumulation so that cultural production is profit- and market-oriented. . . . However 'political economy' does not merely refer solely to economics, but to the relations between the economic, political and other dimensions of social reality. The term thus links culture to its political and economic context and opens up cultural studies to history and politics. It refers to a field of struggle and antagonism and not an inert structure as characterised by some of its opponents. (Kellner 1997: 105)

Even so, in the UK tradition of cultural and media studies the interaction between commodity production and content has not been all that widely explored; those in the field of music industry research, such as Hesmondhalgh, Born, Frith and Negus, stand out for the way in which they demonstrate the impact of commercial structures and organisations on the ways music is selected and produced for distribution to listeners. Rather I would refer to David Hesmondhalgh's volume *The Cultural Industries* (2002), which successfully combines the two areas. Hesmondhalgh points to the way in which the characteristics of commodified cultural production require a method capable of analysing the production of meaning that is frequently undertaken for the purposes of economic exchange.

When considering technological developments, such as the iPod, it is important to recognise the particular characteristics of capitalism as an economic system. As a system, capitalism creates the ability to overcome scarcity via the massive development of the means of producing goods and services. There is also a tendency towards concentration (it helps to be bigger when in competition with other companies or corporations). This process of competition also tends towards oligopoly (a small number of firms dominating a market) and on occasion, monopoly. The tendency towards concentration is particularly well developed in the fields of computer production and of music. This is not the place to take up this discussion in great detail, but it is important to note that oligopolistic and monopolistic tendencies, and the increased concentration of political influence in the hands of corporations, tend to obscure the continued role of competition in the market place, although it can also be reduced when there are only one or two companies in the field. In these circumstances the process of innovation, of unique development and of original ideas, is only a very minor component in the capitalist mode of production. Rather more important is the process of competition, by which individual firms seek to control the market using a variety of methods appropriate to their particular sector. This is true for old sections of heavy industry, film studios and producers of pots and pans, as well as personal computers and vacuum cleaners. By considering the reality of the production process, such as the use of external developers, the reuse of existing ideas and technology, the redeployment of in-house skills and the management of contracts and intellectual property, we can better understand the commonplace methods used to develop new technologies.

One of the best-known examples of the ways in which competition, technological capability and consumer choice interact is that of the Sony Betamax (Wielage and Woodcock 2003). Introducing their home video cassette recorder in 1975, Sony drew on their background in professional quality video, producing a machine that allowed domestic users to record up to an hour of high-quality video direct from their home television. Almost every other innovation in home video, from front-loading of tapes through to the provision of a timer for programme recording and even a pause button (Sony originally said it would damage the recording heads), was made by their competitors. One of the most crucial innovations was the ability to slow the tape and thereby lengthen recording time. Even here Sony was beaten to it by the owners of licences to produce VHS tape machines, the format developed by Sony's Japanese competitors.[1] Despite Sony's modifications and the benefit of a higher-quality image, VHS overwhelmingly dominated the market. What the Betamax case demonstrated was that development takes place as the result of a complex set of factors including consumer choice, production capabilities, technological capabilities and the adaptive ability of the production company. Indeed it appears that it was the dominance of engineers and their attention to technological excellence that undermined Betamax in the market place; they ignored that actual modes of use that were being practised in homes.

The success of the iPod has depended on the ability of the company to connect music company catalogues, protected by law, to music distribution to a machine developed by an independent development company. It is common to think about the development of technology as the most important influence on the nature of society. It is not difficult to argue that new technologies bring about new social and cultural practices. Paul Du Gay and colleagues outlined this in their work on the precursor to the iPod, the Sony Walkman (Du Gay et al. 1997). Although the study offers a picture of the Sony Corporation, there is little discussion of just what other aspects of the consumer electronics industry Sony were concerned with. The discussion depends to a considerable extent on the model of 'articulation' advanced by Stuart Hall (Grossberg 2002). This model, however, gives little sense of how or why the particular 'unity' of elements should take shape in one way rather than another. In the end the impression is given that production and consumption enter into a single articulated factor but without any particular driving pressures. The existence of competition in the market is not given any great emphasis, in contrast with the impact of competition on the development of, for example, Betamax. In the end there is no analysis in the model of what actually sets this process running. It may quite as easily be the demands of consumers as the desire of the company. The problem with this approach is that it removes the specificity from any particular company and the strategic or commercial interests of that particular unit of capital, yet we know that capitalist enterprises actually have great specificity in their particular fields. If anything, Du Gay et al. give a sense that it is technological development that brings the uses of the Walkman into existence. In fact it is much more likely that it was the myriad uses of music – its mobility, its use as background, the portability of the transistor radio – that offered the opportunity to create a device that was technologically possible and had an existing use. At this point the necessity of competition, accumulation and the search for profits influences and sets the context for the actual development process. Considered in this way it is not hard to bring into the picture the levels of atomisation, long commutes and increased individual living that made a room-filling hi-fi unnecessary. The Walkman as an innovative item of media hardware, albeit directly based on existing tape players, created an entirely new market and therefore an advantage over subsequent entries to the market. The level of innovation may be appreciated from the way in which the Walkman trademark became a generic identifier in the same way as the term Hoover. It might be said that the iPod is also a better MP3 player than its rivals, and for this reason the latter term continues to be widely used. A brief look at some work by Raymond Williams will be useful to delve further into such issues.

In *Television: Technology and Cultural Form* Williams made the oft-ignored argument that to reject technological determination should not mean simply embracing the obverse, the determination of technology. In other words, he wanted to maintain the idea that the structure, form, uses and production of a technologically based medium were determined by social practices as much as was the content. What is important about William's presentation of this response is that he does not simply reject technological determination in order to argue that the forms taken by technology itself are determined by social and cultural causes; rather he argues that

> the reality of determination is the setting of limits and the exertion of pressure, within which variable social practices are profoundly affected but never necessarily controlled. We have to think of determination not as a single force, or a single abstraction of forces, but as a process in which real determining factors – the distribution of power or of capital, social and physical inheritance, relations of scale and size between groups – set limits and exert pressures, but neither wholly control nor wholly predict the outcome of complex activity within or at these limits, and under or against these pressures. (Williams 1974: 130)

Williams was, of course, drawing on theories of base and superstructure, particularly as explored in his essay 'Base and Superstructure in Marxist Cultural Theory', originally published in *New Left Review* in 1973. In his discussion Williams is urging us to recognise at once the materiality of laws, politics and ideology, particularly in their role as the representations of the interests of a sector of society, and not to assume that materiality is only a characteristic of the economic base of society. Williams abstracts a sense of the base from the economic and restates it as the means of production of humanity. For our purposes this means that the outcomes of processes of production, even of something as simple as an MP3 player, have an impact on how we behave as people.

As was pointed out above, the crucial factor in the success of the iPod has been the integration of the right to access, record and use music without its undermining the ownership of intellectual property by large business corporations. In order to understand this we need to examine the way in which the Law interacts with property and commodities. The most successful attempt to do this is carried out in Pashukanis's work on Marxism and law (1989), originally published in 1924. According to Pashukanis the development of law in a capitalist society is rooted precisely in the commodity form, that is, the fact that goods are produced not for a particular individual or group but for sale in the market place. What we get from Pashukanis is an exploration of the way in which law develops out of a need to regulate the ownership of goods. It does not take too much thought to conceive of the ways in which concepts of ownership and non-ownership lie at the heart of law in a capitalist economy. To use a basic theoretical example: as a commodity a music file does not choose its owner. Ownership only exists through the rights of owners. In other words, 'I cannot take your property unless you consent, you cannot take mine unless I consent.' From this simple statement succeeds all contract law, tort and so on. In the case of intellectual property it is helpful to understand law as a pure expression of the rights of ownership. The fact that the rights in a piece of music can be bought and sold – that is, they are a commodity – gives ownership a greater importance than a simple desire to listen. We can extend this view of ownership to show how the rights of ownership of various parts (commodities, whether software or hardware) influence the design and consequently the use of the device.

What this understanding of law allows us to do is to arrive at a mechanism by which the superstructure determines, in Williams's sense, the limits of the growth of technology. In our case the design of the iPod is regulated to a greater or lesser extent by the desires of the designers and manufacturers and how they interact with the technology available to them, the extent of ownership of the commodity by customers, and the interaction with the ownership of the rights in the cultural commodities. Put more simply, the nature of the iPod is an outcome not only of technological capability, but also of who owns what in the form of ideas, including software, and who is prepared to make use of those ideas. To this relationship must be added the linearity of time: who is the first to develop, market, trademark and patent these ideas. The factors in the development of the iPod can be summarised as follows.

- technological capability;
- ability to acknowledge ownership of intellectual property rights, including those of music owners;
- ability to deploy resources for development in advance of the receipt of income;
- existing social practices in the use of music, particularly the Sony Walkman and related devices.

Let us now turn to the iPod itself. It has been possible to buy an MP3 player for some years: Rio, Creative Technologies, Sony and a number of other 'generic' manufacturers have put together machines to play Walkman-like, pirated music. However, as the music was either sourced from peer-to-peer (P2P) sites and denounced as 'illegal' by the music corporations, honest citizens – fearful of piracy and recording industry writs – have been less than keen to join the outlaws. The alternative – ripping CDs to produce MP3 tracks – smacked of a rather geeky technical expertise. Therefore a key element in the success of the Apple iPod is that it has provided an alternative practice that users find both legal and useable.

In comparison with the design process claimed for the Sony Walkman, the iPod was predicated not on the creation of a unique item with a novel set of uses, but on the reconfiguration of a number of existing forms of media, creation, distribution and use. It is possible to identify four elements: creation of songs or tracks, database of content and Internet distribution, Internet connection, and

Table 3 *Types of music delivery*

Precedent	Process	iPod or not
Sony, Universal, Time Warner, Bertelsmann, EMI	Creation of songs or tracks	Sony, Universal, Time Warner, Bertelsmann, EMI
Napster, Limewire, Kazaa, bittorrent	Databasing of content and internet distribution	iTunes
Apple/Microsoft-based personal computer; telecommunications, including Internet service providers	Internet connection	Apple/Microsoft-based personal computer; telecommunications, including Internet service providers
Rio Creative, Sony, etc.	Sony Walkman and equivalents	iPod

the iPod player itself. The original elements and their equivalents can be easily identified in table 3.

The year 2004 was the one when digital music and distribution took off; about 230 services were available online and over a million tunes had been licensed by the record companies (IFPI 2005). From table 3, the current services all depend on licensing material from the majors, who retain their role in A&M, recording and marketing. Apple and other distributors have yet to enter into these high-risk areas, and considering the specialisation of their respective roles, trespassing may be unlikely. In the second row, the effort of Apple and other distributors is essentially to offer mass alternatives to piracy. The P2P networks also depended on the efforts of the record companies, but avoided the necessity of paying tribute in the form of licence fees to the majors. The record industry can now be seen to operate a twin-track approach in using the Record Industry Association of America to prosecute a number of users for copyright infringement and to license their music to businesses such as Apple iTunes. In the third row the operation of iTunes depends on the internet and associated infrastructure for its effectiveness. In the fourth row, the iPod is involved in a fairly straightforward exercise in competition with other hardware manufacturers. It is in this area that the special characteristics of Apple's business methods, particularly the integration of software and hardware, have played a useful role in carving out a share in the sector. Apple, under the leadership of Steve Jobs, always offered computers that integrated the user software with the operating system to a much greater extent than was the case with the Windows/Intel model. By offering a non-Intel-based computer that was required to use the frankly superior Mac operating system, Apple were able to generate a software–hardware mix that locked in users, in comparison with the generic

IBM clones favoured by Microsoft's operating system. However, in terms of commercial success, the result has been that Microsoft/Intel machines account for 97 per cent of the market in personal computers.

None the less, Apple continued to follow this model and integrated the iTunes server with the iTunes client and the iPod machine; the software became a means of selling the hardware and the hardware a means of selling the software service. It is also true that the iPod can be loaded with music from the usual sources of pirate copies, ripped CDs and even, if so desired, original music.

It appears that Apple understood the market and then looked around for ways to integrate the whole process. The problem for Apple was they did not have a digital music player in-house, but fortunately an external organisation did. It will be seen how the development process for the Apple iPod was driven not by innovation (except in integration), but by competition. If Apple were to dominate the market then rapid acquisition of a player was necessary.

In the process of developing the iPod, Apple utilised an approach that IBM had used to develop the PC in the 1970s, also as a result of competitive pressures in the computer industry. For the sake of speed, IBM assembled the PC out of generic parts (Cringely 1993). The Apple iPod is an interesting example of this in that it is actually quite clearly a computer device, using all the aspects of the modern PC: digital storage, operating system, input/output, encoding and interaction with digital networks. In fact, it may be the very specificity of the Apple Corporation with its long-term integration of hardware and software that made it particularly capable of undertaking and achieving the development of a digital music player. As Steve Jobs put it in an interview with *Rolling Stone* in 2003:

> Well, Apple has a core set of talents, and those talents are: We do, I think, very good hardware design; we do very good industrial design; and we write very good system and application software. And we're really good at packaging that all together into a product. We're the only people left in the computer industry that do that. And we're really the only people in the consumer-electronics industry that go deep [i.e. have considerable expertise] in software in consumer products. So those talents can be used to make personal computers, and they can also be used to make things like iPods. (Goodell 2003)

The development process of the iPod was outlined in an interview on the *Wired* website with Ben Knauss, a former senior manager at PortalPlayer, the company Apple Computer approached to help develop the MP3 player that would eventually become the iPod. The idea for an integrated online music store with a dedicated MP3 player came from Tony Fadell, a former employee of the Philips Corporation. Fadell joined Apple in 2001 and was given a team of thirty designers, programmers and hardware engineers. In turn, he sourced the original design from PortalPlayer, who were already offering what is known as a 'reference design' to the consumer electronics industry. Reference designs play an important role in innovation whereby technical issues can be resolved vis-à-vis an actual device. In other words, one component can be changed and the impact measured with reference to all the other components that remain unaltered. When PortalPlayer was approached by Apple they dropped all their other customers, including IBM. Most important for Apple, the PortalPlayer design included an operating system. For the next eight months, PortalPlayer's 200 employees in the United States and 80 engineers in India worked exclusively on the iPod. Apple's contribution was to demand their preferred music format, AAC, as well as the audio-book format, and a five-band equaliser. Apple also wanted a new interface. Overall, Apple's contribution, much of it said to come from the direct intervention of Steve Jobs himself, appears to have been devoted to the look, feel and operability of the device. Not surprisingly, these are precisely the elements for which Apple Macintosh computers, the company's main business, are known. It is interesting to note that FairPlay, Apple's copy-protection technology, was only added with the opening of the iTunes music store. In the end, once the reference design had been turned into the iPod, Apple bought a majority stake in the company.

Except for the exterior physical design, every other aspect of the iPod development and build was obtained through interaction with external companies. These include hard drives from Toshiba, chips from PortalPlayer and others, and an operating system from a small company called Pixo. Apple brought together a range of companies, mixing together evidence of consumer demand with existing capabilities limited by law, and brought about what was possible within those limits. The technological potential, far from driving media hardware development, can be seen to trail a long way behind the interests of existing owners of the rights in both content and technology. The law itself provides instead an extremely well-developed mechanism for the control of the exploitation of the rights invested in their owners.

Clearly a key element in the success of the iPod has been the development of the iTunes server. In effect Apple has provided a source of music files that is 'safe' to use, provides guaranteed quality (at least technical), and will guarantee that the tracks can be played on the iPod. This approach to the use of the Internet, building in highly specific links between sources of data, particular software and special hardware, is anathema to its original design. The Internet and the web browser, with which it is most closely associated, were designed precisely to overcome the problems of moving information between computers when every manufacturer had a file format that could only be read on their specific equipment. In fact it could be argued that in the case discussed above it was precisely the fixed link between Betamax tape and Betamax machines that caused Sony so many problems.

Another important element has been that P2P networks have been successfully characterised by the music industry as pirates. The use of the law to pursue organisations such as Napster, and in recent cases some individuals, has undoubtedly helped create an atmosphere in which legal download systems appear sensible and dependable. In other words, quality and dependability are important elements in the preparedness of individuals to pay 79p a song. The issues of dependability arises because in the absence of indicators of trust – such as brand names and trademarks – it can be difficult for users to determine whether the video, music file or movie is worth the effort of downloading. Media companies have recognised this and have striven to 'pollute' P2P networks with corrupt, damaged and low-grade files. More recent techniques also include running servers that look like P2P nodes but are actually entirely redundant (Maguire 2003). It has to be said that the selective prosecution of private individuals has undoubtedly helped to maintain the image of P2P file sharing as an entirely illegal activity. Therefore, the Apple imprint offers a protection from the worries engendered by the prosecutions of those using pirated music.

What Apple has done technically is again lacking in any great innovation. Essentially, iTunes uses a dedicated browser to obtain information from dedicated servers using a mix of http, the standard web protocol, and XML, which provides data in a list form presented according to a predefined format (a combination also known as a REST interface). The XML file is obtained from an Apple server and this is then displayed using controls native to the Mac operating system and user interface, though obviously the Windows version uses Microsoft controls. Apple's servers need to be able to take huge numbers of hits but the amount of data they hold is relatively small. It is worth noting that relatively low-definition music files, 128 kb compared with the 256 kb necessary for full CD quality, also enable faster distribution over the Internet. Consequently, music files are only about 1 Mb per minute. However, the file-format issue was also important in the way in which digital rights management (DRM) was built into the system, an essential component that allowed Apple to bring the music industry on board; after all, it is precisely the issue of control of distribution and the ease of copying digital music that so exercises the Recording Industry Association of America and their battles against the likes of Napster.

ITunes uses a newer but still open standard file format, AAC, rather than the older Mpeg layer 3 used by P2P and others.[2] It is worth noting that this is one area in which the iPod is undoubtedly an improvement on its competitors and is a direct result of Apple's arrangements with the music corporations. Obtaining digital tracks direct from the owners of the original recordings, iTunes does not have to depend on the more commonly used MP3 files generally swapped across the Internet. The tracks are protected from redistribution by the use of Apple's 'FairPlay' DRM. The iTunes software on the users PC installs a key in the downloaded file that can only be replaced twice more, enabling a restriction to the users of PC and iPods, and prevents redistribution over the Internet. Thus the safety and security element in the overall design of the integrated Apple music experience is backed up by a secure interaction of software that limits the uses to which the user can put their purchased music. What can be seen here is a redefinition of the music purchase, from ownership of the object or a CD track to licence to use, in fairly limited ways, the music encoded in a track. This approach to licensing has a long history in computing but appears to be entirely novel in other media. In effect, the accurate replicability of digital media is undermined and even destroyed not by technical limitations, as was the case with vinyl or the VCR, or by the ephemeral nature of the single-entry ticket to the cinema or the over-the-air broadcast of the television programme, but deliberately by the proprietors of the tunes.

In conclusion we can argue that the way in which law protects ownership and rights in the commodity impacts to a much greater extent on the users of the technology than do the user's preferences. It is the way in which the technology allows the management of every user's legal rights and obligations to be expressed via the technology. The determination indubitably stems from the economic base; economic interests are paramount, but the technology becomes an expression of the use to which the rights-managed music may be put. There is in effect an inversion in where the authority lies. It appears to stem from law, but law expresses precisely the requirements of the owners of the commodities vis-à-vis each other. The imposition of limits of use does not lie in the object but stems from the interests of the owners of those commodified objects, in this case the right to make limited uses of infinitely replicable digitised sound. In this way, the existing relations of production, i.e. who owns what, limit the uses of the technology. However, it is important to note that the word used is 'limit'. Alternative uses and practices may well develop amongst users and these may feed back to providers. The point is that the development process will be guided by concerns with ownership, where those uses touch on the commercial concerns of the producers of commodities involved in the reproduction of either the music or the devices for playing it.

In contrast with the problems generated by hackers, the biggest challenge to Apple's iTunes security so far came comes from another media interest, the proprietors of Real Player, which is widely used to play video and audio on personal computers. The company broke Apple's digital rights protection using a method known as reverse engineering. This form of non-market competition is common in the computer industry, with companies avoiding patent and copyright problems by ignoring the content of a piece of hardware or software and simply developing, by trial and error, an object that will do the same thing as the original. It was precisely this method that allowed companies to develop computers that would operate software compatible with the original IBM PCs.

Finally, what can be said about the relationship between music and media technology is that it is not only a function of the technological capabilities of music producers. It is a much more complex picture of limits and determinations that exist through commercial structures which themselves are limited by ownership of rights and the licence to exploit those rights. The technological capability of music distribution and replicability is partly a technological issue, encompassing, for example, file size, download times and hard-disk capacity. However, the right even to access the file in the first place requires the user to enter into a complex and highly structured relationship with a variety of property owners. The determinant is not, therefore, what is the best way to listen to music, but what method of listening to music is congruent with a huge variety of factors that are as much economic, legal and social practices as they are technical or even simple issues of taste.

NOTES

1. Sony were advised by the US television manufacturers, RCA, to make it possible to record an American football game lasting around four hours; however, Sony insisted on a one-hour tape, suitable for a standard US programme or two half-hour slots.
2. The standards for digital encoding of still images, 'jpeg', and moving images, 'mpeg', are determined by expert groups that draw their personnel from a wide variety of organisations.

REFERENCES

Cringely, R. (1993), *Accidental Empires* (London: Penguin).

Curran, J. (ed.) (1999), *Media Organisations in Society* (London: Hodder Arnold).

Day, J. H. (2005), 'Inside iPod', *Electronic Design*, 20 January, http://elecdesign.com/Articles/ArticleID/9500/9500.html (accessed August 2006).

Du Gay, P. (1997), *Production of Culture/Cultures of Production* (Milton Keynes: Open University Press).

Du Gay, P., Hall, S., Janes, L., Mackay, H., and Negus, K. (1997), *Doing Cultural Studies: Story of the Sony Walkman* (Milton Keynes: Sage).

Eagleton, T. (ed.) (1989), *Raymond Williams: Critical Perspectives* (Boston: Northeastern University Press).

Frosh, P. (2003), *The Image Factor: Consumer Culture, Photography and the Visual Content Industry* (Oxford and New York: Berg).

Gaines, Jane M. (1991), *Contested Culture: The Image, the Voice, the Law* (Chapel Hill, NC: University of North Carolina Press).

Garnham, N. (1997), 'Political Economy and the Practice of Cultural Studies', in M. Ferguson and P. Golding (eds), *Cultural Studies in Question* (London: Sage).

Goodell, J. (2003), 'Steven Jobs: The Rolling Stone Interview', *Rolling Stone*, 3 December, http://www.rollingstone.com/news/story/5939600/steve_jobs_the_rolling_stone_interview (accessed August 2006).

Grossberg, S. (2002), 'On Postmodernism and Articulation: An Interview with Stuart Hall', in D. Morley and K. Chen, *Stuart Hall: Critical Dialogues in Cultural Studies* (London: Routledge).

Hesmondhalgh, D. (2002), *The Cultural Industries* (London: Sage).

IFPI (International Federation of the Phonographic Industry) (2005), 'Digital Music Report, 2005', 15 March, http://www.ifpi.org/site-content/library/digital-music-report-2005.pdf (accessed August 2006).

Kellner, D. (1997), 'Overcoming the Divide: Cultural Studies and Political Economy', in M. Ferguson and P. Golding (eds), *Cultural Studies in Question* (London: Sage).

McChesney, R. W. (2000), *Rich Media, Poor Democracy* (New York: New Press).

Maguire, J. (2003), 'Hitting P2P Users Where it Hurts', *Wired Magazine*, 13 January, http://www.wired.com/news/digiwood/0,1412,57112,00.html (accessed August 2006).

Malone, M. S. (2000), *Infinite Loop: How the World's Most Insanely Great Computer Company Went Insane* (London: Aurum Press).

Mintel International Group Limited (2006), *Mintel Report: Electrical Retailing – UK – April 2006*, http://reports.mintel.com.

Negus, K. (1993), *Producing Pop: Culture and Conflict in the Popular Music Industry* (London: Hodder Arnold).

—— (1999), 'The Music Business and Rap: Between the Street and the Executive Suite', *Cultural Studies*, Vol. 13, No. 3, pp. 488–508.

Pashukanis, E. B. (1989), *Law and Marxism: A General Theory* (London: Pluto Press).

Schwerzmann, J., and Wilde, E. (2005), *When Business Models Go Bad: The Music Industry's Future*, 31 March, http://dret.net/netdret/docs/wilde-musicicete2004.pdf (accessed August 2006).

Wayne, M. (2004), 'Mode of Production: New Media Technology and the Napster File', *Rethinking Marxism*, Vol. 16, No. 2, pp. 137–54.

Wielage, M., and Woodcock, R. (2003), 'The Rise and Fall of Beta', http://www.betainfoguide.com/RiseandFall.htm (accessed August 2006).

Williams, R. (1974), *Television: Technology and Cultural Form* (London: Fontana).

—— (1980), *Problems in Materialism and Culture: Selected Essays* (London and New York: Verso).

INDEX